Praise for *Scaling up Business Solutions to Social Problems*

"Business must take the lead in reinventing capitalism and making it more inclusive. This book provides business leaders with a hard-nosed assessment of the opportunities and challenges of doing so."

–Dominic Barton, Global Managing Director, McKinsey

"While I have had the privilege of working with Valeria and Olivier for over ten years on concrete projects aimed at inventing new socially impacting business models, and hybrid value chain solutions, this book has broadened my understanding of the myriad of entrepreneurs who are working to change our planet."

–Emmanuel Faber, CEO, Danone

"This book provides business executives with a wealth of concrete cases and deep insights into what it takes to build scalable inclusive business models."

–Jean-Laurent Ingles, Global Senior Vice President Household Care, Unilever

"The huge wall that has separated the business and social halves of the world's operations for several centuries is an especially rich opportunity and is the chief focus of this book. I doubt that there is anyone who can match Valeria and Olivier for depth of experience, insight, or clarity here."

–Bill Drayton, CEO, Ashoka

"The emerging field of inclusive or BoP business has suffered from 'pilotitis'— the proliferation of small pilot business experiments with little prospect for expansion. Kayser and Budinich's book provides both the diagnosis and the treatment regime for taking BoP business to the next level. A long-overdue resource for anyone interested in how to accelerate entrepreneurship for a more inclusive and sustainable world."

–Stuart L. Hart, Professor of Sustainable Business,
University of Vermont Business School;
co-author of *The Fortune at the Bottom of the Pyramid*

"*Scaling up Business Solutions to Social Problems* provides important insights into why the innovations proffered by social entrepreneurs with potential to be truly transformative for poor families rarely reach more than a small proportion of them. It's an exceptionally accessible and relevant read to those from the development and business sectors thinking about how to have greater and more sustainable impact."

–Jamie Cooper-Hohn, Co-founder of the Children's Investment Fund Foundation

"For too long, governments have considered they were solely responsible for tackling the issues facing developing countries. This book is a 'must-read' for public sector executives intending to partner with business in development."

–Pascal Canfin, former French Minister for Development

"Kayser and Budinich have written a fascinating book and an important source for those who want to test the limits of what can be done "within the system" to solve societal problems through market-based, economically sustainable approaches."

–Luiz Ros, Opportunities for the Majority,
Inter-American Development Bank

"This wonderful book is full of so many great stories and rich, practical insights into how frugal innovation can help build scalable and inclusive businesses around the world. It provides a blueprint for how we can help make poverty history, while warning us of the pitfalls along the way."

–Jaideep Prabhu, Professor of Business and Enterprise, Judge Business School, University of Cambridge; co-author of *Jugaad Innovation*

"This book is definitely a landmark in the realm of inclusive business: read it both to become inspired by incredible social entrepreneurs around the world and to gain key insights into understanding how we can collectively accelerate."

–Frédéric Dalsace, Associate Professor of Marketing,
Social Business/Enterprise and Poverty Chair Professor, HEC Paris

A Practical Guide for Social and Corporate Entrepreneurs

Scaling up Business Solutions to Social Problems

Olivier Kayser
Managing Director, Hystra

Valeria Budinich
Leadership Group Member, Ashoka

Forewords by Bill Drayton, CEO, Ashoka, and
Emmanuel Faber, CEO, Danone

First published 2015 by
PALGRAVE MACMILLAN

Palgrave Macmillan in the UK is an imprint of Macmillan Publishers Limited, registered in England, company number 785998, of Houndsmills, Basingstoke, Hampshire, RG21 6XS.

Palgrave Macmillan in the US is a division of St Martin's Press LLC, 175 Fifth Avenue, New York, NY 10010.

Palgrave is the global academic imprint of the above companies and has companies and representatives throughout the world.

Palgrave® and Macmillan® are registered trademarks in the United States, the United Kingdom, Europe and other countries.

ISBN 978–1–137–46652–5

This book is printed on paper suitable for recycling and made from fully managed and sustained forest sources. Logging, pulping and manufacturing processes are expected to conform to the environmental regulations of the country of origin.

A catalogue record for this book is available from the British Library.

A catalog record for this book is available from the Library of Congress.

Typeset by MPS Limited, Chennai, India.

To Marianne and Amaïa, my granddaughters,
and the hundreds of thousands of children born every day.
May they build a world of peace and justice.

Olivier

Para mi Nena – a wise and powerful woman who first taught
me as a child the fundamental injustice of poverty.
And to my parents – who inspired in us compassion and the
courage of our convictions and made my journey possible.

Valeria

Table of Contents

List of figures, tables and illustrations

Figures

Tables

Illustrations

Forewords

Don't miss this turning point
By Bill Drayton, CEO of Ashoka

Missing a big turning point is probably the worst mistake you can make.

Just ask Detroit. Fifty years ago it was the pinnacle of US technology, wealth, and pride. This icon of the assembly line is now bankrupt, has lost much of its population, and must now spend $1 billion to tear down an unsavable 40 percent of its remaining structures.

Remember the world's superpower of its era, Persia, and its great king, Darius? He probably never gave a moment's thought to the primitive fringe tribe beyond even the Greeks, the Macedonians, or their new military phalanx organization (the predecessor of the Roman legions). That was the end of Darius.

Turning points almost always come as a big surprise to most. There's a long buildup, but the old system continues in most things – until suddenly the tipping process takes off. The early innovators begin to succeed and connect. The first books and meetings follow. Large numbers begin to fear not understanding and not being able to respond more than they fear being out in front of everyone else. The press becomes a tipping multiplier as it serves the new mass need to know.

The world is now in the middle of such an awareness tipping process -- for what is almost certainly the biggest change humans have experienced for millennia. Valeria Budinich and Olivier Kayser's excellent, deep book enables the reader to explore and understand one of the most important dimensions of this new world – the fact that the traditional walls that usefully kept differing activities and sectors apart in the old order must now come down. The huge wall that has separated the business and social halves of the world's operations for several centuries is an especially rich opportunity and is the chief focus of this book. I doubt that there is anyone who can match Valeria and Olivier for depth of experience, insight or clarity here.

What is the overarching transformation now upon us that requires all the walls to come down – and many other changes?

Until very recently change was so slow and occasional that for all practical purposes people and their organizations could ignore it. The source of value came from efficiency in repetition. Think the assembly line (e.g., Detroit) or the law firm.

Around 1700, along the North Atlantic, business moved to a radical new "everyone a changemaker" (Ashoka's goal) structure. It would make anyone with a better idea that that person made work wealthy and respected – and it would then copy the innovation. That revolution spread to the citizen sector structurally around 1980 (which is why we launched Ashoka then and also why the field of social entrepreneurship took off at that point). In both business and social sectors, this structural revolution has now spread globally.

The driving force defining our time and the profound changes now needed is the fact that the rate of change has been accelerating exponentially because of these changes for three centuries. The same is true for the number of changemakers and the dimensions on and degree to which they are interconnected.

Now value comes more and more from delivering change. Today it is more dangerous not to change than it is to change.

Increasingly every group's strategic environment is one where a higher and higher proportion of those around it initiate changes and where each change bumps more and more people and groups – causing them in turn to change and to bump others.

It is no longer a world where repetition reinforces repetition as A fits steadily with B. Instead change now begets and accelerates change. This is not just different. It is the opposite of the pattern of the prior millennia.

This fact means that the way we have organized for the old game is failing. And as the tipping process now shifting into gear rapidly brings everyone into the new game, those that fall behind will quickly be in serious danger.

Now each group needs a thousand eyes – each team member watching and understanding the evolving patterns in the part of the world before him or her. Then those thousand eyes need to think and create together – putting all those observations of parts of the environment together and then seeing new areas where the group can contribute significant value.

Then the group must create a new team to seize and develop that opportunity.

Because the opening and clients are probably both new – and indeed constantly changing, success requires pulling together a new team of teams – from wherever the strongest team members may be – that will do the best possible job servicing this new opportunity.

This new game thus requires everyone to be a changemaker. Teams need those thousand eyes that can then think, create and organize together – building constantly changing new teams of teams.

In this "everyone a changemaker" world of accelerating change always requiring new team of teams combinations, the organizational walls that so characterize the past are more and more hurtful. A world of change requires fluidity, not walls.

This is why this admirable book is so important. It requires wisdom and a great deal of skill to know how to tear walls down – and far more to know how to replace them with fluid, open teams of teams cutting right across the old divisions. The authors have decades of thought and experience pressing this leadership frontier forward, and this book will help you not only to see the game change turning point now upon us but also to know how to be a skilled change architect.

A journey towards a better business?
By Emmanuel Faber, CEO of Danone

In my role as a business executive, my ultimate commitment is to help turn the power of corporations into a positive force in the world. At Danone, I have been given the opportunity to stretch the limits of what is commonly accepted as normal business practices and invent new models. In the midst of the financial meltdown in 2008, realizing that a company cannot be successful if its suppliers and distributors struggle (we call it our business ecosystem), we were able to convince Danone shareholders to dedicate 100 million euros to support NGOs working with some of the thousands of small farmers from which Danone sources its milk. A few years before, we had created a joint venture with Grameen Bank to produce and market fortified yoghurts in Bangladesh. But we have not always been successful: in Senegal, with the Slow Food movement and ENDA Graf Sahel, we co-developed Mossteki, a highly innovative, nutritious snack for kids at school, entirely made of local, traditional ingredients, which we hoped to be able to sell and distribute in Dakar suburbs. Yet, after many attempts, we have so far failed to make it a viable social business.

The lesson from Senegal and many other places is that this is an exciting but often challenging task. NGOs we want to work with are often skeptical about our motives. Internally, it is also very hard to build internal resilience so that our initiatives survive through lean years. Finding a dynamic balance between profits and sustainability requires constant attention. You therefore need to learn as much from failures than successes, yours, and others'.

Yet, given the daily pressures of a business job, it is a struggle to stay aware of all the initiatives other corporations or NGOs are undertaking. I had to make a conscious decision to devote a significant part of my time to this field of experimentation, taking all possible opportunities to learn and explore our corporate blindspots: this journey brought me to unexpected places, such as the World Social Forum in Belem, at the very moment our Chairman Franck Riboud was in Davos with Muhammad Yunus. More recently I spent a great deal of time, with a small team, to co-author with my friend Jay Naidoo, from South Africa, a report for the French Government on how local NGO-private sector coalitions could radically change the paradigm and the catalytic impact of Official Development Aid.

While on this journey I have had the privilege of working with Valeria and Olivier for nearly ten years, on concrete projects aimed at inventing new socially impacting business models, and hybrid value chain solutions, and this book has broadened my understanding of the myriad of entrepreneurs who are working to change our planet. And I am convinced that many of their innovations can become exciting opportunities for corporations, too.

This book has also helped me to see that the challenges I face are shared by many other executives and entrepreneurs, and that the successes they have enjoyed are proof that there is hope in what we are doing every day.

My motivation is deeply grounded in my own personal experience, but it is also shared by many others. Social entrepreneurs may not know each other, but they are guided by the shared belief that entrepreneurship can change the world for the better. Hopefully, so can business, provided executives don't lose sight of what their corporation is really good at, aimed at, created for. And that can't just be profit maximization. All companies and every person is larger than this, and quite often, we have rediscovered the core of our mission and why we exist as an institution through the tough reality-check of our dialogue with social entrepreneurs. What they do is a wake-up call for all.

Acknowledgments

The writing of this book is the result of a team effort over a number of years.

The diversity of backgrounds of the contributors to this book and their commonality of purpose is not accidental. It reflects one of the underlying themes of this book: collaborative entrepreneurship.

Jessica Graf is a Hystra network partner based in Zurich, Switzerland. Jessica spent the first half of her career working in development, leading projects on the ground with various CSOs before advising governments in Asia and the Balkans when working with the UN, the OSCE and the Swiss government. She then worked in the private sector, setting up an asset management company in Vietnam and consulting for McKinsey Zurich for many years. She joined Hystra in 2010, where she works at reconciling the best of the non-profit and corporate worlds. Jessica wrote the chapters on water and financing.

Lucie Klarsfeld is a Hystra project manager based in Paris. She joined Hystra in 2009 after short experiences with Bain & Company and the United Nations Development Programme (UNDP) and Environment Programme (UNEP). She has led Hystra's work on marketing, information and communications technology (ICT) and nutrition. Lucie wrote the chapters on cooking, lighting, banking, housing, marketing and conducted most of the social entrepreneur interviews featured in this book.

Simon Brossard, a consultant with Hystra, conducted the research for the Financing chapter of this book. Robin Bonsey, a consultant with Hystra, played a critical role in managing the process of editing the manuscript. Guillaume Ginèbre was a junior consultant with Hystra in 2010 and is now a consultant with the social action tank of HEC in Paris. Guillaume contributed to the chapter on sales and distribution.

Laurent Liautaud, a former project manager with Hystra and now the founder and CEO of Niokobok, a social business in Senegal, contributed to writing the chapters on cooking and lighting.

Current and past members of the global Hystra network have provided invaluable insights and critique based on their hands-on experience of working on hybrid strategies in emerging markets, in particular Jim Ayala, former head of McKinsey in the Philippines, founder of Hybrid Solutions and an innovative distributor of essential goods for the Bottom of the Pyramid; Alexandre de Carvalho, former CEO of Sanofi-Aventis for Africa and former COO of KickStart in Kenya; Ed Jardine, founder of Procter and Gamble's Low Income Consumer Learning and Innovation Center in Latin America; François Lepicard, former partner with McKinsey in France and CEO of Occam Capital, a venture capital fund; Avik Roy, who worked with the late C. K. Prahalad and now runs 2007 Re-emerging World out of Kolkota; Jack Sim, a serial business entrepreneur from Singapore, founder of World Toilet Organization; Francisco de la Torre, former McKinsey consultant and senior executive in Mexico, is the chair of FUNDES.

Both authors leveraged several case studies prepared by Creativ'Entrepreneur, an organization created by Alexandre Guinet and Mathieu Esprit, which conducted site visits of social entrepreneurs in Latin America and Asia in 2008–09, with the sponsorship of Société Générale Credit and Investment Banking, Groupama and Maiz'Europ.

Listing the names of all our clients here would be impractical and diplomatically unwise. Yet, they have been our companions in this journey of hope, learning and action. We are forever grateful for their support and friendship.

This book would not have been possible without the support of the Ashoka community. Ashoka Fellows who were interviewed for this book and/or contributed with their knowledge and insights include André Albuquerque, Rodrigo Baggio, Jeroo Billimoria, Jean-Marc Borello, Caroline Casey, Carlos Cruz, Isabel Cruz, Haidy Duque, David Green, Harish Hande, Jean-Guy Henckel, Franck Hoffmann, Rajendra Joshi, Satyan Mishra, Ron Layton, Faizel Rahman, Jack Sim, Thorkil Sonne, Felipe Vergara and Rebecca Villalobos.

Current and past members of the Ashoka Full Economic Citizenship (FEC) team contributed by sharing their experiences in building hybrid value chain (HVC) partnerships in Colombia, Brazil, Egypt, India and Mexico. In particular, Stephanie Schmidt of Ashoka France was a constant and valuable presence throughout our learning process, generously sharing her extensive field experience in small farmer agriculture, recycling and food distribution. Vishnu Swaminathan, head of Ashoka India and Shivana Manakthala – former head of Ashoka FEC India – made possible a field visit and learning exchange among Ashoka and Hystra teams, a pivotal moment in our co-creation process. In addition, Vishnu contributed his amazing journey in developing affordable housing in India.

Maria Lucia Roa, former head of Ashoka Colombia, enabled access to cases such as Colceramica and Codensa as well as Ashoka Fellows. Linda Peia drafted the Zurich and Danone experiences in Chapter 13. Rochelle Beck, Ashoka FEC communications director, contributed to writing part of Chapter 13. Arnaud Mourot, Co-Director, Ashoka Europe, and Konstanze Frischen, Ashoka leadership group member, shared their valuable knowledge and insights on social entrepreneurs in Europe and beyond. Mark Cheng, Ashoka UK, shared his reflections on the future of impact investment. Felix Oldenburg, head of Ashoka Germany, contributed his experience pioneering hybrid finance in Germany. We are also grateful to Bill Matassoni, former McKinsey partner and Ashoka advisor, who was the first to suggest that a book could emerge from our collective hybrid value chain (HVC) work.

We want to thank Potencia Ventures for believing in our project and providing critical support that made the writing of the book possible.

And last but not least, Bill Drayton, founder and CEO of Ashoka, who has continuously inspired and challenged us to change the world.

List of abbreviations and acronyms

BoP	Base of the (economic) Pyramid
BU	business unit
CEO	chief executive officer
CFO	chief financial officer
COO	chief operating officer
CSO	citizen sector organization
DFI	development finance institution
FMCG	fast-moving consumer goods
FTE	full-time equivalent
GAO	US Government Accountability Office
HFA	Housing for All
HVC	hybrid value chain
ICT	information and communication technologies
IP	intellectual property
IPO	initial public offering
KPI	key performance indicator
M&A	merger and acquisitions
MDC	micro-distribution center
MFI	microfinance institution

MNC	multinational corporation
NGO	non-governmental organization
NVCA	National Venture Capital Association
PE	private equity
PH	Patrimonio Hoy
PPP	purchasing power parity
R&D	research and development
SHG	self-help group
SHS	solar home system
SKU	stock-keeping unit
STUP	specially targeted ultra poor
VC	venture capital
VTC	Viste Tu Casa

About the authors

Olivier Kayser is the founder and managing director of Hystra, a consulting firm specializing in hybrid strategies (www.hystra.com).

At age 23, Olivier went to Mexico and bought a sailing boat from a fisherman in Belize, with the intent of trading fruits. These plans were altered as the boat sank at Sarteneja, a small Mayan village on the northern coast of Belize. Olivier and Christine (now his wife) were saved by the villagers and spent the best part of a year repairing the boat. This life in a village with no running water or electricity proved to be a seminal experience for Olivier.

Olivier joined McKinsey & Company in 1985. He was eventually elected a senior partner and spent 18 years in Europe, the USA and China, advising some of the largest multinational companies as well as state-owned enterprises. He is currently a board member of two multi-billion euro multinational corporations.

The excitement and rewards of his business career did not protect him from the questioning of a mid-(professional) life crisis. At age 46, he made an unchartered entry into the world of "philanthropy." After meeting with Bill Drayton, Olivier eventually started Ashoka operations in France and the UK, and founded the Ashoka Support Network (a global network of now close to 400 business people supporting social entrepreneurs).

Working closely with Valeria Budinich in Ashoka's Full Economic Citizenship Initiative, he realized the role that corporations can play in scaling up innovations developed by social entrepreneurs and, in turn, created Hystra in 2009. Hystra has worked with over 40 clients, large corporations such as Unilever, Danone and Total, major foundations and aid agencies as well as leading social entrepreneurs. Olivier likes to describe Hystra as a "for profit tool for social change."

Valeria Budinich is a leadership group member at Ashoka, the leading global community of social entrepreneurs (www.ashoka.org).

Born in Chile, Valeria lived in the 1970s in Nicaragua and at the age of 21 joined the newly formed Sandinista Government. Those amazing years started with hope and idealism, only to end with disillusion and a pragmatic appreciation of the power of markets. In 1982, Valeria moved to the USA to pursue graduate studies in business and engineering at the University of Texas.

For 16 years, she focused on stimulating the creation and development of businesses, first in the USA and then in Latin America. She worked at Appropriate Technology International (a global NGO supporting small producers) where as its chief operating officer, Valeria led a major transformation of the organization, which in a few years increased its impact and outreach tenfold to over half a million people annually. In 1991, Valeria met Bill Drayton – ATI's chairman – who helped her realize that she was not an engineer but a social entrepreneur. This triggered a journey of exploration that started with her joining Endeavor – a group enabling venture capital in emerging markets – and then "The Entrepreneurship Club" where she co-developed several start-ups designed to cultivate entrepreneurial abilities and enable collaborative entrepreneurship.

In 2003, Valeria decided to return to the USA to join the Ashoka team to "merge" her business and social experiences. She founded Ashoka's Full Economic Citizenship (FEC) initiative to develop and spread system change innovations designed to transform markets for social impact through scalable business/social alliances. As the chief entrepreneur of FEC, she conceived and led the implementation of the hybrid value chain (HVC) approach in five countries. This has encompassed 50 partnerships with leading companies and citizen sector organizations in Asia and Latin America as well as mobilizing close to $10 million in philanthropic and $120 million in commercial investments.

In 2012, she received the Harvard/McKinsey M-Prize for management innovation for the articulation of a new vision of capitalism based on business and leadership models innovations enabling collaboration across society. In its new phase, this work is now focused on spreading a new vision of leadership based on open and fluid teams of change-makers collaborating across industries for the good of all. Valeria's challenge is to enable commercial and change-making partnerships with leading universities, management consulting firms and business media groups.

In addition, Valeria is a member of the Advisory Boards of the Lemelson Foundation and Leapfrog Investments.

Introduction

A silent revolution is underway initiated by social entrepreneurs – pragmatist visionaries who are challenging prevalent notions of business motives and methods to invent market-based solutions to eradicate social injustice. Yet, to succeed and reach scale, they need help from within the social and economic systems they intend to change. This book is a call to arms, encouraging each of us to join this mutiny.

This is not a dramatic wholesale change led by a single, well-organized movement. Instead, this transformation is made of a multitude of tweaks and fixes promoted by single-minded individuals who have decided to devote their lives to solving a particular social problem that they have turned into an opportunity.

Not all problems have been solved, far from it. But since the 1980s, thousands of social entrepreneurs across the world have invented and tested as many solutions. While many have failed, this massive thrust of innovation has produced an impressive set of solutions that work; that is, which solve the social problem they tackle in an economically sustainable way. In this book, we put the spotlight on dozens of these solutions, ranging from solar lanterns to financing schemes for home-improvement projects. We trust the number and potential of these solutions is such that even a skeptical, hard-nosed observer will admit that there is a strong case for hope.

This begs the question as to why these solutions are not scaling up to their full potential. In other words: why is the lab for social innovation full but its globalization plant so empty? In our research, we have analyzed why these solutions fail to scale up. The short-term incentives of corporate executives lead them to miss out on the opportunity to serve the needs of the four billion poorest customers. Giveaway programs funded by well-intentioned philanthropists or governments often distort markets that social entrepreneurs attempt to serve. And social entrepreneurs themselves are often encumbered by ideology or limited by their own capabilities. The obstacles that prevent these solutions from reaching scale are indeed remarkably common. All the players in our ecosystem (companies, citizen sector organizations, philanthropists, investors and social entrepreneurs themselves) who are somehow part of the problem can also be part of the solution. This book goes beyond these obstacles to scale and suggests strategies to overcome them, inspired by the actions of hundreds who, within corporations, governments or foundations, are testing the limits of what can be done "within the system."

Addressing these obstacles inevitably leads us to challenge the traditional division of labor between "for profit" business that creates economic wealth and the "not for profit" public and social sectors that attempt to mend its social or environmental consequences.

Profit is not necessarily good for society. The world's most prestigious corporations pay billions of dollars in fines every year because their pursuit of short-term profits leads them to strategies that are bad for society. Yet this is only the visible part of the proverbial iceberg, as the real issue is: "What are the actions that corporations could take to help the world, but that they don't?"

"Not for profit" is not necessarily good either. Because of the relatively small pool of philanthropic financial resources – public and private – giveaway programs cannot reach all people in need. Using such scarce resources to solve problems that can be tackled through market-based solutions is economically and morally wrong.

Ethics are conveniently excluded from our daily lives as consumers or executives. What we need to question is the nature of the social contract between business and society. The statement "the business of business is business" is increasingly seen as simplistic, opening the door to new theories and experimentations that are trying to design a world where market forces can be harnessed to serve society best.

Challenging this comfortable division of labor between "for" and "not for profit" leads us to a tricky terrain where all of us must ask ourselves the question of what is right. As Gandhi said, "we need not wait to see what others do."

The financial crisis that started with the demise of Lehman Brothers in 2008 has provoked a crisis of conscience among many Western business people. It is ironic that it is because their wallet was hurt that they started wondering whether long-held beliefs – about what made capitalism good for society – were fundamentally flawed.

The combination of the maturing of the social entrepreneurship movement and the sudden awakening of the traditional business community creates a unique opportunity for change, an exciting time for entrepreneurs to truly change the world. The purpose of this book is to provide these entrepreneurs with a hard-nosed assessment of the potential to solve societal problems through market-based approaches, trying to stay away from ideological debates and drawing lessons from the experience base that is available today. We are writing the book we would have liked to be able to read: a road map for entrepreneurs (in business, citizen sector or government) in our changing world.

We hope this book will offer a road map for all of us, mutineers who want to make the world a better place.

* * *

Part 1 of this book will provide an inventory of "solutions that work" in some critical areas such as access to energy, safe drinking water, housing and financial services as well as enhancing the income of small producers. While we highlight the limitations of these market-based approaches, we make the case that they provide effective, scalable solutions to a sufficiently large part of our world's problems to warrant attention.

Part 2 of the book focuses on understanding why these solutions are not scaling up to their full potential and what can be done to get these innovations out of the lab and into the plant. Starting from social entrepreneurs themselves, we review how each of the key players (corporations, financiers and philanthropists) are part of the problem *and* can be part of the solution. The second part of the book is less grounded on existing experiments: we venture to propose our own ideas on how to overcome these obstacles.

Part **1**

Solutions that work

chapter 1

Faces of poverty

This book is about children born in a favella in Rio or a rural village of Bihar, women and men who struggle to make a living and sustain their families. Their lives are so different from our lives in rich countries and yet so similar, filled with joy and pain, love and loneliness.

Their struggle invites our sympathy and admiration but also raises many questions. Does being economically poor mean being unhappy? Isn't there happiness in slums? Are they really trapped in poverty, surrounded by insurmountable obstacles? Aren't these sufferings partly self-inflicted? And even, are we right in using our own rich-world values to judge their lives?

We wonder who we would be if we had been born into these families. These lives touch us because they could have been ours.

The reader will find in the next pages some of the prevailing definitions of poverty as well as a summary of the attempts to put numbers on this multi-dimensional problem. But we wish to start this book by portraying three poor families from rural India, urban Brazil and rural Kenya.

A rural Indian family[1]

Bhogi Mukhiya, 45, and his wife, 35, have four children aged 14, 12, 10 and 5. They live in the village of Saurath in Madhubani District, Bihar. Bhogi has a job as a cleaner, his wife is a housewife. The entire family income is provided by

ILLUSTRATION 1 / Bhogi's home and family

Bhogi's work: he earns 2700 Indian rupees (INR) or $45 per month;[2] he also occasionally works on a farm and gets paid in kind, with wheat and rice.

Boghi uses his government-issued Below Poverty Line Card to buy subsidized rations of food at half the standard price at the local grocery store. He spends over 80 percent of his income on feeding his family, a typical situation in poor households. The family has free access to drinking water at the village pump but they have to pay $11 per month for the irrigation water used to grow their own vegetables.

Only 2 percent of Boghi's income is spent on electricity, buying it from a local diesel generator that powers one light bulb from 6 pm to 10 pm. The family also spends $2 per month buying kerosene, in particular to allow Boghi's children to study in the smoky light of a wick fitted into a glass bottle.

No money is spent on cooking fuel as Bhogi's wife and children spend several hours a day collecting the wood and leaves that fuel the traditional smoky *chulha* (cookstove). Boghi owns his house and pays no rent, but the walls are made of *kuchcha* (mud) and need to be repaired each year after the rain season, costing around $17. There is no sanitation in the house, and the family defecates in the neighboring woods.

ILLUSTRATION 2 / Studying by candlelight

The youngest boy and the eldest daughter go to the local school. Admittance is free but parents have to spend $0.7 per month on books and notebooks. This $0.7 is an important expenditure but these illiterate parents are hopeful that their children will be better off in the future as a result of their education. Health expenses are roughly $10 per year. There are health-care services in the village or nearby. The local chemist gives consultations and sells medicine. The government runs a free Primary Health Clinic about 3 km away.

Boghi owes $58 at an interest rate of 2 percent per month (around 27 percent annually) to the village moneylender, whom he pays back in $1.1 monthly installments. In addition, this family of six spends $2 every month on clothes, $0.7 on travel, $0.5 on social events and $4 on cigarettes and other treats.

Recently, Boghi was given a valuable present: a cow (worth $170 on the market). Selling the milk will provide the family with an additional $50 for about eight months per year, nearly doubling the family's earnings! It comes as no surprise that when asked what he would do with credit of $1000, Bhogi answers that he would invest in cows or buffalos and pay back the money by selling milk.

Today, approximately 35 percent of rural people in India are living at or below the income of Boghi's family.

TABLE 1 Boghi's family monthly P&L in current dollars

Expenses		Income	
Food	36.6	Cleaning support	45.0
Irrigation	11.1	New income from cow	32.0
Cigarettes (if money left)	4.1		
Clothes	2.1		
Energy	2.0		
Home improvements	1.4		
Loan servicing	1.1		
Health	0.8		
Education	0.7		
Travel	0.7		
Social events	0.5		
Total	**61.1**	**Total (current)**	**45**
		Total (with cow)	**77**

Notes: Average profit and loss (P&L): all non-monthly expenses or income have been computed annually, then divided by 12. Current total income: the net loss incurred before milk from the cow became available was bridged by recurring loans from informal sources, such as moneylenders or known people in the community, a prevalent practice of other families in Boghi's village.

THREE DEFINITIONS OF POVERTY

"Low income, low levels of health and education, poor access to clean water and sanitation, inadequate physical security, lack of voice, and insufficient capacity and opportunity to better one's life."[3] The World Bank

"If an individual possesses a large enough endowment or portfolio of capability he can, in principle, choose a specific functioning to escape poverty." "Capability" refers to access to nutrition, health, education, shelter, clothing and information, but also refers to "freedoms" (from oppression, of religion, of expression), "security, and the degree of discrimination and social exclusion below which an individual is thought to be deprived."[4] Amartya Sen, Nobel Prize in Economics

"Individuals, families and groups in the population can be said to be in poverty when they lack the resources to obtain the types of diet, participate in the activities and have the living conditions and amenities which are customary, or are at least widely encouraged or approved, in the societies to which they belong."[5] Peter Townsend, *Poverty in the United Kingdom* (London, 1979)

An urban family in Brazil[6]

Pedrina da Costa Antonio, 55, is a single mother living in a slum in Paranaguá, south Brazil. Pedrina's first husband died; her second husband left her, along with their daughter, now aged 16. Pedrina has also adopted two abandoned children, five-year-old old girl and a 17-month-old toddler.

ILLUSTRATION 3 / Pedrina's family in their new house

As a widow, Pedrina receives a monthly allowance of 400 Brazilian reais (R$) ($179) from the state. She occasionally adds to this income by working as a cleaning woman, providing her with R$120 ($54) each month.[7]

Her house is made of plank boards and old wood. It was hurriedly and illegally built after Pedrina's previous house was destroyed in an accidental fire. It is connected to the electric and water grids, and to phone landlines. There are no sewers; waste water flows straight into a septic tank in the yard. Pedrina cooks on a wood stove, fuelled by old timber collected locally.

She struggles to pay $166 in monthly bills, over 60 percent of her average monthly income: $80 for utilities (electricity, water and telephone); $31 payable for seven years in order to become the legal owner of her house – her life dream; $54 to repay a loan. Fortunately, schooling and health are free public services – the nearby health center is quite crowded but the consultation is free.

This barely leaves $67, less than $2.3 a day to feed a family of four. This is a challenge when 1 kg of rice costs $0.7, beans $1.3 and 1 ltr of milk $0.8.

ILLUSTRATION 4 / **Pedrina and child in her new house**

TABLE 2 Pedrina's monthly P&L in current dollars[9]

Expenses		Income	
Food	67.3	Widow's pension	179.4
Loan repayments	53.8	Income (cleaning)	53.8
Electricity	31.4		
Housing (payments for land ownership)	31.4		
Phone	26.9		
Water	22.4		
Total	233.2	Total	233.2

Pedrina improves the family diet by collecting fruits and vegetables that the local supermarket throws away. Clothes and household goods are second-hand.

Pedrina considers she is better off than her parents, because at least she will own her land and house. She is also hopeful that her children will make a better living, because they are going to school.

If she had money, she would fix the roof, find a house for her mother, and pay the bills on time. She would love to open a children's day-care center, but has no idea how to make this dream come true.

Today, one in ten Brazilians live with equal or lesser earnings than Pedrina's family.[8] The United Nations estimates that by 2020 1.4 billion people will live in slums throughout the world.

MEASURING POVERTY

Metric

The complex reality of poverty is typically reduced by economists to one single number: daily consumption per capita measured in purchasing power parity (PPP) dollars.

To enable international comparisons, economists use the PPP exchange rate, i.e. "the rate at which the currency of one country would have to be converted into that of another country to buy the same amount of goods and services in each country."[10]

As these numbers change over time, economists have been using 2005 as the base year for all their calculations. When you read about the $2 poverty line, it refers to the purchasing power of $2 for someone living in the USA in 2005.

Continued

Continued

In addition to technical challenges in producing accurate statistics, this measure only takes into account the cash economy, without considering that, especially in rural areas, subsistence producers consume part of their own production.

Poverty lines and BoP

The bottom of the (economic) pyramid (BoP) designates the poorest group in a population, living below a certain level of income or poverty line.

To set objectives for poverty reduction, the World Bank has established two poverty lines:[11]

- Extreme poverty: $1.25 PPP 2005 per day
- Moderate poverty: $2 PPP 2005 per day

The size of the market of the BoP is estimated by Al Hammond in "The Next Four Billion" (2005) with the same metric, but at a level set to $3,000 per year:

- BoP: $8 PPP per day

Note: C. K. Prahalad had defined the BoP as consumers earning less than $1500 PPP per year.[12]

A rural Kenyan family[13]

Boniface Kinungi is 38 and lives in the village of Gatundu, Thika with his son Dennis Mari, 14, and his two daughters Irene Wanjiku, 12 and Winnie Wanjiru, 9. Their mother died five years ago.

Boniface works as a mason 20 days per month on average, making around $137.[14] He grows coffee on his one acre of land and sells his two harvests (200 kg of berries) to the local cooperative at $0.6 per kg, adding $8.5 per month.

The Kinungi family grows maize, beans and potatoes, but still spends over 75 percent of its cash on food bought from the local mini-shop. Usual meals are *ugali* (milled maize with vegetables, stew), *githeri* (a mixture of maize and beans), rice and *chapati* (flat bread, only during major holidays).

ILLUSTRATION 5 / Boniface's home and family

ILLUSTRATION 6 / The kitchen

The family cooks on a traditional three-stone stove, using firewood bought for $10 per month. A small lantern popularly known as a *karabai* is the only source of light in the house, burning $5 worth of kerosene each month.

There is a shared pipe for water but it runs dry most of the year. All family members fetch water from a river that is said to be clean, spending two hours a day carrying four containers of 20 ltr.

Education is very important to Boniface, who only went to primary school. Dennis failed to join secondary school and attends a youth vocational training centre. To pay for the $120 two-year program, Boniface took out a loan from a "*Ngumbato*" (a merry-go-round group where contributions from all members are pooled together as savings from which members borrow in turn, offering lower rates than banks). He pays back $7 per month.

The primary school that Irene and Winnie attend is free, but each child has to pay $9 per year for the private teachers employed by the school to cope with the lack of government-employed teachers. Other recurring expenses are transportation to the local market and phone expenses for Boniface to enquire about employment opportunities. Health issues cost $23 per year, while clothes are purchased at Christmas for about $23.

TABLE 3   Boniface's monthly P&L in current dollars

Household expenses		Household income	
Food (only cash part, maize, beans and potatoes come from Boniface garden)	114.2	Mason income	137.3
Energy (kerosene for lighting and firewood)	15.0	Coffee harvests (paid twice a year)	8.5
Debt servicing (for older child's education)	6.8		
Cell phone	2.3		
Travel	2.3		
Health	1.9		
Clothes (paid once per year)	1.9		
Education (teachers)	1.4		
Total	**145.8**		**145.8**

Notes: Average P&L – all non-monthly expenses or income have been computed annually, then divided by 12.

In addition to his land and house worth $4,300, Boniface owns a sheep that he rears for animal manure and eventual sale value. He plans to buy a grade milk cow to lower his expenses on milk ($4 per month) and sell the extra milk to processors. He hopes to save some of the $850 required to buy the cow – and to borrow the rest. His dream is to own ten dairy cows.

Today, approximately 55 percent of the Kenyan population is living at or below the income level of the Kinungi family.

DYNAMICS OF POVERTY

Since 1981, the proportion of people living below the $2 poverty line has been reduced from 55 percent to 35 percent of the world population but the number of poor people has barely been reduced from 2.6 to 2.3 billion. The real progress has been achieved by reducing the number of the extremely poor by 800 million.

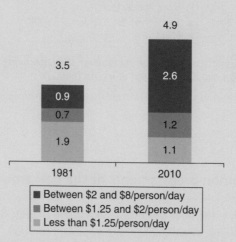

FIGURE 1 Global evolution of the poverty headcount between 1981 and 2010 (billion)

Source: World Bank (2009) *PovCalNet,* iresearch.worldbank.org/PovcalNet/povcalSvy.html.

Continued

Continued

China has been the primary positive factor behind these results: 30 years of close to double-digit growth have enabled the country to lift 700 million people out of poverty.

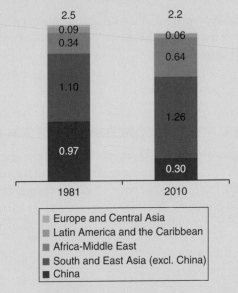

FIGURE 2 / Regional evolution of the number of people living with less than $2 PPP per day, between 1981 and 2010 (billion)

Source: World Bank (2009) *PovCalNet,* iresearch.worldbank.org/PovcalNet/povcalSvy.html.

The common predicaments of the BoP around the globe

As we have seen in the three portraits set out in this chapter, BoP communities are incredibly diverse. Mainly urban in Europe and the USA, they are mostly rural in Africa and Asia, although their urbanization is exponential.

Yet these families share a similar predicament, as they are trapped in poverty and excluded from the benefits of economic development. They are fairly representative of the nearly six billion people living at the BoP, comprising over 80 percent of the world population, and whom the solutions presented in this book attempt to serve.

Our three families represent different levels of poverty (measured in $ PPP 2005):

- Boghi's family lives in India with well under $1.25 per day per person, the upper limit of extreme poverty (they could become "moderately poor" if and when their cow produces milk).
- Boniface's family in Kenya lives with $2 per day per person, at the upper limit of moderate poverty.
- Pedrina's family lives in Brazil in the upper segment of the BoP, thanks to the state allowance.

TABLE 4   **Daily per capita income of BoP families**

Family	Per day (local currency)	$ 2014	$ PPP 2005
Boghi	20 Indian Rupees	0.3	1
Boniface	105 Kenyan Shilling	1.2	2
Pedrina	4.2 Brazilian Real	1.9	2.9

As we saw in the three family portraits, these poor families are also consumers. "The Next Four Billion" report led by Al Hammond estimated this market to be $5 trillion yearly in purchasing power parity (PPP).[15] This has grown according to 2010 estimates to over $6 trillion today,[16] a little more than the US consumer expenditures in PPP terms.[17]

As these family portraits show, families living at the BoP face four main obstacles within the walls of the poverty trap:

The poor generally pay more by unit of spending than those living at the higher levels of the pyramid

1. **They suffer from the "BoP penalty."** First, the poor generally pay more by unit of spending than those living at the higher levels of the pyramid. For instance, in the slums of Jakarta, people pay up to 60 times the official utility tariff for water sold by water vendors that serve their neighborhoods.[18] In rural Cambodia, poor households spend at least twice the amount every year on boiling water than what it would cost them to purchase a quality-certified filter.[19]
2. **They lack access to basic infrastructure and services.** More than two billion poor people still lack access to safe water, which has devastating health consequences, causing almost 2.5 million deaths per year.[20] 2.6 billion people do not have access to adequate sanitation; 1.25 billion people do not

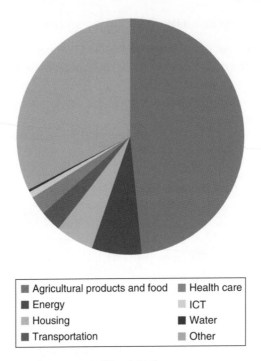

Legend:
- Agricultural products and food
- Health care
- Energy
- ICT
- Housing
- Water
- Transportation
- Other

FIGURE 3 / BoP spendings 2010 (million $ PPP)

have access to electricity;[21] 2.5 billion adults are unbanked.[22] Subsistence and small-scale farmers and fishermen do not have the capacity to protect themselves against adverse events and are extremely vulnerable to the depletion of the natural resources they depend upon.

3. **They are vulnerable to exploitation.** Small producers lack access to formal distribution channels, often having no choice but to sell their production to middlemen (*coyotes* in Mexico, *arthis* in Pakistan) who exploit them – indeed, as the latter finance the cash flows of operations, they have the power to convince farmers to supply them at the arbitrary price they fix. This is precisely the reason why Amul – a successful social business and the first Indian dairy industry – was created: "*remove middlemen*" was its first motto.[23]

4. **They are deprived of basic rights.** Close to one billion people live in slums, most of them with no legal ownership titles.[24] They cannot mobilize these assets as collateral and lack the incentives to invest in their homes. Most poor people do not receive paychecks (95 percent of the Indian workforce) as they are self-employed and are thus deemed ineligible to receive loans.

Government programs destined to hand out subsidies to the poor are confiscated by corrupt government officials because the poor lack proof of identity.

Given this situation, many have lost confidence in the future and in their own ability to change it. Caught in their day-to-day struggle for survival, they have no time to think about or plan for such an uncertain future. Yet many are still hopeful and ready to seize the opportunities that life will bring.

It is easy to feel compassion for these lives and share their sorrow. But the purpose of this book is to demonstrate how these problems can be turned into opportunities. Indeed, one can think of the poor as being surrounded by opportunities for improvement: this is how social entrepreneurs see them. Such social entrepreneurs are the focus of the next chapter.

chapter 2

Social entrepreneurs and "system change" strategies

A particular breed of entrepreneurs understands the systemic nature of the causes of poverty and has designed effective strategies to tackle them. While they may be tackling a particular issue, as we will see in this chapter (rural distribution for Satyan, property rights for André and intellectual property for Ron), they understand the complex, interwoven set of obstacles faced by the poor. The following stories of these three social entrepreneurs will make this argument better than we ever could.

Satyan – making goods and services accessible to rural communities

Satyan Mishra is the founder and CEO of Drishtee, a network of kiosks providing rural Indian communities (around 70 percent of India's population) access to products, financial and health services as well as secure internet-based services. The network as of 2014 counts 2000 internet kiosks and 14,000 retail points in three Indian states, serving close to 15 million people in rural communities.

Satyan's intense gaze shines behind his spectacles as he articulately connects the story of Drishtee with his own life:

> I was born in 1973 to a middle-class family of Bihar, where I spent my childhood in rural villages before moving to New Delhi for college. I started working in the stock market and wanted to become really rich. But in 1994, there was a major financial crash, and in one day, I lost everything.

ILLUSTRATION 7 / Satyan Mishra

When I started my MBA at Delhi University the following year, I knew that I wanted to do something different afterwards. I started an IT training company in Bhopal. Thanks to the IT boom, I was able to earn good money. In 2000, I had a car and a house and I did not need that much money any more. I happened to win a project from the government, called Gyandoot ("knowledge"), to set up rural kiosks for government services. It gave me the chance to go back to rural villages. It was like coming back home.

Gyandoot made me realize that access in general was a fundamental issue for these communities. I thought that technology could provide such access and I was really keen to see how it could play a catalyst role.

However, many state-led initiatives like Gyandoot – setting up ICT centers for the masses – failed because the government simply gave out equipment instead of focusing on the value of the actual services. I thus realized that the approach needed to be bottom-up, customer driven. We learnt from the community what they really wanted.

It took us three years to realize that the main challenge faced by our clients, such as the family of Bhogi Mukhiya, was a lack of access to quality products at affordable prices. Because they are far from urban centers, they have to pay a "BoP penalty" coming from multiple intermediaries and inef-ficient transport and supply chains. Once we provided easier access to prized consumer goods, we quickly became commercially and socially viable. The core idea remains solving the access issue for rural people, yet the range of services, now community-focused, has changed.

If I relied on grants, I could only go so far before I run out of money. Philanthropy does not create entrepreneurs proud of their own business. It tends to make you think more about what your grant partners want than what your customers want.

My dream at the end of my life is to have kick-started sustainable communities who can experience the same type of growth as the richer parts of the country. I don't have the full path ready – I'm just taking it step by step and seeing where life takes me to achieve this goal.[25]

André – mediating land title disputes

André Albuquerque created Terra Nova in Brazil in 2001 to solve conflicts between landowners and illegal dwellers. Terra Nova works closely with all stakeholders – landowners, squatters and government authorities – to settle through mediation conflicts deadlocked in the courts.

Philanthropy does not create entrepreneurs proud of their own business

ILLUSTRATION 8 / **André Albuquerque**

Landowners receive fair compensation for their property, informal dwellers acquire land titles through affordable monthly installments, and government agencies avoid costly and never-ending land expropriation procedures, and use public funds more effectively to address municipal development needs.

In 2012, ten years after its inception, Terra Nova had reached more than 22 communities and over 12,000 families across three states of Brazil (Paraná, São Paulo and Rondônia). André wants to replicate Terra Nova's methodology in several other developing countries before 2020.[26]

André speaks in Brazilian Portuguese with such heart and passion that his vision of reconciliation and harmony becomes as enticing as the tempo of samba:

> I was born in 1966 in Curitiba, Paraná. I've always been very active – I have always felt like an entrepreneur. I grew up with the sense that I was on Earth to make a difference to the lives of my fellow Brazilians.
>
> As a young boy, I had the reputation of being a conflict mediator by nature. After a law degree and studies in urban and environmental management, I began working for the Housing Secretariat of Pinhais (Paraná). There, I played a central role in developing the mediation of conflicts between landowners and squatter communities on behalf of the city administration. Life had driven me to land regularization. I realized it was a cause I could carry on working for to make my dream come true and trigger social change in people's lives. Convinced that the energies used for conflict could be turned into positive energy for the community, I created Terra Nova.
>
> The best way to assure that people's living standards really improve is to make them realize they have the power to change them themselves. No change can be real and lasting if it comes from the outside.
>
> The Terra Nova approach is different because we provide people with opportunities and make them part of the process of change. When someone takes part in a process of regularization, they have to contribute financially. This contribution is key to empowering individuals; it proves to them that they can do things for themselves. It not only gives them a property right that they were deprived of so far, but it also builds back dignity and confidence in the fact that they can change things.

*I created Terra Nova as a business because when social
change is a business – and a profitable one – a lot
more external resources can be gathered than in
philanthropy. People realize that by investing
resources they can both act for good and get
fair returns on their investment.*[27]

Ron – fighting for the intellectual property of small farmers

Born in New Zealand to a family of civil servants and social workers, Ron started his career as a civil servant in economic development, working in a remote part of the Pacific where he discovered the need for developing countries to overcome isolation and weak negotiating positions. Choosing to train in the business methods of intellectual property (IP) ventures by forming his own company, he built skills over 15 years as an IP businessman. In 2001, he founded Light Years IP, a nonprofit organization with the goal to help large groups of poor, small producers in Africa to reposition themselves by using IP to improve their export income.

ILLUSTRATION 9 / Ron Layton

Ron's laid-back style and charming Kiwi accent when he talks about rugby (which happens often) quickly fade away when he gets involved in an intellectual debate (which happens even more often):

> I was influenced by both my parents regarding the importance of public service. It was entrenched in them to see what they could do for others, and I learnt from that.

> When I was 15, I became a social activist as part of the New Zealand anti-apartheid movement, and in 1972 I stood for parliament with a small group of activists in the first "green" party of New Zealand.

> In 1975 I joined the New Zealand foreign service and, in 1977, asked to be seconded to the government of Niue, a minuscule Pacific island nation. My role was to initiate development, to find something that worked and develop the country's economy. While I was working there, I realized that such a country in geographic isolation can't trade in markets for commodities, because those markets don't cover the cost of shipping small quantities by sea – the only way to overcome isolation is to sell higher-value products and reposition producers to capture some of that higher value in the same way as a producing corporation would position itself. So I turned to study intellectual property (IP) as an element in this positioning for Niue. Niue licensed unique designs and denominations for the philatelic market, which earned it export income without being limited by high shipping costs.

> My professional life has been driven by this awareness of the business skills needed to help the most isolated, such as African producers over 500 miles from the nearest port. The isolated farmers that I work with today are like islands; geographic isolation means that they can't live off their products unless we make sure they can capture the intangible value generated by the products at retail and not just their international commodity market price.

> Fine coffee farmers living in western Ethiopia have suffered from their coffee beans earning only the world commodity coffee export price and the cost of shipment to port taking up a large share of the export price. Until 2007, the Ethiopian coffee export sector could not negotiate to secure a share of the high retail price generated by their fine coffee.

> Ethiopia makes many of the best coffees in the world, which retail for about five times as much as commodity Arabica coffee, meaning that there is a lot of intangible value paid by consumers due to the superior taste, body and other elements valued by consumers. The country of origin of these

fine coffees, and in particular the farmers, needed to capture a share of this intangible value. By using corporate methods, Ethiopia could increase negotiating power. Ethiopia was helped to take control of the retail brands of the three most valuable coffees and to take some control of distribution of the coffees from import to retail stores in developed countries, including the USA and Japan and in Europe.

Ethiopia earned an extra $200 million over the first three years of brand-owning, without increasing production. This is why I created Light Years IP in 2000, and what I am striving to replicate in other large initiatives for isolated African producers of high-quality products valued by global consumers.[28]

* * *

Satyan, Ron and André have devoted their lives to helping the poor get out of the poverty trap. They are "social entrepreneurs." Even though such entrepreneurs come from all walks of life (business, citizen sector, aid agencies, governments) they share some essential characteristics. They:

- Trust in the ability of the poor to transform their lives if given the opportunity to do so. They see the poor as being surrounded by attractive investment opportunities and focus on tackling the external conditions that prevent them from activating these opportunities.
- Start without any resources but for their energy and networks. They recognize they will not be able to buy their way out of the problem and have to be creative in leveraging the key stakeholders (government, corporations and so on) that control the resources they need. They are thus able to create win–win relationships within their "ecosystem."
- Focus on solving a problem (such as health), not promoting a solution nor building an institution. This makes them agile and ready to partner with others who share the same goal.
- Choose carefully the strategy and means for reaching scale while maximizing impact. While for some this is about operating social enterprises that scale directly, for many others it is about playing the role of a market enabler who operates as a nonprofit organization. Increasingly, social entrepreneurs use hybrid approaches and focus their scaling strategy on changing the mindsets of key industry players.

Satyan, Ron and André have all been elected Ashoka Fellows, which was the first and is now the largest and most preeminent community of social entrepreneurs in the world. We will introduce many other social entrepreneurs in the pages that follow, whose life stories, similarly, cannot be separated from the solutions they have designed. Whilst they undoubtedly have strong personalities, their lives also point to the fact that individuals, and each of us, can indeed change the world.

chapter 3

Why focus on market-based social innovations?

This book has been "in the works" since 2008. At that time, "business" approaches and "market-based" forces were all the rage. Development aid was deemed "fatal,"[29] and "philanthrocapitalists" were welcomed as the new saviors.[30] One major financial crisis later, government intervention is back with a vengeance and capitalism has turned from a superhero into a villain to be rehabilitated with a healthy dose of regulation.

Bearing that in mind, the authors of this book are pressed to be humble in pretending not to be influenced or unbiased while taking a stance to answer the question: "why (still) focus on market-based social innovations?"

Many believe that it is wrong to hope that market forces will promote social change. Right-wing critics challenge whether business should worry about these issues. Milton Friedman famously stated that the "business of business is business."

Left-wing critics doubt whether business can really solve the problems that they think were created by business in the first place. While acknowledging the dynamism of business, they think it is misguided. They point out that short-termism and the dictatorship of capital markets make business a rampaging behemoth that is destroying the planet without thinking about tomorrow. A heartless one also, as the limitations of business approaches are clear: reducing human interactions to what can be monetized leaves aside what are probably the strongest motivations of mankind – love, patriotism, desire for recognition – as well as some of its most potent levers such as social capital and collaboration.

Indeed, many of the largest-scale changes in society have nothing to do with "market forces," but with the willingness of people to fight for their loved ones, for what they believe is right. The fights for democracy, for women's rights and against apartheid have changed the world. Yet it doesn't seem practical to create such global movements to promote specific solutions to the large number of development issues the world faces, from providing poor people with access to safe water to enhanced cookstoves, reading glasses or fair markets for their produces. Providing tailored solutions to specific problems is what market-based approaches are good at, as individual entrepreneurs focus on each specific issue, design innovative strategies, raise social and financial capital and focus on making change happen.

We also wish to stress that this book is about how to make markets work for the poor, not about effective government and democracy, two very important topics that we do not feel qualified to address. This is not to say that governments cannot have a huge influence on markets by creating enabling conditions. In Chapter 5, we describe how IDCOL, a Bangladeshi government entity, has played a fundamental role in promoting the development of a local solar home system industry that serves over one million families with a combination of effective subsidies, concessional finance and quality standards.

This book is about how to make markets work for the poor

Such catalytic government interventions are unfortunately as rare as they are impactful. We will see that in most of the cases reviewed in this book, entrepreneurs have not waited for governments to create ideal situations: they have managed to work within the existing – or slightly modified – political and regulatory frameworks. While a wholesome reform of rights would be a very welcome happenstance, pragmatic entrepreneurs have found smart ways to get around these constraints and still enable the poor to gain access to essential services. Patrimonio Hoy (see Chapter 6) manages to sell home improvement packages on credit to illegal residents in slums. Manila Water (see Chapter 7) negotiated with local governments to be allowed to provide water services to illegal residents in Manila slums.

The two most important reasons why market-based solutions are worth investigating are that they are *scalable* and *empower* the poor.

Scalability

The sheer scale of the problems the world faces requires financial resources that only market-based, economically sustainable approaches can hope to reach. Such scale is simply beyond what taxpayers and philanthropists can muster.

In 2010 a group of executives in a major building material company was discussing whether their "affordable housing to the BoP" program should be considered as a philanthropic or a business initiative for the company. Conservative estimates of the global housing deficit pointed to a need for the refurbishment or construction of 180 million homes from 2010 to 2020, for a total annual financial cost in the order of €72 billion.[31] So if this company chose to address 1 percent of this deficit through charity (which may seem grossly insufficient for a leading global player in the sector) it would require spending €720 million per year, or over 70 percent of its total net profit.

With "economically sustainable" operations (that not only reach operational break-even, but also cover their cost of capital), necessary funds can be sourced from capital markets, avoiding the dependency on limited philanthropic resources or taxpayer money.

Deciding *not* to rely on market-based forces implies having to choose which poor people will be saved and which will not. This moral dilemma is generally brushed away by CSOs who prefer to focus on the ones they save and stay within the moral comfort of not "making money off the back of the poor." Yet it is difficult to leave the moral high ground to programs that deliberately exclude a majority of the people in need.[32]

Empowerment

Treating the poor like customers who have a choice (and not as the lucky beneficiaries of charity) ensures they feel empowered and respected. Having to "sell" a product to the poor ensures that this product corresponds to their needs and wants. This is not the case when products are given away. For instance, philanthropists prefer to pay for new installations of hand pumps as opposed to building a sustainable solution for maintenance and spare parts provision. It is estimated that out of the 600,000 to 800,000 hand pumps installed in sub-Saharan Africa over the past 20 years, approximately one-third are nonfunctional, resulting in a total failed investment of more than $1 billion.[33]

What is given away is also typically not valued. For example, it is this lack of accountability that plagues the thousands of free toilets built in Asia that were never used as such but immediately "recycled" as henhouses and storage; or the hundreds of social housing units that remain empty in flood-struck Pakistan. Because the goods were given away, the "needs and wants" of their future users were less (if at all) relevant. While the truth is, even slum dwellers value their neighborhood as much as a roof over their heads. Without the friend next door to look after the kids, and the relative to share a drive to work with, moving house – even for cheap and high-quality accommodation – becomes a lot less attractive. If suppliers of products and services see the poor as customers to be served, then they will compete against each other for better service and lower cost, fostering innovation and productivity gains that the poor will ultimately benefit from.

Lastly, using public and philanthropic resources to tackle issues that could be addressed by market-based mechanisms is not only structurally limited in impact, and inefficient in designing appropriate solutions: it is also morally wrong. Funds from taxpayers and donors are dramatically needed in fields where government or charity actions are indeed the only solution: in public services such as education and health, and where and when local economies have been destroyed, by disasters of human or natural origins. Social entrepreneurs have no business trying to sell their products after a tsunami, nor in a refugee camp; similarly, it makes no sense for a charity to be "dumping" goods and services on people who could afford to pay for them. Not relying on market-based mechanism represents a cost of opportunity for humanitarian action.

* * *

In the chapters that follow, we will see that market-based solutions start from the apparent paradox that poor people are surrounded by attractive investment opportunities.

For a family that lives with less than $8 a day, *spending* does not always mean *increased consumption* but can also rhyme with *shrewd investments in productivity* or *cost savings*. While buying a bicycle may be an act of consumption for the rich, it is an investment for the poor that will increase their productivity and income. This is what leads us to argue that the poor are surrounded by lucrative investment opportunities. Many of the products they currently do not possess (such as water purifiers, solar lanterns, eye glasses and so on) would make a big difference in their ability to save money or generate income. This begs the following question: if such attractive investment opportunities do exist, why don't poor people capture them?

A range of other systemic obstacles impede these decisions: lack of access to the products, bad quality, lack of knowledge, absence of credit, uncertainty about the future, lack of property rights, expectation of free help and so on. These systemic obstacles are the walls of the poverty trap.

Innovative entrepreneurs have cracked these walls. Chapters 4 to 8 describe some of the most successful solutions that have been developed for five key needs of BoP families: cooking, lighting, housing, water and financial services. Each of these chapters describes market-based solutions that work and analyzes the obstacles that prevent them from being scaled up and replicated. This selection is based on our expertise of five domains that we have studied in depth between 2008 and 2014, analyzing over 1000 projects across the world.[34]

In Chapter 9, we will see how market-based approaches can increase the income of the BoP by improving productivity and enabling fair market access to micro-entrepreneurs, and by offering fair employment to disadvantaged segments of the population.

Undoubtedly, these solutions are still far from covering all existing problems (Chapter 10 focuses on their limitations), but the various solutions set out in the coming chapters are already extensive enough to prove the size of the opportunity: in terms of gaining new markets, improving or creating products and services, and improving the lives of billions.

4

Cooking

However little there is to put in the pot, all families have to cook. In many different places all over the world, to braise, broil and boil food, open fireplaces are fueled with some form of biomass: wood, charcoal or dry cow dung. This traditional practice, which seems to define humanity, is possibly one of its most devastating. Close to three billion people spend a share of their daily schedule or income in obtaining this cooking biomass: in India, for example, biomass represents more than 5 percent of household expenditures – and that is not even including the time spent collecting "free" biomass, with women and girls gathering wood for two to three hours each day.[35] Worse still, cooking on an open fire creates toxic fumes, causing asthma and other respiratory diseases. According to the World Health Organization, indoor air pollution kills over four million people each year, mainly women and children – more than malaria does![36]

Cookstoves cost from $5 to $35, which is paid back by fuel savings in less than six months

Yet there are simple and cheap solutions to avoid these deaths, free-up the time spent on gathering fuel, and reduce pressure on the environment; improved cookstoves that reduce by 30–50 percent the quantity of biomass used and by up to 98 percent the emission of toxic fumes. These cookstoves cost from $5 to $35, which is paid back by fuel savings in less than six months.

Several organizations have developed such cookstoves, selling several millions of them over the last decade. Some – such as First Energy or Envirofit – rely on central manufacturing of modern cookstoves that are then distributed in multiple countries through CSOs or traditional hardware distributors. Others – such as Toyola – have set up entirely local value chains, training and employing local people in using locally available materials to build the stoves, which are then sold through local channels.

First Energy

It is appropriate to start this chapter with BP Oorja as it is the brainchild of the late C. K. Prahalad, who started discussions with BP top management and convinced John Browne, the CEO who had crafted the "Beyond Petroleum" vision of BP, to engage in a groundbreaking initiative to capture the "Fortune at the Base of the Pyramid." BP selected an international team of high-flying executives who worked with Prahalad and his team of consultants, called TNP (The Next Practice), and gave them six months and a budget to come up with a new business idea to provide energy access to the "underserved" through a profitable and sustainable business model – and plans to turn it into reality.

Roberto Bocca, now with the World Economic Forum, was the leader of this BP team. He recalls: "We spent five months exploring the market to define what our model would be. We stayed in rural villages, observing how the people cooked, their habits and behaviors in energy consumption, doing all of the social and ethnographic research that was very rarely done by large companies back then."[37] The team partnered with the Indian Institute of Science to further develop an exciting device, found lying on a shelf: an enhanced cookstove that could improve fuel efficiency and drastically cut toxic fumes emission. They decided to set up the BP Emerging Consumers Business that commercialized its product with the brand Oorja ("oorja" means "energy" in Hindi). Avik Roy, now a Hystra network partner and managing director of Re-emerging World, was part of C. K. Prahalad consulting practice and he recalls how they worked with local CSOs, a pioneering move for BP at that time: "CSOs helped us all along the project, their role evolving at each step. They were first a perfect intermediary in the local communities to get the product right, then a crucial bridge in creating and keeping the trust with local communities (and also a buffer, a shock absorber when things were not perfect...), and finally our distribution partner."[38]

The commercial launch took place in 2006. It started with three home models sold for between $15 and $30: today only two models are sold, for $40 and $50. They all run on pellets of compacted agricultural waste. Roberto Bocca explains: "This was an innovation: we were providing an integrated offer, not just the stove but also a fuel made from locally available material, with no need for an expensive supply chain and imported products." This system also incentivizes stove sellers as they could expect recurring sales of pellets. The team also innovated to overcome what they had learnt to be one of the major challenges for operations: distribution in rural areas. "The selling model was also unique at that time for a large company: we trained 'village entrepreneurs' to do the sales, marketing and maintenance, basically being our ambassadors in the village."

In 2007, John Browne's sudden departure marked the end of the "Beyond Petroleum" era. Roberto recalls: "BP had invested a considerable amount in it because it believed this could become a profitable business with significant positive impact for both society and the environment. Unfortunately, with the change in leadership within BP, the emerging consumer business was not considered strategic any more and we were asked to discontinue it." So BP sold the Oorja brand and activity to its Indian management team and additional partners, and in 2009 it became First Energy.

Thanks to its strong local distribution network and a vast initial marketing campaign, the company sold nearly 40,000 cookstoves in the financial year 2010 (for a total of 450,000 since inception). Since 2010, in order to reach break-even more rapidly, First Energy has also been renting stoves to restaurants, which pay the price of fuel and a small fee (around $20) for usage. First Energy takes care of all the maintenance and upgrades. It sells 30,000 tonnes of pellets per year, resulting in a global annual turnover of $2 million. The company's activities have been profitable since April 2012.

Envirofit

Envirofit is another model of a centralized manufacturing entity selling cookstoves, this time based in the rich world. A nonprofit organization started in 2003 in the USA, it has developed a range of high-efficiency clean-burning stoves selling for $15 to $35 in India, Nepal, Pakistan, the Philippines, Peru, Honduras, Guatemala and several African countries (including Kenya, Tanzania and Uganda). Envirofit extensively tests its products in the lab and then in the field to make sure it "finds and fixes problems before they become your problems."[39]

Envirofit managed to sell over 700,000 units by the end of 2013, thanks to various distribution networks, the most efficient being traditional hardware distributors. Envirofit also partners with CSOs, governments and microfinance institutions (MFIs) to conduct awareness campaigns to spread the word about its products and sell them.

When consumers spend $10 on an Envirofit stove, they save 50 percent of money spent on fuel and/or time collecting it. Moreover, the stove lasts several times longer than traditional stoves.

Envirofit is betting a lot on carbon credits to improve its financials (more about this later in this chapter). The accreditation is in process with Eco-Securities. Sales are expected to become profitable once revenues from carbon payments kick in.

Toyola

Central manufacturing with external distributors is only one way to provide the BoP with efficient cooking solutions. Toyola, a small Ghanaian business, has instead chosen to create a local integrated value chain from stove manufacturing to last-mile distribution. Toyola is leveraging a network of existing craftspeople to manufacture $8 to $12 cookstoves that are then distributed through local entrepreneurs. Only the ceramic lining – the key component for quality – is manufactured by Toyola. Employing specialist artisans in the production of specific components has increased their productivity by 500 percent.

In terms of marketing, the powerful strategy of Toyola relies on word of mouth to turn satisfied early adopters into "evangelists": generally women who collect and regroup orders from their village and surrounding ones.

For the poorest of its clients, Toyola has designed the "Toyola box." This recycled metal can is left with the client with the following recommendation: "tomorrow you will find out you have some charcoal left, so instead of giving money to your child to go and buy charcoal at the local shop, just put these coins in the little box." Sales agents typically come back to pick up the box within three months, by which time the full cost of the stove has been saved on fuel as the cookstoves use 40 percent less charcoal than traditional stoves. This allows customers to purchase the stove without taking out a loan. Toyola now sells 90 percent of products with such flexible paperless arrangements, with an end customer repayment rate of 95 percent.[40] However, this requires working capital and it was only when Toyola got its first loan that it could start giving flexible payment terms, which made its sales jump from 3000 to 20,000 items in a year. Many Toyola clients could actually pay cash, but this deferred payment allows them to make sure that their stove works as well as the one used in the demonstration by the very persuasive salesperson.

Toyola has expanded to several other West African countries and is now selling about 100,000 stoves per annum, generating over $1 million in revenue, and an attractive profit margin.

INTERVIEW WITH SURAJ WAHAB, CO-FOUNDER OF TOYOLA

ILLUSTRATION 10 / Suraj Wahab

As a kid I used to go around selling fish door-to-door, and I was selling around three times what my mother could sell at the shop. So you could say that door-to-door marketing is my background. That's how I knew how to train my sellers. Advertising, TV or radio cannot effectively reach people: if you want to introduce something new in this environment, you need to give people the opportunity to ask questions.

My mother borrowed money to send me to school, and she was always very careful about repaying. That's how I was later sure that my clients would repay me. We do not ask for legal documents: in Africa social pressure works best. Some people pay late but they always pay. I never had default.

We Africans know the solutions to our own problems, but we lack financing to make it happen. I had this loan from E+Co:[41] I'm sure many others could have done the same if they had had the same opportunity.

Obstacles to scale and replication

Even though various affordable models exist for improved cookstoves, 73 percent of people who use solid fuels to cook still rely on open fires or traditional cookstoves. What is preventing the practical solutions described above to cover the close to three billion people who need them today?

1. **Lack of awareness and trust:** people are not aware of the risk that the fumes generated by old-fashioned stoves represent for their health. Even when they are aware, people often do not realize that alternatives exist. Shell Foundation conducted a study in southern India that found that only 10 percent of respondents spontaneously mentioned improved cookstoves as a way to reduce smoke from cooking.[42] Most respondents were unsure about how to use them, and would need to see them work for long enough before believing their benefits and durability.

2. **Lack of cash:** clients require a way to finance the $5 to $35 investment needed to buy cookstoves. Most clients do not have access to MFIs, which would likely turn down the request for a loan, as a cookstove is not considered to be a productive investment.

3. **Lack of technical capabilities:** producing efficient cookstoves at scale requires technical capabilities that are rarely found in developing countries. Overcoming these obstacles adds expensive training costs to the investments of local companies.

4. **Lack of cost-efficient last-mile distributors:** reaching remote rural areas adds significant logistic costs to products that are already sold on small margins, forcing retailers to increase the price for end users in order to remain profitable.

Yet the first three of these four key issues have found answers or are on their way to being solved.

1. **Awareness and quality certification** can be created by branded campaigns, both making the product aspirational and explaining its benefits. The marketing campaign of BP Oorja, (now First Energy) over two years explains its current success. Toyola pays specific attention to its early adopters to make them "evangelists" of the product, naturally promoting it to their acquaintances and turning them into the next generation of distributors. Recognizing the urgency for scaling up these solutions, former US Secretary of State Hillary Clinton launched the Global Alliance for Clean Cookstoves in 2010, a public–private partnership that includes Shell, the US government and the UN Foundation and aims at selling 100 million cookstoves by 2020.

The initiative is in the process of creating global standards and labels such as "Room to Breathe," which is awarded to stoves that reduce fuel use by over 40 percent, emissions by over 55 percent, and come with at least one year of guarantee, timely delivery and local servicing.[43] Yet all these efforts would probably be trumped by a well-known consumer brand willing to endorse the cookstoves.

2. **Access to credit** has been provided by some entrepreneurs through third-party partners who can provide credit (MFIs, cooperatives and so on). Some of Envirofit's local distributors are partnering with MFIs or have set up their own financing schemes in order to increase their sales. Market research led by Shell Foundation found that the most cost-effective way to market cookstoves was indeed to do it through MFIs, associating a stove promoter with a loan officer who will immediately be able to offer the corresponding loan, achieving a marketing cost of $4 per cookstove sold. Other manufacturers are providing credit themselves, which means transferring the financing need to their own books. Distributors then pass it on to their clients, raising the price of the stoves by a few dollars in exchange of credit payment terms (see Chapter 14 for more on marketing and financing).

3. **Building technical capabilities** has already been taken on by CSOs, philanthropists or governments. For instance, the initial training by the CSO Enterprise Works, as well as the loan funding provided by E+Co, has allowed Toyola to train its more than 200 local workforce as needed in order to manufacture 50,000 to 100,000 stoves per year.

As we can see, there are practical solutions to overcome the obstacles to replication of these improved cookstoves. Furthermore, a major breakthrough could dramatically accelerate their spread: carbon credits. Carbon credits are certificates or permits representing the right to emit one tonne of carbon dioxide or equivalent: projects that reduce carbon emissions can claim such credits and sell them to third parties who need these credits to cover their own carbon emissions. Indeed, an efficient cookstove is estimated to save over one tonne of carbon emissions per year. A number of cookstove projects have registered to receive carbon payments.[44] As each stove, costing as low as $8, can generate around $20 of carbon credit in its lifetime, there is vast potential to pass on some of these benefits to customers, and allow its wider spread.

We Africans know the solutions to our own problems, but we lack the financing to make it happen

It took Toyola two years, close to $200,000 and the support of energy investment fund E+Co to register under the Gold Standard, a high-quality carbon credit certification, which had already allowed the selling of more than 51,000 tonnes of carbon credits in February 2011.[45] Some companies are working as facilitators and aggregators for carbon credits. C-Quest Capital, a carbon investment company focused on creating and supporting energy companies that provide energy to the poor, is now working in Nigeria on what could be the largest cookstove carbon program in the world. Yet it's a risky business requiring high upfront investment, as explained by CEO Ken Newcombe:

> *We are paid only on the carbon credits earned by the companies we work with. In Nigeria, by the time we get the registration (in 2012) we'll have spent over two years and $1.5 million before selling stoves. It will then take another 18 months before we receive any money from carbon credits. Carbon prices need to be high enough, firstly to reimburse all these initial costs, and secondly to pay for the difference between the stove costs and what people are ready to pay for them... We need at least $30 of carbon benefits per stove. The amount we effectively get depends on the efficiency of the stove we select, on how much it is used, on whether we can find it, and on the price of carbon – which is the big uncertainty. Prices of certified emission reduction units (CERs) in the EU Emissions Trading Scheme should reach and remain at or above $8/CER over the medium to long term to make this kind of cookstove project viable. Under these conditions, the carbon market can provide an extraordinary opportunity to bring private capital to deliver services to the poor.[46]*

* * *

With all the good fairies surrounding the enhanced cookstove, one can hope that it will flourish and reach the hundreds of millions of families who need one. As we can see, the two obstacles that remain in the way of a rapid spread of enhanced cookstoves are:

1. The ability to effectively leverage carbon credit mechanisms, namely the predictability of the price of carbon credits and the simplicity of the certification process.
2. The existence of effective "last-mile" distributors able to promote, finance and maintain these devices.

We address this last issue in Part 2 of this book.

5

chapter

Lighting

Nearly 20 percent of the world's population, 1.3 billion people, live without electricity, most of them in rural sub-Saharan Africa, India, Bangladesh and Pakistan.[47] In addition, one billion more suffer from very poor service from the local electric utility, with frequent electricity cuts that plague cities in the developing world.

Traditional kerosene lamps, candles and batteries for lanterns are ineffective, expensive and unsafe. Staying in an un-electrified rural village, one can experience the immediate idleness that grips the village when the sun sets, wasting four precious hours of work, or of homework for children who struggle to read under the pale flame of a small wick. Lighting also means improved safety and comfort.

Conventional solutions to bring electricity to the unlit – as in investing in generation and connecting distant villages to electricity grids – would take a long time and require a staggering investment of $665 billion, or six times the total amount of annual international official development aid.[48] Yet this may be the only solution to provide cheap electricity in amounts sufficient not only to cater for lighting but also to power fans, fridges, air conditioning and machines.

In the meantime, however, innovative entrepreneurs have designed reliable and environmentally sustainable solutions to provide lighting to BoP families, at a price actually lower than candles or kerosene lamps. Some of these entrepreneurs address individual household needs by selling solar home systems (such as SELCO and Grameen Shakti) or solar lanterns (such as d.light), while others provide collective village mini-grid solutions (such as HPS). In this chapter we will also look at the obstacles they face in order to scale up and replicate.

SELCO – or the power of patient local value chains

Bringing electricity to rural families through individual solar home systems (SHSs) has been a long-time dream. The typical SHS consists of a solar panel, a battery, four lamps and a 12V plug that can recharge a cell phone and even power a TV. Conventional development wisdom was that the poor could obviously not afford the investment required, but that they should be able to pay for the low running cost of maintenance and change of battery.[49] Well-meaning foundations and aid agencies have given away SHSs across the world, convinced that a one-time gift would then allow for sustainable lighting over the years. The awakening was sobering. Organizations that went back to their beneficiaries a year or two after having installed SHSs found out that they had stopped working for lack of care by their users or unavailability of proper maintenance; or they had disappeared, having been stolen or sold.[50] Additionally, these programs discouraged entrepreneurs from setting up solar businesses.

A few pioneers believed that it was only by *selling* SHSs to the poor that the service could become sustainable. These pioneers and their solutions have been around since the 1990s and yet only a few years ago many "experts" of rural electrification and solar practitioners in large energy multinationals had never heard of them. In 2009, we interviewed three leading Western players (a manufacturer, a foundation and an aid agency) who had been involved for years in rural electrification programs in Africa. They were all convinced that the only available solution was a $1000 SHS that had to be given away, given its price. They were simply not *aware* of the existence of economically sustainable SHS models that had been selling in the hundreds of thousands for $300 to poor families in India and Bangladesh.

One of the pioneers selling SHSs is Harish Hande, an Indian engineer who founded SELCO in 1995. Harish turned the mainstream logic on its head, starting from how much his target customers were currently spending every month in kerosene and candles. He then figured out they could afford to buy a $300 SHS with a credit, with monthly installments that would be equivalent to their current monthly expenses. At that price, he could provide a high-quality solution that would give his clients four to five hours of lighting at night. The price reduction came from a smaller battery and PV panel. As a result, the system needed to be recharged every day and would not be able to produce electricity on the few days of the year when it was so cloudy that the panel could not work. On these days, the customers had simply to revert to their old kerosene lamps.

One of SELCO's other innovations – that would scare most managers of large corporations for its operational complexity – is that the installation of SHSs is locally tailor-made. Technicians spend time with clients discussing where to install the lamps in each room.

To reach their current 45 percent penetration of households, SELCO relies on patient marketing tactics that focus on "early adopters" (small local businesses in the marketplace that make the product highly visible), demonstration effect (demonstration devices in schools, clinics or in the homes of religious or political leaders) and "word of mouth" to convince poorer and more risk-averse customers.

Harish also solved the maintenance issue that plagued the subsidized programs. SELCO set up 38 service centers in rural India, each with at least two technicians who visit customers every three to six months. Maintenance fees vary with the client or the circumstances. This flexibility would seriously trouble any normal auditor but is a key success factor in cases where it is hard to build trust within a highly risk-averse community. Ensuring a superior after-sales service is paramount when your marketing strategy relies on word of mouth.

An SHS would enable a typical family to save $5–6 per month in kerosene, candles and batteries – the amount of the monthly repayments requested by SELCO. The $300 investment and even subsequent battery replacements (around $50 every five to eight years) become economically justified even for poor clients.

However, most of SELCO target customers did not have the cash readily available and needed a financing solution adapted to their informal situation (absence of collateral, informal and irregular revenues without proof of income). Harish finally succeeded in convincing 42 rural banks to provide credit: "Some people cannot even afford the 15 percent upfront payment and need a credit on the full price. So we created a fund that guarantees the loan on the additional 15 percent."

Nineteen years after inception, 90 percent of sales are made on credit, with repayment rates of 90–98 percent, testifying to the satisfaction experienced by clients. This makes SELCO a profitable company. It has raised $1.4 million on the basis of a business plan targeting 200,000 new customers within four years, and is now earning $3 million in revenue per year, with a net margin of 5–8 percent entirely reinvested in its business.

As of 2013, SELCO has installations in more than 135,000 households, 80 percent of them rural, in five Indian states.

Grameen Shakti – creating an entire industry

In Bangladesh, Grameen Shakti has done even better. With nearly 1.5 million SHSs installed as of June 2014, Grameen Shakti can rightly proclaim to be amongst the largest inclusive businesses in the world. The organization employs 13,000 people and has built a network of 1300 village branches.

Run as a not-for-profit company (all profits are reinvested in the business), Grameen Shakti has developed an end-user finance solution of its own, without attempting to work through its sister company, Grameen Bank. To purchase a 50W system powering four lamps, cell phones and a TV, a Grameen Shakti customer has the option of paying cash or making a down payment with monthly installments for three years, which covers a monthly mainte-nance visit. Interestingly, the 15 percent implied interest rate is not visible to clients as Grameen Shakti communicates its price as a 6 percent annual service charge over the amount of the loan.

In Bangladesh, several companies are now replicating the Grameen Shakti model. Rahimafrooz, the main Bangladeshi battery manufacturer, notably got into the business in 2006, achieved break-even in as little as six months and is now fully profitable, with more than 440,000 SHSs installed and sales of around 6000 units per month.

Overall, SELCO, Grameen Shakti and their followers have profitably sold over 1.5 million SHSs, a success that demonstrates the power of customer-focused and innovative entrepreneurs. And sales are still accelerating. The penetration rate of SHS into the addressable markets (as in where companies are present) is now estimated at 45 percent.

Obstacles to scale and replication of SHS

What is needed to replicate these very successful models throughout the world?

Phil LaRocco, the founder (1994) and retired CEO (2009) of E+Co, a social investment fund for energy that played a pioneering role in the sector, answers this question with a smile: "The only thing you need is to find more Harish

Handes."[51] SELCO and E+Co decided to give this solution a try and worked on an incubation program to train the next generation of entrepreneurs and take the SELCO model to new Indian states and beyond.

Yet the SHS approach might not work so well in other parts of the world. The key conditions of this success lie in the specific business environment of South and Southeast Asia: (1) a densely populated area that enables a maintenance team to serve more than 1000 families within a 25–100 km radius;[52] (2) a well-developed field of microcredit and a well-developed culture of paying back the loans; (3) the availability of trained technicians. These three conditions are not easily found elsewhere. In Africa, for example, the low population density alone makes sustainability much more complicated at the branch level: Karnataka (where SELCO started) has a density of 318 hab/km^2, while Senegal has a density of only 62 hab/km^2.

Even when these key conditions to success are met, replication has been desperately slow. The deep local roots of these business models make them very resilient locally, but also extremely complex to replicate. Hence the need to look for radically different business models for other parts of the world.

Solar lanterns – a solution for less dense environments

An alternative to locally built SHS, ready-made solar lanterns have a more limited use (a simple source of light and a phone charger) but are also substantially cheaper. Over the last five years, price reduction in small-size PV panels, improved performance and price reduction of lithium batteries, and emergence of cheap, reliable and energy-efficient LEDs have brought down product costs dramatically, with quality products selling from less than $10 for the simplest ones (only providing lighting) to $30 or even $50 for larger, more powerful models with a phone charger.

A multitude of manufacturers of such products have emerged in the last decade, with different degrees of quality. A study conducted by Hystra in 2010 already counted over 100 different models of solar lanterns from 25 different brands, nearly all of them manufactured in China. Among quality brands, companies such as d.light design and Greenlight Planet have led the growth of the solar lantern markets in developing countries, each passing the mark of a million lanterns sold.

In 2006 d.light was founded by two students in a Stanford Design MBA class, Ned Tozun and Sam Goldman, with the remit to bring safe, bright and renewable lighting to customers without access to reliable power. The company designs, manufactures and sells solar lanterns that can also charge a cell phone, at prices ranging from $10 to $45. The company now also sells SHSs on top of solar lanterns, via existing channels (liquefied petroleum gas – LPG – stores in India, Total gas stations in various African countries and so on) with different levels of marketing and sales support from d.light depending on geographies. As of mid-2014, d.light design had sold more than six million products in over 60 countries through some 12,000 outlets, impacting the lives of over 33 million people.[53]

Greenlight Planet is a for-profit company based in the US, started in 2005 with the objective to provide poor Indian households with solar energy. They have created a range of products (called Sun King™) sold for $11 to $40. In addition to selling to global distributors, Greenlight has created a fully owned sales network in India, counting over 4800 sales agents as of 2013. They reach a penetration rate of up to 70–80 percent in villages where they are active, selling about 40,000 lights per month, even though a Sun King™ product often represents two weeks of income for its clients. Overall, Greenlight Planet has sold over one million lanterns.

Manufacturers such as d.light and Greenlight Planet have grown significantly over the past few years, and are now profitable with sales of hundreds of thousands of units per year across the world. They have managed to create strong enough brands thanks to their product warranty and the strong after-sales service that they request from all their distributors, to keep cheap low-quality copycats at bay. They keep evolving their products to better answer their clients' needs.

Between SHS and lanterns – plug and play products

While SHS is moving one step at a time in its slow tailor-made spread of distribution, lanterns are potentially moving much faster. When we started writing this book in 2009 there was no clear road in place for their distribution. Today more and more large-scale distribution channels carry these simple devices to the mass of customers who can use them.

Between SHS and these simple lanterns, a new trend has emerged in recent years. Companies such as Barefoot Power, d.light, Duron, Sundaya or SunTransfer have developed new technology solutions: plug and play complete solar home systems. These present several advantages:

- They do not require such complex local distribution operations as SHSs. As Maurice Adema, the founder of Sundaya (one of the most innovative and successful companies manufacturing plug and play solar home systems), explains, his new modular solar home system is "plug and play, extremely easy to install, not requiring a trained technician. It is also very easy for after sales, as you can just unplug a light and bring it to the service center (instead of requiring a technician visit)."[54]

- They are easier to finance than SHSs as they are modular – lamps can be bought separately and added to the system one by one, limiting credit needs by spreading the purchases over time.
- Over time, they allow people to acquire a whole system with more function-alities than solar lanterns alone (for example, they can power a fan or TV).

Today even the smallest units of these solutions remain more expensive than single lanterns, but they are starting to make a compelling case for themselves: in May 2014, d.light hit the milestone of 125,000 modular SHSs sold. On top of being maintenance-free, its system comes complete with wall switches with high and low settings, providing a real grid-like experience to the user.

Key success factors of individual solutions – quality, brands and distribution networks

Manufacturers of these key products need:

- Investment in product quality and in building the corresponding trusted brands to reassure risk-averse customers.
- For solar lanterns and plug and play products, investment in large-scale pro-duction (most, if not all, are today outsourced to China), significantly lower-ing product costs and making them affordable for larger numbers of people.
- To find or build adequate "last-mile" distribution channels that reach BoP customers, offer financing solutions and guarantee maintenance. Manufacturers will have a competitive advantage if they collaborate with their distributors to stay close to their customers, and if these distributors can find the right awareness and communication strategy to convince end users to purchase their products (see Chapters 14 and 15 on marketing and distribution).

A remaining potential competition threat for the entrepreneurs described above could be a large multinational whose brand is already known and trusted, who could take these markets out of entrepreneurs' hands once the distribution channels have been built and customers know enough about solar energy to buy large volumes rapidly. Large players in the consumer electronics and lighting industry such as Philips, Siemens-Osram or Samsung have significant competitive advantages: technological capabilities, bargaining power over suppliers, experience in outsourcing manufacturing and – most importantly – the power of their brands spread over a broad catalog of related consumer products: radios, TVs and so on – but so far they have not interfered with the success of the companies described above. Some have actually supported these lantern manufacturers by carrying their products in their distribution networks, for example, Total selling d.light, Greenlight Planet and Sundaya products in their gas stations.

Another possible competition might come from the other types of products described here. These three types of products have mostly been distributed in different geographies so far. But as many of them become more and more mainstream, some start competing. SELCO sees some of its potential clients turn down the offer for an SHS as they already possess a lantern and know they could not afford an SHS powerful enough for a television set – the main additional advantage that an SHS still brings. Harish and other founders of SHS companies are wary that these technologies may undermine the empowerment of local communities and local job creation that are at the heart of their programs, as opposed to made in China solar lanterns, imported and sold in a box.

So, what is the right solution for development? A more local, labor-intensive integrated solution, yet more expensive and slower to scale up? Or a disintegrated supply chain manufacturing in Asia and delivering cheaper ready-made products for local partners to distribute faster throughout the world? The jury is out to see which solution will light the developing world. But the light could also come from yet another solution: mini-utilities.

Mini-utility solutions – the attractiveness of collective solutions

Existing individual solutions are limited in the power they can bring. The largest systems cannot yet power a radio, a small TV or a fan all at once, although rapid technological progress may render this possible in the near future.

For now, collective solutions are required to bring larger amounts of power. A typical mini-utility powered

Collective solutions are required to bring larger amounts of power

by a diesel generator would serve a few thousand customers who would pay less than $10 per month to get 10–15 kWh, enough for lighting, a fan and a TV. While the use of diesel might raise a few eyebrows among environmentalists, it is a significant improvement over the use of kerosene lamps. In countries such as Cambodia and the Philippines, such mini-utilities are serving hundreds of thousands of rural families and are generating healthy returns on equity for local entrepreneurs.

Other mini-utilities use local renewable energies (such as solar, biomass or hydraulic power). One of the most successful mini-utility initiatives to date is Husk Power Systems (HPS), a company set up in 2007 by a group of entrepreneurs in India. Gyanesh Pandey, co-founder and CEO of HPS until 2013, had worked in the power management industry in the USA and thus knew how to bring costs down to a minimum. In addition he had a true drive to go back to and help the region where he was from: "I had always wanted to work in the development of rural areas, one of which I call home. I decided to work on rural electrification because of my experience at home. I used to feel embarrassed by the lack of facilities in the villages and how people didn't do anything about it."[55]

HPS had the idea of going back to a decade-old overlooked technology of biomass gasifiers combined with a dual-fuel (diesel and biomass gas) power generator and tweaking it to run fully on biomass gas. They managed to bring down its installation cost to $750/kW, about half that of solar power. The system can run on any type of biomass, including rice husk, a waste product of rice production largely available in East India. The generator is then wired to any household that has paid for the connection, and is run for six to ten hours per day to provide lighting and other electric services.

After a few trials installing the machines for CSOs in rural Bihar (one of the poorest areas of India, with plenty of rice husk), the technology was ready. The team then refined its business model to become fully self-sustainable through sales of electricity, by-products – char from the husk gasification process that can be used to make incense and other products – and carbon credits. For Gyanesh, these were all ways to enhance his business: "I did not know I was a social entrepreneur before investors and the international community started calling me that. To me I'm an entrepreneur doing business in Bihar, the region I come from and where until now I was unhappy with the state of affairs."

Before construction of a new plant starts, the sales and marketing team of HPS markets its benefits to the local inhabitants. Construction starts when they have found a local manager and a minimum of 400 households signing up for electricity installation. Clients can choose from one lamp shared between two households (very popular to light a courtyard between two houses and be able to see snakes at night) to several lamps and fans for a single house.

As of 2013, HPS had more than 90 plants in operation, serving around 200,000 people. They had also trained and recruited 250 women for incense stick manufacturing and 150 operators. They received more than $2 million in financing in 2010, and convinced philanthropists to donate funds: Shell Foundation has awarded them several million dollars since inception, notably for research and development (R&D) and to set up adequate training programs. They convinced the government of their cost-efficiency compared to alternatives to bring electricity to rural areas: local governments provide a 50 percent subsidy for any new installation. And, of course, they convinced their clients of the value of their offer, as the doctor of the first rural village electrified by HPS, sitting on a plastic chair on the mud floor in front of his house, testifies:

> *Thanks to electricity, I am now able to see more patients as I can work later hours, and I have made my office more comfortable for them, with a fan. My three children can study at night. The whole village has improved thanks to HPS: the market is now open until 9 pm, and 300 households out of 500 have electricity here. The ones who do not have it choose not to because they lack the education to understand the benefits from it, not because they do not have the money. HPS electricity costs only 100 to 200 Indian rupees ($2–4) per month, it is affordable for anyone here. Actually, we used to spend more on kerosene.*[56]

Mini-utility solutions – obstacles to scale and replication

Mini-utilities such as HPS still face two key challenges for expansion: (1) operating a large network of decentralized, small-scale plants; (2) obtaining a favorable regulatory environment.

How should a network of hundreds of decentralized utilities be managed? Monitoring these operations to verify consistency of service quality and adequate payments becomes increasingly difficult. HPS has already developed smart meters to overcome that challenge, and is now working on smart grids that would allow more efficient allocation of the power load, and follow all plants from one centralized location.

The second obstacle to geographic replication is an unfavorable regulatory environment. In most countries, the sheer existence of a mini-utility is made impossible by the national monopoly granted to the state-owned electric utility. In others, countrywide tariffs make it impossible to have commercially viable mini-utilities serving small villages at prices based on the cost of serving large urban centers.

David Ehrhardt, the CEO of Castalia and a global expert in mini-utilities, explains: "We are so used to the regulation of utility prices that the notion of not regulating mini-utility tariffs may seem quite wrong at first. But really from an economic point of view it is quite reasonable. Regulation of prices is used for monopolies. But a mini-utility entering a market is competing with many other energy sources: kerosene, batteries, solar lanterns, solar home systems, and individual generators. So competition, not regulation, will protect consumers."

Finally, such collective solutions have the advantage of being able to bring more power per household than individual solutions, allowing clients to use more electrical appliances and consequently create additional social impact. Actually, in the case of HPS, some local entrepreneurs are already using the plant to power electric mills or other agro-tools during the day when villagers do not need lighting, thus bringing additional wealth to their village.

* * *

Even if the various technology solutions and business models described in this chapter might need adaptation to work in other parts of the world, there should be a solution adapted to every location and to nearly every budget. Anyone who was previously spending money on "traditional lighting" (such as candles or kerosene) will actually save money by purchasing a small solar lantern, compared to spending money every month on consumables. Similarly, even the poorest can afford to rent a light from a mini-utility for $2 per month. For individual solutions, the challenge of social entrepreneurs is mainly to ensure maintenance, provide financing if needed and convince risk-averse users to invest – all challenges that have found solutions (see Chapters 14 and 15 on marketing and distribution). For collective solutions, in places where there is no rice husk, other technical solutions (such as hydro, large solar plants or others) might work instead. Just as for individual solutions, the main challenge does not lie in technology, but rather in getting community buy-in, and monitoring and enforcing payments.

We no longer have an excuse to leave 1.3 billion people in the dark

Social entrepreneurs such as those described in this chapter – by adapting their products to local environments and needs, learning from best practices in marketing and distribution, and lobbying for an effective regulatory framework – have the power and capability to enlighten the world. We no longer have an excuse to leave 1.3 billion people in the dark.

6

Housing

Today close to one billion people live in slums, and this figure could grow to three billion by 2050 if nothing is done.[57] Indian urban areas alone need over 22 million new homes – and this is only counting households earning $82 to $491 per month who might be able to afford a home.[58]

And yet the BoP already spends more than PPP $400 billion on housing[59] – the third largest item in their budget after food and energy – be it in rents or in building, repairing and improving their dwellings.[60] A 2014 study done by the Inter-American Development Bank estimates the current investment by the BoP in its housing solutions at close to $60 billion annually in Latin America and the Caribbean, thus confirming the buying power in this sector.[61]

Indeed for a BoP family, a home is not just a home. As Manjula-ben, an incense stick maker in Ahmadabad, India says: "My house is my workshop, my savings and my place to rest." Thus improving it means not only more comfort, but also a better income and overall enhanced opportunities.

If you have ever visited a slum or a low-income neighbor-hood in a developing country, you must have witnessed "work in progress," rooms being built or (at least) stacks of bricks or bags of cement. This is how poor neighborhoods are built: bit by bit depending on their inhabitants' irregular cash flows and time availabilities. Some organizations have created ways to make this progressive home improvement faster, cheaper and safer. Others have chosen to build and sell affordable new homes. Both approaches are needed, and both can be commercially viable, as the examples below illustrate.

Home improvements – Cemex

During the Mexican Tequila crisis at the end of the 1990s, executives at Cemex, one of the world's largest cement producers, were intrigued when they saw that while all commercial construction had stopped, cement bags continued to be sold to poor neighborhoods. This segment appeared to be immune to the cyclical swings that hurt the profitability of high fixed-cost industries such as that of cement. To understand this phenomenon and the building habits of slum dwellers, Cemex sent several of its staff to the slums of Guadalajara. When they came back a few months later, they had learnt a lot.

They had found out that progressive home improvement for these people was a very slow process: families needed four to five years to complete an extra room in their house, at the tortoise pace of 2 m^2 per year and with up to 40 percent wastage of material. And it was also ineffective, as the final result was unsafe, low-quality buildings.

The reasons for this unfortunate situation are multiple. In this segment 80 percent of Mexicans lack a formal contractual property title that can be used as collateral to obtain loans from banks.[62] Most people lack the technical skills to properly design and estimate the cost of a project, select the right materials and use them appropriately. "They have all the capacities, they only lack the opportunities," as Israel Moreno explains. Israel was the general manager of Patrimonio Hoy (PH) for many years. This program, launched by Cemex in 1999, organizes and facilitates the self-construction process through an integrated offer, enabling their clients to build and pay $1000 for a 10 m^2 room in 70 weeks, with weekly payments of 240 pesos (MXN) ($17).

In order to get PH known and trusted, 1200 local women called Promotoras conduct door-to-door sales and marketing and motivate their neighbors to register in the program. When a family enrolls, PH first assesses their needs and calculates the corresponding material package in the right quantities. The 240 pesos weekly payments include 190 pesos of building materials and 50 pesos of "membership fee," for designing the room, calculating the bill of materials, breaking down the project in achievable steps and giving advice on construction techniques. It also guarantees fixed prices for building materials for the 70 weeks, and offers phased home delivery (depending on progress of the works) in order to avoid wastage of unused material. Lastly it offers credit without requesting any collateral other than proof of ID. As Israel puts it: "These families may not have formal collateral but they have *verguenza*, pride in their good reputation." PH leverages this verguenza, providing growing

ISRAEL MORENO
TRANSFORMING LIVES,
NOT SELLING PRODUCTS[63]

Born in 1965 in Mexico, Israel Moreno founded Patrimonio Hoy in 1998 and was general manager from its inception until 2012.

ILLUSTRATION 11 / Israel Moreno

When I started to work for Cemex, I grew wary about the fact that we did not know how our end clients were using our cement. When I spent time with these families, I had the opportunity to see how difficult it is to live as a family in just one room. Working in the exploration and design of a solution to that issue made me feel that I was doing the right thing.

You really need to live in these communities. If you don't, how can you earn their trust, and understand their concerns and expectations, their strengths, capacities and weaknesses? If they don't trust you, and if you don't prove that you trust them as well, they will not buy your product. We have to succeed together.

People are living in those conditions because they don't have access to solutions or to people who could help them find

Continued

Continued

solutions. They are poor because of their ignorance, because the education model set up by the whole society is not helping them. Everything seems difficult for them, they are fighting against all types of problems. Fathers give the impression to their sons that they were born poor and will remain poor.

Philanthropic approaches do not change this mindset. If you give 1000 houses then you will have 1000 families living in a better place, which obviously is good. But when you give someone something, they will not value it to its real price because they have not chosen it or made any effort for it. If you give, you are not transforming the family, you are not changing their mindsets into "you can do things for yourself," instead you give the message that they need someone to come and help them. If you ask them to pay, if the house costs them money and it is a product of their own work, if at the same time they are learning how to plan and how to build, and showing these values to their children, then you are creating much more than through giving them a house. For people who get free houses, the message is that a better life will come through begging. This is not the message I want to give.

The most important thing is to remember that these people are not just customers you want to sell something to, but they are people whose lives you want to help transform, in order to have a better community, a better country.

amounts of credit as families demonstrate their ability and commitment to pay on time.

PH demands that people deposit the weekly requested amount for five weeks before making the first material delivery for the value of ten weeks of payment, in effect providing credit for five weeks. Once the full ten weeks have passed, clients must pay the following two weeks in advance, before getting a delivery corresponding to 12 weekly payments' worth of materials. The ratio "payment in advance" over "credit" diminishes as the cycle progresses.

Payment discipline is strictly enforced: a 30 pesos "fine" is levied if the weekly payment is one day late, but families who pay on time can have access to up to $8000 of credit. Interestingly, PH doesn't require refinancing, as the saving of the families that ask for deliveries to be deferred are sufficient to fund the credit extended to the ones who don't.

Since its inception, PH has served more than 380,000 families, allowing them to save about one-third of the cost and two-thirds of the time previously needed to build a functional room – and to build one that is now much better.

What is striking in the way that Israel Moreno speaks about his clients is the huge respect he has for them and the importance he gives to establishing mutual trust. As for his clients, they speak with pride about PH and the achievements it has enabled. To understand what PH is really about, one could, for example, simply witness the pride visible in the eyes of a 12-year-old Mexican girl looking up to her mother who, after her father had left them, managed to get her a new room all by herself thanks to the PH program.

PH is not only a remarkable social success: it is one of the most profitable distribution channels of Cemex today. With sales of $45 million in 2011, 40 percent of it in Cemex building materials, PH generates several incremental millions of dollars in profit every year.

Home improvements – Viste Tu Casa

Colceramica, a large tile manufacturer in Colombia faced with threats from low-cost imports from China, has won 28,000 new clients in four years through its program "Viste Tu Casa" (VTC, literally "dress up your home").

Colceramica brought down the cost of its tiles without affecting quality by limiting the range of colors and styles, but the most drastic innovation had to do with its distribution strategy. In 2004, Colceramica approached Haidy Duque, a social entrepreneur and Ashoka Fellow, to survey low-income customers to identify their specific needs. In February 2005 Haidy Duque started training women in local communities as community sales agents or *promotoras* of Colceramica products, a model similar to Patrimonio Hoy. *Promotoras* talk to housewives about the hygiene benefits of having tiles in a kitchen or bathroom; women in turn convince their husbands to enroll in VTC.

As most clients would not have the $600 needed for a typical project, Colceramica started offering payments in 12 monthly installments with 1.5 percent monthly interest rate. After a period of rapid growth, the company decided to outsource the financing of these loans to third-party finance providers and focus its efforts on building its own commercially successful distribution system.

With the support of other citizen sector organizations, Viste Tu Casa has expanded into six Colombian cities, and has managed to reach combined sales of $20 million since 2007, with over 40,000 client families.

New homes – Housing for All

The construction sector for "new urban low income homes" has just started to emerge, offering prices typically from $6000 to $20,000 for a one- to four-room apartment. In India the phenomenon can already be called a boom: real estate developers have built at least 30,500 such private social housing units between 2011 and 2013 and a million more are planned in the coming years.[64] These programs are proving that BoP families are able and willing to invest these large amounts in a new home, with loan repayments of $30–80 per month, an amount that is usually equivalent to half of what they are paying already in rent.

As an example, let's travel to the slums of Ahmadabad. For families living there, crammed in with often three children in a one-bedroom space, owning an apartment in a new building is a dream. And recently this dream has become a real possibility for households earning as little as 9000 rupees ($150) per month.

Owning an apartment in a new building is a dream

Ashoka's Housing for All Program (HFA) has successfully brought together DBS Affordable Home Strategy Pvt Ltd, a real estate developer, and SAATH, a CSO founded by Ashoka Fellow Rajendra Joshi, to build and deliver houses to these households.

Vishnu Swaminathan, director of the HFA program, attributes this success to the cross-sector collaboration of all the partners required to facilitate the purchase of an owned home for "untraditional" customers: financial institutions, community organizations and real estate developers.

Finding the right finance partners proved a challenge. The loans required in housing are part of the financial "missing middle" that no current financial structure has the tools to service: the amounts required are too large for microfinance institutions but too small for traditional banks. Additionally, as slum dwellers are working in the informal sector and do not have property rights nor pay slips, the housing financial institutions involved in the project had to adapt their loans and creditworthiness assessment methods for these new clients.

To avoid the social and economic dislocation of the relocated families, SAATH and other local organizations helped to design the new building to make sure it fitted the needs and lifestyle of the targeted clients (such as community spaces, garage space to park rickshaws and so on). They also provide their social services in the new buildings.

The critical piece of the puzzle was real estate developers. As Vishnu explains: "Developers are the ones who negotiate with the government to receive a construction permit and be entitled to deliver ownership titles to their clients. In order to do so, developers must share with public authorities all the data that they collected on a community through CSOs, and provide them with their plans and designs (each flat must already be attributed to a specific buyer). This system may sound complex but it allows better transparency and limits corruption. On such projects, developers typically invest $13 million for a 1000-homes project, including land purchase, land development and construction cost as well as access to public utility services. The investment is usually broken down into two to three phases as the project is sold off, and the developer uses a percentage of down payments collected to offset certain costs and/or uses it as collateral to take a construction finance loan."[65] If real estate developers make a 15–25 percent gross margin per unit on average – that is, lower margins than in the traditional construction sector – they plan to make up for it with shorter project time, gaining overall a higher return on their investment than with projects targeting richer populations. By 2012, developers participating in the Housing for All initiative had built 10,000 new homes.

In 2014, Ashoka India and its local partners established the Indian Housing Council (IHC), a nonprofit organization with the mission to fill the gaps in the affordable housing sector and redefine the way the sector can reach scale and maximize impact. IHC is introducing CASA, the first national building standards for new housing projects targeting low-income families in India. The CASA certification is designed to provide incentives across the housing ecosystem to balance housing quality and costs as well as to provide consumers with choice and quality assurances.[66] The standards have been developed over the last two years by TÜV Rheinland, a global provider of technical, safety and certification services, in close consultation with key housing industry leaders, CSOs and the Indian government. While CASA will be a voluntary standard that developers can apply to for certification, it is designed to increase the confidence of all stakeholders involved in the ecosystem to bring more investment into this sector and hence contribute to accelerating the expansion of the Indian housing market.

Obstacles to scale and replication

Both Patrimonio Hoy and Viste Tu Casa have amply demonstrated that it is possible to create a profitable business that enables poor urban families to improve their homes faster, cheaper and more safely. While HFA is more recent, it is showing a promising avenue for harnessing the commercial construction industry to serve the BoP.

So, given that these models work, and are profitable… why don't they scale up? There are four main reasons for this, as outlined below.

1. Lack of financing

The financing challenge is indeed formidable: closing half of a very conservatively estimated urban housing deficit of 180 million units by 2020 would require creating and operating housing finance institutions representing in total the size of 22 Grameen Banks![67] As Patrimonio Hoy has shown, providing financing to households without collateral can be profitable thanks to very high repayment rates.

Yet existing financial institutions are not geared to provide such loans:

- MFIs focus on providing small, relatively high interest short-term loans to finance productive investments. Thus one or two years, low interest $1000 loans for home improvements fall outside of their remit.
- Banks or housing finance institutions selling mortgages are simply not able to provide loans without collateral and means to verify income (i.e. payslips).

To address the finance bottleneck will require creating new refinancing lines. A new microfinance housing fund could be created to refinance institutions that provide housing loans for home improvements to households excluded from the traditional banking sector, while offering a positive return on investment to investors. A $500 million loan portfolio would allow for the equivalent of five "Patrimonio Hoy," i.e. 150,000 families per year. It is an open question whether this fund should invest in new homes, which is a much larger social and financial need (for example, providing 150,000 new housing loans per year would mean a $3 billion loan portfolio) but a less proven business model.

In 2000, the Peruvian economist Hernando de Soto demonstrated how the absence of property rights was a primary driver of poverty: "the majority of entrepreneurs are stuck in poverty, where their assets – adding up to more than $10 trillion worldwide – languish as dead capital in the shadows of the law."[68]

2. Lack of property rights

Many families have lived for decades on their plot on land but do not have the necessary slips of paper to testify their ownership. To answer this "relatively simple" issue, the government of Karnataka, India, decided to act upon the length and cost of the process to get an official property-right paper, which was deterring most farmers and preventing them from benefitting from the rights attached to it. The government launched the Bhoomi project, which digitalized 20 million land records for 7 million farmers in 27,000 villages. In 2002, after the roll-out of Bhoomi, these records were available for print in 202 village kiosks managed by government officials for around $0.5 per record. The system had 700,000 users per month and had provided 70 million copies of land records since its launch, allowing farmers to use their land as collateral.

A Brazilian social entrepreneur, André Albuquerque (already mentioned in Chapter 2) has designed and tested a pragmatic solution for the more complex issue of illegal squatters. Terra Nova, the private company he has founded, specializes in securing land rights for low-income populations in Brazil, resolving stalemates between informal squatters and legal landowners through the negotiated settlers' acquisition of the plot they live on.

Local settlers gain property rights by paying amounts often equivalent to what they were paying as illegal rent. For them, this means obtaining an asset and collateral, the first step to access loans. Additionally, those who were in unhealthy or risky zones get relocated. Finally, part of the transaction amount is set aside for local infrastructure development.

Even if they do not get the entire market value of their land, landowners recover some value for it, which they had often given up hope of realizing (some illegal settlements are more than 15 years old).

Local authorities solve the issue of illegal, insalubrious and sometimes dangerous settlements at a lower cost and faster than the landowners could on their own. They are also able to levy taxes from these newly formalized areas.

Thanks to Terra Nova, since its first project in 2001 more than 12,000 families have become owners of their plots. The resolution of illegal settlements is estimated to have saved the government over $80 million in relocation costs.[69]

While Terra Nova is a commercial entity (its revenues are a percentage of the transactions that they make possible), André regards his role as transformational within the community, showing families that they can help themselves out of poverty and giving them the opportunity to work together on community planning. Through this system Terra Nova has proved it possible to unlock the capital hidden in illegal settlements and redistribute the value fairly among low-income communities, landowners and government, improving the lives of all.

3. Lack of trained masons

A minimum of seven million masons would be needed to build new homes and help improve existing ones in order to close half of the urban housing deficit in the coming ten years to 2024.[70] This translates into a need for training centers on the one hand, and, on the other, financial possibilities to start as a mason, such as microloans to buy the material needed. Neither exists on a large scale today.

As an example of a business model for such training centers, Lafarge India has set up training programs for gypsum installation to address a skill shortage that deterred some clients from purchasing gypsum products. The young masons get a loan for their three-month traineeship period in order to cover food, board and living expenses; then a loan to set up their company. Once they are trained, Lafarge recommends them to its client for gypsum installation, ensuring that they get their first contracts. The costs of the program are borne by Lafarge's marketing budget and are not linked with corporate social responsibility (CSR). And Lafarge can now tap into its own pool of masons to install its products in India, increasing its gypsum sales.

4. Fragmentation of the construction industry

Though home improvement programs such as PH or VTC have been initiated by specific building materials manufacturers, effectively addressing the needs of the customers requires a full product offering, including financing, technical assistance and possibly access to skilled labor. This is the natural role of a retailer, not that of a manufacturer. The problem is that the building material retailers in developing countries are still highly fragmented and conservative. Becoming the "Home Depot" for the BoP is an attractive opportunity yet to be seized.

The HFA case has shown the need for an intermediary able to convene the host of different parties involved, which are mostly small, local actors: real estate developers, building material suppliers, CSOs, retailers and finance institutions. Not only are all these players hard to identify and convince to participate, but they also struggle to work together. Building trust takes time and has to be done all over again in each new location.

We are facing a typical case of market failure that economists call the *free rider* problem: each industry player would benefit from the investments made in developing the BoP market but none would gain sufficiently to justify making the investment alone. Players used to competing and expected to do so would need to collaborate. This is not an easy task for commercial companies but one that public, philanthropic and development players might take on. Instead of spending money in programs that give homes away, they could use their unique position to catalyze markets by investing in setting up the needed ecosystem. This would include providing technical assistance to MFIs willing to develop a housing microfinance division, funding BoP mason-training programs and providing guarantee funds for microfinance institutions that are helping starting masons.

This would be a high-leverage way of partly redirecting the large public funds dedicated to social housing programs that are needed for the poorest (launched in 2009, Brazil's Minha Casa Minha Vida program aims at building 3.4 million homes by 2016; South Africa targets 500,000 new social houses per year but struggles to deliver). The Mexican government has already started leveraging PH's operational set-up to serve poorer Mexican households, providing up to an additional 40 percent of material for free to PH clients (it was previously giving cash to people, which was rarely spent on improving homes). Such initiatives should be encouraged.

* * *

As we have seen above, the market case to build new and better homes for the poor is emerging, yet it still needs time in which to scale and validate its business model.

The model for profitable home improvements, however, has been fully cracked by Patrimonio Hoy. And, as Israel Moreno says, this is not just about building an extra room, it is about transforming lives.

chapter 1

Drinking water

Today, more than one in three people do not have access to safe water.[71] This partly explains why diarrhea remains so widespread, and kills over 760,000 children every year.[72] Given that an estimated one-half of the world's hospital beds are filled with people suffering from water-related illnesses, diarrhea could cost over 73 million working days per year to the Indian economy, and 20 percent of Nigeria's GDP. But lack of safe water also has many other implications: in Africa and Asia, women walk an average of 6 km per day to fetch water for their family. Tens of millions of children skip school to help their mothers with the water chores.

The "have-nots" pay a lot more money to get safe water

Despite this urgency, money to fix this crisis remains scarce. It is estimated that water-borne diseases, which account for 20 percent of the global disease burden, receive less than 1 percent of total public and private funds devoted to health research. Even when significant financial resources are mobilized, traditional philanthropic approaches (based on grants or subsidies) fall short of fixing the problem for good. For instance, it is estimated that 600,000 to 800,000 hand pumps were installed in rural sub-Saharan Africa over the past 20 years by CSOs and donors. But over one-third of them are now nonfunctional due to lack of a sustainable maintenance solution. In urban areas of developing countries, utility operators deliver piped water to 1.7 billion people but too often, only poor quality water is available for just a few hours a day. Furthermore another 300 million urban dwellers do not have any water connection at home.

The result of this situation is that the "have-nots" pay a lot more money to get safe water. In the slums of Jakarta, for instance, families spend over $7 per cubic meter for water sold by the local water vendors who serve their neighborhoods, while the official utility tariff is about $0.1 per cubic meter. In rural Cambodia, poor households spend up to $180 per year on fuel to boil water, while an equally effective filter costs around $40 to own per year. This situation will become even worse with the explosion of the urban population in Africa and Asia. Estimates predict that there will be an additional 1.3 billion people living in cities by 2030, most of them poor.[73]

Fortunately, in recent years, innovative entrepreneurs have found approaches to provide safe water to the poor – reliably, sustainably and at an affordable price. These cover the full spectrum of situations facing the poor: sustainably functioning water pumps for small, remote villages; home water treatment solutions for rural families or families with unsafe tap water; sophisticated mini treatment plants in places where the water is highly contaminated; and independent water networks in suburbs and small towns that are not connected to the main utility.

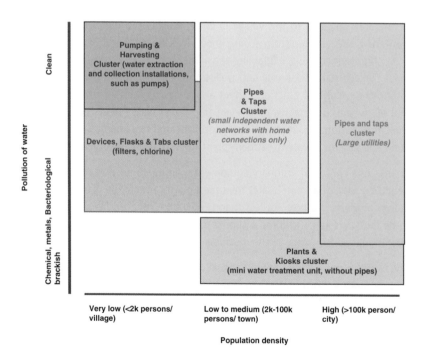

FIGURE 4 / The scope of safe water solutions, in terms of appropriateness and cost-effectiveness

Our work on water shows that these solutions, should they be scaled-up to their full potential, could reach approximately 50 percent or one billion of poor people in need of safe water. But this scaling-up has not happened yet. In this chapter, we try to understand why, and what could be done about it.

We look in particular at two types of solutions: mini water treatment plants (usually known as "kiosks") and decentralized water networks.

Mini water treatment plants – Sarvajal and Naandi

It is 9 am in the small Indian village of Kava. Kokila Ben is carrying her "bigrou" – the traditional iron water container in Gujarat – on her head to fetch her daily water supply at the Sarvajal mini water treatment plant. At the kiosk, Kokila is joined by men: fetching water has traditionally been a woman's chore, but since the water has come out of taps linked to sophisticated water treatment machines, men also come proudly to the plant to buy water. Most of them use monthly prepaid cards in order to both improve convenience and reinforce regular use.

Before Sarvajal came to this village in 2009, Kokila used water from the well. Back then, she suffered from aching knees. In Kava, the local water source has a very high salt content, explaining the ailments of Kokila, and of many of her fellow villagers. Brackishness and pollution by arsenic or fluorosis, driven by intensive agricultural practices, affect an increasing number of areas in India and elsewhere. Boiling water or even traditional water filters won't do: this level of pollution requires much more sophisticated treatment. But who would build and pay for a water treatment plant for a small village in remote Gujarat?

Thanks to a couple of visionary equipment manufacturers and social entrepreneurs, the idea of a "mini" water treatment plant came to life. Sarvajal can now deliver a "plant-in-a-box" for less than US $3000 – reduced from over $15,000 some five years ago, including a remote monitoring device, which can track the operational performance of the machine.

The founder and former CEO of Sarvajal, Anand Shah, is one of these visionary change-makers. Born in 1977 in Texas, Anand returned to India in 2001. He explains his journey:[74]

> *I grew up in America in a family of Indian immigrants. My father was keen on making us understand what poverty was like: he made us visit India when we were little and sent each of us for a year after graduation to work on social issues. I eventually moved back to India in 2001*

and ran a foundation for the Piramal family who was interested in health care: with water quality having a direct impact on health, we began looking into it.

My starting point was to acknowledge that there are things out there that already work. We analyzed Naandi (who already had hundreds of kiosks in India) to learn from their great work and try to adapt their model to make it faster and easier to replicate. We lowered the cost of the technology, and chose an economic model based on private franchises instead of raising financing.

Funding was available, but I needed to engineer my solution so that it fitted the way in which investors think

My end point was that I wanted to build a large business, and not another CSO project: in India, people get excited because their CSO brought clean water to ten villages. If you are trying to do business like we do, one needs to reach 1000 villages to make it work economically.

So, the question was how to reach that scale. There are models that work to scale up, but mainly in the "rich" world. So far nobody has looked enough into how to take these solutions into rural, poorer, more complicated environments. For this, you need smart people (which we had) and funds to pay for the development of these large-scale approaches. I realized that the funding was available, but that I needed to engineer my solution so that it fits the way in which investors think. I also struggled to attract the attention of governments and large corporations, because we were still too small. They do not know how to deal with smaller-scale but high potential innovations, and expect us to invest further and further. I wish that the state government instead stated that it seeks to crowd-source some public services and announces: "solve this problem in 1000 schools, and we'll give you the contract for the whole state." This would give innovators an incentive to reach the minimum scale required to be relevant for governments to take best solutions to the national level and for large corporations to replicate them globally.

Today, mini water treatment plants such as the ones of Sarvajal are successfully running in over 1000 Indian villages. These plants typically treat 500 to 1000 liters per hour, for sale at a price of $0.2 to $0.6 per liter. Given that most families consume about 20 liters of safe water per day, this represents less than 4 percent of even the poorest families' income.

In the case of Naandi, which started its operations in 2005, the full installation represents a cost of between $10,000 and $20,000. This is financed through a mix of grants, village contributions and state authorities' investments;

ultimately, it is either the village or the state authorities that own the plant. It is nonetheless operated by Naandi staff and the water sales contribute to pay for Naandi's operational costs.

Sarvajal started three years later, and managed to lower the initial investment to between $2000 and $3000, notably by using existing buildings to host the plant and reverse-engineering a "bare-bone" version of the equipment. Sarvajal owns the plants, but offers "micro-franchises" to local entrepreneurs to operate them: they have to pay $950 upfront to buy the franchise, and 40 percent of their monthly revenues to Sarvajal. The kiosks generate sufficient revenues for many village entrepreneurs to find this an attractive business opportunity. Sarvajal also invested very early in technology in order to lower its operational costs and better control the performance of its franchisees. Its remote-monitoring device (integrated into every machine) can track in real time the condition of the machine and its production.

In India, Sarvajal and Naandi provide safe water for more than 700,000 people but the number of their plants has remained stable for the last five years. Albeit impressive, this is still short of the estimated 30 million Indian villagers who would need a mini water treatment plant in order to have clean water every day. So, why don't they scale up?

The reasons differ between Naandi and Sarvajal. Naandi struggles to finance its cash-heavy growth. It needs to raise grants for each kiosk it builds, or alternatively secure public money by lobbying governments. It also finds it increasingly challenging to oversee its employees in hundreds of remote locations.

Sarvajal has found a nimbler way to grow, but now faces a different problem: it struggles to retain its franchisees who quickly realize they would make more money by setting up their own kiosk. After Sarvajal has helped them set up the kiosk and learn the trade, the value of being part of the Sarvajal franchise quickly decreases. Having learned operations and basic maintenance, kiosk operators would prefer to purchase and operate their own equipment and pocket the full profit.

Both Naandi and Sarvajal are threatened by the proliferation of low-quality water kiosk operators, piggybacking on the success of branded kiosks. There are not yet well-defined or well-enforced quality standards and regulations in this new industry: as a result, established players are increasingly challenged by small independent operators who compete on low price but are often unable to guarantee consistent water quality. These operators put at risk the health of their users, and threaten the reputation of this whole nascent industry.

What architecture is needed to move from small networks of kiosk operators to a thriving kiosk industry?

Sarvajal and Naandi are successes in their own right: the technology is working, villagers drink safe water and the operations are (at least partly) financially sustainable. However, there is an opportunity to transform the architecture for the whole, and unleash at scale the potential demonstrated by these early players. Such an architecture would comprise:

a) Public authorities that set and enforce quality standards for water kiosks.
b) Kiosks paid for, owned and operated by village entrepreneurs, as it is a profitable business to be in, requiring limited skills and investment. Loans for the purchase of the equipment could be provided by microfinance institutions.
c) Industry support platforms set up to facilitate and accelerate the dissemination of kiosks among local entrepreneurs. The platforms would provide a number of services including:
   – "Turn-key" packages for new kiosk operators, including training and licensing (if required by law), sourcing and installation of equipment, and support for the launch of promotional and user education campaigns.
   – Maintenance contracts.
   – Intermediation for financing from third parties (including helping entrepreneurs to submit business plans and loan requests).
   – Auditing operations, where mandated by public authorities.
   These platforms would function like social businesses, whereby the paying services would cover operating costs, and any profit would be reinvested in supporting even more kiosks.
d) Manufacturers of water treatment equipment competing to offer adapted, low-cost technology for these water kiosks, through these platforms.

This framework would help rural villages with heavily polluted water sources. Let us now turn to semi-urban areas.

Decentralized water networks – Balibago

Balibago Waterworks System Inc. (BWSI) is a privately owned Philippine water company, specializing in setting up and operating small, decentralized water networks providing safe water at the home tap to communities of a few hundred to a few thousand families.

In the Philippines, the responsibility for public water infrastructure lies with the local municipalities. Balibago has become a medium-sized operator by obtaining from municipalities the right to operate (and sometimes build) a water network, ideally for a long period of time (35 years on average), after which the ownership and operation of the network revert to the municipality.

Small, independent water networks are nothing new. Often managed by the municipalities themselves, or by local private operators, they often tend to be hardly profitable and poorly run, hence unable to invest into new equipment and expand the service.

Balibago's cost structure and organization allows it to finance its own growth. As it now operates 42 water networks, it achieves profitability by combining economies of scale (for instance in sourcing equipment) with lean, local management operations. In 2013, Balibago served sustainably about 90,000 households with high standards of service, and generating more than $15 million in revenues and $3 million in profit, while investing in new infrastructure and improved operations. It is able to offer a whole set of services, ranging from refurbishing an existing network, to installing a new one, or simply taking on the operations in an area where public authorities do not yet have the capabilities to run the infrastructure.

Still, Balibago keeps a "pulse" on the communities it serves; the locally hired teams have a lot of independence to run day-to-day operations and the door-to-door payment collection allows the team to know all the users personally. These local teams are the ones to call the shots when it comes to better responding to the customers' needs and ability to pay.

The Balibago model also relies very little on cross-subsidies in order to grow. The logic of cross-subsidies (that is, the rich pay a premium so that poorer customers pay less) lies at the heart of the functioning of most water operators – public and private. While they have been very effective at enabling cash-constrained authorities to serve the poor, they tend to "freeze" the situation. Indeed, the more a utility expands into peripheral or poorer areas, the more difficult it is to maintain a sound economic balance. The premium paid by the richer segments cannot be increased sufficiently to finance new infrastructure and compensate for the discounts offered to an ever-increasing poor population. As a result the poorest have to buy bottled water from resellers at a much higher price.

In contrast, Balibago is allowed, thanks to a progressive regulatory framework, to negotiate the price it charges for water with each municipality, based on two criteria: the level of investment required, and the duration of the contract. Such arrangements allow Balibago to make each of its water networks profitable, incentivizing Balibago to grow as much as it can. That would not be true if Balibago was obliged to apply the same tariff across the country. It would shy away from the higher cost to serve municipalities, where the operations could not be profitable.

Thanks to this arrangement, Balibago customers pay on average $.050 per cubic meter (while bottled water is about 1000 times as expensive). Average water consumption is 140–160 ltr per day per person for middle-class households and about 30–40 ltr per day per person for the poorer ones.

How to scale up a Balibago

According to our estimates, the Balibago model could provide safe water to 70–90 million people living in semi-urban areas without safe water access, and to 390 million people in urban areas who will not be covered by the main utility in the mid-term. In fact, the strength of the Balibago model is that it functions in a decentralized manner and can start where needs are greatest. Its networks are sufficiently modular to be directly connected to the main water supply once it reaches the area.

We still need three essential ingredients to replicate Balibago at scale:

- Capital: each new decentralized network (of about 1000 family connections) costs at least $250,000, while pay-back takes from five to ten years. Social impact investors – that is, investors who are ready to forego some financial return if the social impact is high – might be willing to provide such patient capital.
- Legitimacy: it is crucial to position "Balibago-like" operators not as competition for the main utility operators, but rather as "complementary solutions" for remote areas. "Balibago-like" operators would also be different in the sense that they would adopt a "hybrid" governance model, to reflect the dual social and commercial purpose of the company (for instance by having public and development sector players represented at the board).
- Political support at many levels: it is needed to lift the regulatory hurdles associated with connecting families living in informal neighborhoods (which often lack property titles); to support each municipality in negotiating a contract and tariff that are tailored to local conditions; to channel subsidies

if and where needed; and finally to facilitate the work of operators in difficult areas, where the water business may be controlled by local mafia.

* * *

Over the last decade, social entrepreneurs, CSOs and corporations have implemented alternative and innovative approaches to provide safe water to millions of poor people in ways that are (for the most part) economically sustainable.

Were these innovative approaches to scale up in every developing country and reach full potential, they could effectively reach approximately one billion people in need, in other words, around 50 percent of today's total poor population without access to safe water.

Significant funding will be required to make this happen: over $6 billion in equity and loans will be needed to accelerate the development of BoP-focused safe water industries across all clusters. But, more importantly perhaps, given the size and complexity of the problems at hand, there is a need for unprecedented collaboration between public, nonprofit and private players, so that solutions are made available to all, where and as needed.

chapter 8

Financial services

There are 2.5 billion adults in the world who are unbanked.[75] Two out of three adults worldwide cannot access credit in order to grow their business, finance the acquisition of a home or any appliance that would make their life easier.

But banking is not just about loans. Unbanked families do not have access to even the simplest of banking services: savings. Mary, a self-help group leader in the Dharavi slum in Mumbai, India, explains: "When we had money from a good day of sales we used to hide our savings under our beds to keep some of it for less happy days, but then at some point our husband would take it. Sometimes he would buy something useful but sometimes he'd just spend it on drinking with friends. Bank accounts are the only way to make sure our savings are in a safe place."[76] Unbanked emigrants cannot send money back cheaply and safely to their relatives; unbanked families cannot benefit from insurance protection against the uncertainties of life.

Traditional banks find it unattractive to serve the BoP market: first, they perceive a high risk of default; their credit assessment procedures are unable to deal with customers who are self-employed and receive no paychecks, have an irregular income and do not possess any formal property titles to offer as collateral. Second, they see it as too costly to serve: the individual transactions are much too small to bear the marketing and administrative costs of business models designed for affluent customers.

Turning conventional banking logic on its head, MFIs have pioneered a radically new approach that has successfully addressed the problem of perceived lack of creditworthiness of the poor. Microcredit is known for achieving high repayment rates (99+ percent) by focusing on women, offering group lending and linking the amount of credit extended to the track record in timely payments. Despite this achievement, interest rates charged to the poor remain surprisingly high for the casual observer, with a global average of 35 percent in annual rates: so, are MFIs generating undue profits?

Bank accounts are the only way to make sure our savings are in a safe place

A paper from MIX (the leading source of information about the microfinance industry) provides some very useful information: "For all costs that must be covered by interest rates and fees paid by borrowers, operating expenses represent 63% on average, financial expenses 21%, and profits less than 8%."[77] Clearly, the primary driver of high interest rates are the operating expenses of MFIs, not their levels of profit.

In 2013, MFIs reached around 195 million people worldwide, or 8 percent of total unbanked people.[78] This remains a mitigated success after 30 years of existence. High operating expenses and resulting high interest rates are undoubtedly a reason that explains the slow growth of the microcredit industry and the fact that it can only serve "productive investments" and loans of short duration.

MICROFINANCE

Like all great inventions, microcredit has many inventors, yet Professor Muhammad Yunus (Nobel Prize for Peace in 2006, founder of Grameen Bank) was undoubtedly the promoter in chief of the microcredit movement that started in the 1970s. Over the years, the model has been refined and microfinance institutions now bring financial services directly to the doorsteps of poor people, along with employment opportunities and security against adverse events. Microfinance goes beyond microcredit – in countries where the legislation allows MFIs to do so – and also provides savings, insurance and fund transfers to low-income clients or solidarity lending groups.

The 10,000 MFIs (including state banks, agricultural development banks, savings banks, rural banks and non-bank financial institutions) around the world total outstanding loans of $65 billion for 195 million borrowers, of which 124 million live with less than $1.25 per day and 75 percent are women.[79] Among the largest microfinance institutions today are the National Bank for Agriculture and Rural Development in India, which finances more than 500 banks that in turn lend funds to over eight million self-help groups covering 95 million poor rural households;[80] Grameen Bank in Bangladesh, which lends money to 8.6 million clients (96 percent women);[81] and Bank Rakyat of Indonesia (BRI), which serves 6.5 million microloan clients and 25 million small savers.[82]

Fortunately, other media than microfinance institutions have brought efficient financial services to previously unbanked clients: electricity bills, cell phones, mobile agents equipped with adequate technology, small shops and post offices.

The hidden power of the electric utility bill – Codensa

How could an electric utility become a successful and profitable MFI? Codensa, the Bogotá electric utility since 1997, had managed to reach electrification rates above 99 percent in its concession. In 2002 they realized that poor clients were not spending much on electricity because they could not get loans to buy electrical appliances: 66 percent of Codensa's clients were unbanked and lacked credit history. Codensa built a complementary business called Codensa Hogar to offer household credit, including the repayments in the borrower's electricity bill.

Codensa Hogar was actually the perfect structure to solve the two key issues that traditional MFIs face:

- Assessing client credit risk when they do not have regular, formal and proven income: Codensa's database of electricity payment history provided accurate credit scoring.
- Keeping administrative costs low, in particular regarding payment collection for small amounts each week: Codensa could invoice and collect small amounts at a very low marginal administrative cost by including it on the monthly electricity bill.

And indeed the credit offering was so successful that Codensa then offered magazine subscriptions, micro-insurance and home improvement. In 2009, Codensa covered 31 percent of the market for electronic appliances in Bogotá.

Not only did Codensa "do good" by providing this new service to its clients, but it also turned its intimate knowledge of their payment history into a – very – profitable business line, even more so than business as usual for Codensa. Non-energy services including revenues from its 730,000 credit clients in 2008 represented 12 percent of total revenues for Codensa. While serving low-income people, the default rate was only 5 percent. Such success explains the $529 million paid by Multibanca Colpatria to Codensa to buy Codensa Hogar in 2009.[83]

The conspicuous magic of cell phones – M-PESA

And what about using cell phones? Safaricom, the Kenyan mobile operator, started its now world-famous M-PESA mobile money scheme in 2007, initially targeting the vast internal remittance market in Kenya. The service spread virally – with over 18 million active users by 2014, of which at least two-thirds were previously unbanked. This success notably stems from its simplicity of use: absence of registration fee, deposit fee, minimum balance, simple user interface, and easy access to a dense agent network of 40,000 points for "cash in and cash out." The service offers the possibility to send money to anyone, including non-registered users, but with higher fees for the latter, in effect encouraging them to register as well.

M-PESA generated revenues of $300 million in the financial year (FY) 2014, an increase of over 22 percent compared to the previous year, now accounting for more than 18 percent of Safaricom revenues.[84] Today, M-PESA is innovating through provision of new services (such as links to bank accounts), or possibilities to pay in installments via its system for goods such as Kickstart irrigation pumps. We will analyze why this model struggles to replicate outside Kenya on pages 81 and 82.

The ubiquitous chip card – FINO

Even those without a phone can be served through innovative technologies. Biometric smart cards have enabled FINO to become a major financial inclusion player within a few years. Founded in July 2006, it is now providing a full suite of financial services to 28 million (now actively transacting) customers in India – of which at least 80–90 percent were previously unbanked.

Anwar Shaikh and Alen Cransvarsis are two examples of these new bank clients. They live and work in Dharavi, the largest slum in Asia, hosting more than one million people with an estimated yearly turnover of over $500 million (due to its numerous informal manufacturing activities). They regularly need to send money to their families who live in other states. From the moment they enter a FINO shop, it takes them no more than five minutes to deposit the money (via the point of transaction terminal that the shop employees help them to use), get a receipt for the transaction and leave. When asked about FINO, their answers are as immediate as similar: "Transactions can be made very fast, this is great. In the bank we used to stand in queues for two to three hours, sometimes several days in a row, to do one transaction, and the transfer itself took several days." When asked what more he could ask from FINO, Anwar said he would like to have a FINO system in his own shop and become a FINO agent. What better proof for FINO that its clients are satisfied than when they want to become its employees?[85]

FINO effectively acts as the intermediary between financial institutions and the unbanked. In dense urban areas such as Dharavi, FINO has set up small shops where customers can conduct their transactions within minutes. In rural areas, mobile agents carry these terminals and visit their customers door to door when they need to make transactions. This has dramatically reduced the cost of money transfers between urban workers and their families who stay behind in rural areas: by using the FINO system it can cost as little as 25 Indian rupees (INR) ($0.5) per transfer of up to $200 (fees vary by slabs of sum being remitted). The family members residing in rural areas are serviced by FINO agents by opening no-frill savings accounts, enabling debit-credit transactions right on the doorstep.

In addition to money transfers, in 2010 FINO launched microloans of up to $200 and life and accident insurance schemes specifically designed for the poorest. FINO has also managed to smartly diversify its revenue sources through government payments (social benefit transfers), bank payments (commissions on account opening and transactions), micro health insurance (beneficiary enrollment and claim management), enterprise payments (wage disbursals and cash management services) and technology sales.

This has allowed FINO to break even in 2011, to generate $55 million in revenue in 2012–13, and to reach over 80 percent market share (defined as number of clients) on the Indian financial inclusion market.[86]

Even banks can provide banking services! – Bradesco

Similarly channeling government payments, Bradesco is one of the three main banks in Brazil that has extended its reach to remote regions, to deliver government social payments as far as remote Amazonian villages. Its outlets

RISHI GUPTA, CHIEF OPERATING OFFICER OF FINO[87]

ILLUSTRATION 12 / Rishi Gupta

Born in 1969 in Kolkata, Rishi is one of the pioneers who founded FINO within the largest private Indian bank ICICI.

Things went very fast. We decided to set up FINO In May 2006: three months later it was seed-funded and officially launched with a team of ten people. We were passionate about setting up a company that would make a difference. We have gone through many storms, and now the company is doing well. Now the next step is to make it shock-proof: five to ten years from now, I want to see this company able to withstand all issues, and endure for tens of years.

Above all, FINO is a business. We are backed by international investors like Blackstone and the IFC, and Indian investors like ICICI Bank and LIC. If we want to do financial inclusion for 700 million people (the scale of the need in India alone), the only way is

> to have a sustainable business model. If we were a CSO we would not have enough donor funds to serve even a million people.
>
> We are in the business of enabling banking services, and banking is heavily regulated. However, the focus of the principal regulator (RBI) on bank-led financial inclusion has helped set up a regulatory framework with enough freedom for us to develop a viable system to enable a bouquet of financial services to the remotest corners of India. The RBI continues to introduce evolving models and regulations, to address challenges based on prior learnings. Hence the payments domain continues to remain an exciting place to be in.
>
> We are running a marathon. We must not try too many things at once, but go slowly and be patient in building the right structure for these results to be optimal ten years from now.

piggyback on nearly 50,000 existing independent retailers, shops and post offices.[88] The necessary investment to equip existing outlets with banking hardware (limited to a computer with internet connection, a barcode reader and magnetic card swipe reader) and software amounts to $2000 maximum, while a fully fledged bank branch set-up costs $250,000.[89] As in the case of FINO or M-PESA, limiting these costs via appropriate technology allows the bank to profitably serve previously unbanked customers at affordable costs for them. Bradesco is also one of the channels that the Brazilian government has chosen to undertake the transfer of social benefits. Beforehand, pension beneficiaries would spend as much as one-third of the benefits on transportation to the place where they received the payment.

Obstacles to scale and replication

We estimate that within less than five years solutions such as Codensa, FINO, M-PESA or Bradesco have served a total of 120 million new users, bringing essential financial services to the unbanked in an affordable and profitable manner. This is quite an acceleration compared to the 195 million clients acquired by MFIs in 30 years. Yet 2.5 billion adults remain unbanked. Why do these innovative solutions fail to scale up and replicate faster?

As we have seen, critical to these new approaches are very low operating costs that enable such solutions to profitably serve the very small transactions of low-income customers. This can be achieved by piggybacking on an existing infrastructure (as Codensa did with its utility bills) and leveraging new technology (as M-PESA or FINO). In both cases, three challenges need to be addressed: (1) getting the existing owners of the infrastructure to agree; (2) quickly gaining a critical number of customers; (3) winning government regulatory support.

The need for existing infrastructure limits the number of entities that can start such services to those that have both sufficient fame and trust among the targeted populations, and relevant physical assets. Codensa, M-PESA and Bradesco leveraged their existing customer base or network and already trusted brands. Nationwide telecom companies have their prepaid card seller network; utilities benefit from an established billing system for a large customer base; far-reaching distribution networks (retailers, post offices and so on) offer a range of services and can easily add one more; technology companies only need a first large client (in FINO's case, the government) to pay for the technology infrastructure to reach remote customers, and can then leverage that infrastructure for additional services. But the owners of such large-scale infrastructure are typically large incumbent players that are wary of jeopardizing their operations for the sake of serving an untested market.

In terms of quickly reaching a critical mass of users, channeling government payments did the trick for FINO and Bradesco. M-PESA benefited from a "perfect storm": a large and dense internal market with a high amount of national remittances due to split family between urban and rural areas; a Safaricom customer base of 80 percent of mobile banking users in Kenya; a crisis situation when 600 bank branches had been closed for security reasons; and a decisive multimillion dollar advertising campaign. In the absence of such favorable circumstances, it is very difficult to reach scale: very few of the more than 80

THE FAILED PROMISE OF MOBILE BANKING (SO FAR)

Mobile banking solutions such as M-PESA seemed to have a bright potential, as out of the four billion unbanked people in 2009, a full billion people owned a cell phone, and this number was expected to grow to 1.7 billion by 2012.[90] McKinsey estimated that the market potential for mobile banking was $5 billion by 2012 in direct revenues and $2.5 billion from reduced churn for mobile operators, expecting 290 million unbanked people to be served.[91] Yet in 2011 there were still "only" 45 million mobile banking customers in developing economies, 30–40 percent of them previously unbanked.[92]

mobile money services created in the wake of M-PESA have passed the one million active user mark.

Relying on non-banking players to provide financial services introduces the regulatory issue of how to authorize them to conduct financial transactions. In Brazil and India, regulators pushed for these new models to increase financial inclusion and even paid the service providers to do so, contracting them and becoming their first source of revenues, in effect kick-starting their businesses. In Kenya, the Central Bank watched passively while M-PESA unfolded outside of the banking laws before deciding to support it and include it in the banking framework. So if regulators managed to adapt the laws in Brazil, India and Kenya, why could it not work elsewhere?

* * *

The unconventional banking initiatives discussed in this chapter approach the financial inclusion issue with a very different angle than microfinance does. Microfinance grows slowly but surely through local networks; it does not require vast initial investments or infrastructure. And when it does require start-up capital to build local capacity, this has usually been provided as seed capital and/or grants by international development organizations and foundations.

The initiatives seen here, on the contrary, require "big bucks for big bang": they do not work every time but when they do, thanks to the leverage of existing large-scale networks, they spread extremely fast, as FINO's 1.5 million additional clients per month show.

The two approaches are complementary: combined, they can actually accelerate their scaling-up as well as deepen their impact. M-PESA in Kenya has started working with MFIs, offering them a platform for loan reimbursement to lower their operating costs, while FINO recruits its agents among trusted members of the communities where it operates, such as self-help group leaders, formalizing and professionalizing the financial operations that were already happening in villages, and offering new services on top.

If, in each country, companies assess local demand and build their marketing approach around a local unanswered need, and leverage the adequate infra-structure (including MFIs) to provide that specific service, while regulators monitor their progress and give them freedom to experiment new ways of doing banking, then there should be no barrier to bringing financial services to the unbanked – all 2.5 billion of them. This should be attractive to businesses.

9

Boosting profitability of small farmers and micro-entrepreneurs

As we have seen, there are ample opportunities to improve the lives of poor families by providing them with valuable, affordable products and services. While the boundaries between domestic and economic uses are often blurred (such as the photovoltaic lamp that helps children to study and parents to work at night), the products and services we have described so far were not *primarily* aimed at improving income generation. This chapter turns to some of the solutions that focus on enhancing income generation by boosting the profitability of small farmers and, more generally, micro-entrepreneurs.

The livelihoods of most families at the BoP depend on their success as (micro) entrepreneurs. Be they farmers, craftspersons or traders, most people at the BoP must earn a living from high-risk, entrepreneurial ventures rather than from a paycheck.[93]

Effective strategies to increase the income of these micro-entrepreneurs often aggregate them in large clusters so that they can access the market under more equitable conditions and increase productivity. Since the 1980s most of these local initiatives have been supported through grants from international development organizations, foundations and also governments. While these projects benefit the participating micro-entrepreneurs, they rarely reach a significant impact – at least one commensurable to the need – as they tend to require subsidies to grow and/or fail to continue expanding commercial alliances with buyers.

An example of such an approach is "fair trade," a marketing strategy that allows poor farmers in developing countries to get a better deal (price and purchasing conditions) for the goods they produce (coffee, bananas, tea, rice, cotton and so on), through the use of a "fair trade" label. Two of the most successful fair trade initiatives are Max Havelaar in the Netherlands and Fair Trade USA (called TransFair USA before 2010). They both have already played an important role in improving the lot of many small farmers, by giving them back a larger share of the profits than traditional agro-buyers. The fair trade market is growing (10 percent rise in France in 2011; and some fair trade goods, such as coffee in Ethiopia and tea in Sri Lanka, now represent 20–50 percent of total sales in their product categories in developing countries) but it is small: it represents less than 1 percent of world trade in physical terms; and in 2012, out of the one billion farmers around the world,[94] only 1.2 million were engaged in fair trade.[95] The limitation of fair trade is that farmers remain dependent on the somewhat "discretionary" (one may say "charitable") goodwill of fair trade intermediaries, retailers and, ultimately, consumers.

The livelihoods of most families at the BoP depend on their success as (micro) entrepreneurs

Some initiatives have gone beyond the fair trade approach, by empowering farmers to make informed decisions on what crop to grow, and whom to sell to. These initiatives focus on bringing transparency on prices and demand, as well as improved access to markets (and avoid traditional intermediaries who also often wear the "loan shark" hat). Interestingly, these approaches are promoted both by not-for-profit activists and private players, who see this as a "win–win" game.

Amul – mobilizing three million Indian farmers

A great example is the "mother of all cooperatives," the formidable Amul. Begun in 1946, it now has three million members and has fundamentally transformed Indian dairy farming. Amul is also proof that a grass-roots, farmer-led initiative can give birth to what is today a leading Indian brand.

The Indian dairy market 60 years ago was highly dysfunctional: farmers typically lost hours in queues to sell their milk and were left at the mercy of local traders. During winter, when more milk is produced, dairy farmers would often be left with unsold milk. Such irregular and insufficient incomes made it difficult for them to afford sufficient fodder, and the lack of access to credit prevented them from making any investment. Also, because they lacked modern husbandry practices and access to technical support, their cows produced very little milk.

Additionally, lack of mechanization, automation and refrigeration infrastructure all along the value chain caused wastage of up to 40 percent of the production and made it difficult to guarantee the quality of the product, which was often adulterated by middlemen who added up to 50 percent water to the milk!

As a response to the exploitation of dairy farmers in the state of Gujarat, Amul (from the Sanskrit *Amoolya*, meaning priceless) was founded by Tribhuvandas Patel in 1946 with an initial base of two cooperatives collecting 200 liters of milk per day in the region of Anand. Grounded in the story of the Indian independence movement, Amul grew rapidly to become today's first dairy brand in the whole Asia-Pacific region, ahead of well-established brands such as Nestlé, and thus making India the largest milk producer in the world.

One man in particular made Amul what it is today. Considered as the father of the "White Revolution," which multiplied by five the milk production in India since 1950, Dr Verghese Kurien joined Tribhuvandas's team in 1955, transforming milk from a commodity into a brand through the creation of the Gujarat Cooperative Milk Marketing Federation. Valeria Budinich recalls how Kurien, a great storyteller, found the money to make the organization take off: "Kurien crashed into a cocktail bar uninvited in order to talk to Robert McNamara, the then World Bank president. That night he managed to convince Robert to finance the first $25 million, which would make Amul come to life."

Beside the outstanding personality of Amul's early leaders, the organization's extraordinary success is built on four pillars:

- A vast network covering the entire milk value chain: the first in a three-tier structure, 16,000 dairy cooperatives collect milk in each village. They are affiliated to one of 17 milk unions at the district level that procure the milk from them and process it. In turn, milk unions are federated into the Gujarat Cooperative Milk Marketing Federation (GCMMF) that takes care of the branding, marketing, sales and transportation to the warehouse or retail points. In peak period, GCMMF is able to purchase 12 million liters per day. It has a distribution network larger than any other fast-moving consumer goods (FMCG) company, composed of nearly 50 sales offices, over 5000 wholesale dealers and 700,000 retailers.
- The use of information and communications technology (ICT) is critical to improve productivity and transparency: according to Dr B. M. Vyas, who set up the ICT systems in the company, "Amul is not a food company, it is an IT company in the food business."[96] Indeed, as Amul markets perishable goods, it is essential to have 24/7 information flows between GCMMF and all the nodes of its supply chain. In addition, technology at the cooperative

level allows transparent and fair purchasing from and to the farmers, which is a critical factor to create trust in the system initially. The technology – a computerized collection point including an electronic weighing system for up to 5000 liters, a milk analyzer, a PC, and accounting and management software – is bought by village cooperatives for $3,300 on average, financed by farmers' membership fees and, if necessary, by credit from government agencies and paid back within two years.

- "Utterly Butterly Delicious Amul": despite a communication budget far below that of many other companies, it would be extremely hard to find an Indian today who is unaware of the Amul name. The brand's mascot (a cute and chubby girl – which has not changed since 1967) became iconic in Indian advertising. To build the equity of its brand, GCMMF barely uses traditional media, but promotes it through word of mouth, posters and ads in rural areas, and through web-based promotions and competitions in urban areas.
- Shared value at all levels: farmers receive part of the profit generation by Amul in the form of dividends, and the rest (actually the larger share of profits) is part redistributed to cooperatives and part used to promote the growth of milk supply and improve yields.

Cooperative membership tends to double where the Amul system is introduced, as its transparency and fairness creates trust among farmers and motivates them to join the cooperative. Over time, these same farmers typically reap more benefits: 88 percent of them sell more milk and 73 percent own more animals than before.

eChoupal – a rural supply chain

Most of India's 600 million farmers are smallholders. Their subsistence is put at risk every time an adverse event hits their harvests, be it drought or flood, crop disease or pests. When the time comes to sell their produce, the main marketplace is "mandis" (government-regulated wholesale market), where harvest lots are sold by auction. As they have to travel, and cannot store their produce, farmers often end up selling at a very low price. Intermediaries at the mandis reportedly make margins of up to 80 percent on the price given to farmers. Agro-purchasers also suffer from these inefficiencies, as they cannot source commodities directly, and do not have much control over quality.

ITC Ltd, one of the largest Indian conglomerates, decided to create an alternative direct-sourcing channel: eChoupal. It negotiated with local authorities the right to set up its own marketplace, whereby ITC could purchase directly from farmers. Farmers only have to bring a handful of grains to the eChoupal intermediary, a trusted farmer called *sanchalak*, who performs basic quality tests and proposes the ITC-set price for their product. ITC also set up e-kiosks: internet-connected computers installed in the houses of sanchalaks, which provide free information on the prices of various crops at neighboring markets, on the weather and on cultivation practices.

Understandably, the most important aspect of this system is the trust established with the farmers, "the one fundamental of eChoupal" as Mr Shailesh Naik, the general manager of ITC eChoupal Channel, puts it.[97] To gain this trust, eChoupal selected sanchalaks among trusted farmers to be responsible for the e-kiosk, while providing the hardware and applications for free, as proof of good intentions. The sanchalak also had to take a public oath that he would not charge for the use of the kiosk and would share it for the good of his village.

Are you changing the power situation between the small producers and the corporate world?

Today, eChoupal has 6,500 e-kiosks, and ITC can source a range of higher quality commodities at a lower cost. ITC also uses the eChoupal infrastructure to sell $100 million worth of products (ranging from fertilizers to toothpaste) directly to villagers, guaranteeing product quality and reliable supply compared to previous alternatives. Since 2008, it has added a suite of services, such as crop loans and insurance services. As a result, eChoupal has managed to create one of the most integrated supply chain models in India, investing in farmers' knowledge and education, offering them transparent and fair prices, and sourcing for them

THE STORY OF KISSAN TEODALE, A FARMER USING AN ECHOUPAL CLOSE TO NAGPUR, INDIA

Kissan is a farmer who lives with his wife, daughter and two sons. He owns and cultivates 12 acres of land. Now that he has a cell phone, he calls his sanchalak about once a week to get information on prices and farming best practices. Since he started using eChoupal, he has changed his approach to cultivation, saving on the cost of inputs and improving his yield. Today his family earns $6000 per year. Kissan has already invested in a water pump and other equipment. He wishes eChoupal could offer loans so that he could buy a tractor on credit.[98]

quality goods and services. eChoupal's vision was to make farmers more educated and able to produce and trade quality produce, so as to grow the pie that ITC could get a share of. Today, eChoupal increases the profits of farmers by an average of 2.5 percent a year simply by improving their access to the market (while only purchasing 10–12 percent of a given harvest), while enhanced productivity through education and natural resources management, as well as diversification of crops, have considerably increased their income (up to 300 percent).

Interestingly, in India, not only large corporations but also CSOs and entrepreneurial ventures have taken similar approaches to establishing better links between small farmers and large buyers of crops and staples such as supermarkets or food processors. ACDI VOCA, a USAID-backed CSO, is supporting a new kind of buyer at the supermarket level, equipped with smart phones, linked to local aggregators with cell phones at the village level, who pass the orders directly from supermarkets to farmers and ensure that demand matches supply efficiently every day. As in eChoupal, the ICT infrastructure is also used to get weather information and agro-advice.[99]

eKutir is a small venture launched by the incubator Grameen-Intel, which has developed a suite of applications licensed for a one-time $800 fee to local entrepreneurs equipped with at least a laptop and a camera, who then provide relevant paying services to farmers. As of December 2013, eKutir had set up 106 kiosks serving a total of 50,000 farmer families, with kiosk entrepreneurs earning a decent living and farmers reporting improved income from increased and improved production as well as better prices obtained for their products.[100]

In Africa also, similar services are developing: the "Community Knowledge Worker" initiative was started in 2008 in Uganda by the Grameen Foundation; the Kenya Farmers' Helpline was launched by Kencall, an outsourcing company, in 2009.[101] As these projects develop, they should allow farmers to have more certain income and allow them to better plan for the future, while the web record of their transactions could help to gather information on their cash flows and grant them access to credit.

Light Years IP and Ethiopian coffee growers

Small farmers capture on average only 2–10 percent of the final retail value of their exported production. This percentage does not change much, including for those who produce rare or high-quality crops, because the difference in price accrues mainly to those who own the brand and market the product as a specialty or premium good. The "intangible value" that comes from the uniqueness, reputation and quality of a product is almost entirely captured after it leaves its country of origin.

Light Years IP aims at changing that through strategies based on intellectual property. Light Years IP crafts different strategies for each product and geography, offering a range of legal and branding tools from licensing trade secrets to brand management.

The most advanced project of Light Years IP is that of Ethiopian fine coffee trademarking and licensing. In Ethiopia more than 15 million people depend on the coffee industry, including six million farmers cultivating some of the world's finest coffees: Sidamo, Yirgacheffe and Harar. Before Light Years IP intervention in 2004, farmers were getting around $1 per kilo of coffee, and exporters $2 per kilo, while the average retail price hovered around $20–28 per kilo, of which the distribution post export was getting around 50 percent. Light Years IP worked with the Ethiopian authorities to secure trademark registrations that forced distributors to purchase a license to sell these products in over 30 countries. Farmers' income doubled in a few years, and Ron Layton, Light Years IP founder, (already mentioned in Chapter 2) hopes that it will triple to $6–8 per kilogram in the coming years. He explains:

> In most cases Light Years IP model is not a win–win model in the short term, but a fight. Most companies do not see the advantages-to-be of having a better-paid sustainable supply, and must be forced to comply and to give up part of their current margins to their suppliers.

> Fair trade barely touches on the issue, despite the number of projects done under that principle. As long as the question "Are you changing the power situation between the small producers and the corporate world?" is not addressed, there is no structural change and the corporate remains the one that dictates the rule.

> Local governments are doing their share in grants, paying for advice, training and techniques for IP value capture. Most international agencies advocate conventional strategies, advising countries to start non-traditional exports and value-added processing. But moving to products without history and expertise is questionable if there is high intangible value being generated by heritage exports but not captured. International agencies should recognize the much higher returns from the Light Years IP interventions, far exceeding returns from conventional strategies. Western governments on their side should revise their trade and price policy to avoid the current unfair distribution of product revenues among value chain actors. So, basically, it

is a systemic change that is needed. And, in the short term, not all actors will be positively affected by it.

Light Years IP's systemic approach has led to large-scale results in two countries, where it could influence national policies. It is not risk free, though, as it requires producers to build collaboration among significant numbers of small farmers and be assisted to build competitive importing businesses. This is hard work and it can only succeed where there is a critical mass of well-organized producers who are empowered and able to sustain their competitive advantage achieved through IP control over time.

But changing national policies is not the only way to act: as we discuss in Part 2, companies on their own can decide to make a difference and change the distribution of profit in their value chain. In our work around the world, we are already seeing evidence of this change where corporations such as Walmart, Nestlé, Danone and others are engaged in exploring how to better integrate small producers in their supply chains and finding that it is not just good for their brands but also for the competitiveness of their business in the long run.

chapter 10

When markets fail

The reader will undoubtedly have noted the conspicuous absence from the preceding chapters of some of the issues included in the Millennium Development Goals: hunger, universal education, child health, maternal health or gender equity.

As highlighted in Chapter 2, business is no panacea: for many social problems, market-based solutions are ineffective and government or philanthropic intervention is indispensable. In addition, while we have shown that market-based approaches may help people, we have not considered whether they inadvertently hurt the planet.

This chapter will hence discuss:

• The limitations of market-based approaches.
• The need for regulations.
• The issue of whether fighting poverty will lead to hurting the planet.

The limitations of market-based approaches

Limitations to market-based approaches can stem from: (1) the too extreme poverty of the poorest families; (2) the distant and uncertain nature of the benefits promised; (3) the need to get an entire community to agree to pay for a service.

Too poor to be a (fully paying) customer

We showed that 1.1 billion people live in extreme poverty, with a daily income of less than $1.25 PPP. Market-based approaches are useless in fighting such extreme poverty, as BRAC's "Challenging the Frontiers of Poverty Reduction, Targeting the Ultra Poor" program will show.

Founded in Bangladesh in 1972, BRAC is one of the most impactful CSOs in the world. With over 120,000 staff members and a $728 million budget in 2013, it provides microloans to 4.5 million families, health services to 25 million pregnant women through a network of 110,000 front-line community health workers, school to 1.3 million children and improved access to sanitation to over 30 million people. This list is not complete and refers only to Bangladesh, while BRAC is also among the leading development organizations in Afghanistan, Uganda, Tanzania and Southern Sudan.

BRAC describes itself as "pioneering a new kind of organization, which integrates development programs with social enterprises and enables BRAC and individuals to become self-reliant." This focus on self-reliance is demonstrated by the remarkable fact that less than 30 percent of BRAC's $728 million expenditure budget was funded by donors. In particular, the microcredit program ("Dabi"), which provides loans of $100–1000 to poor women is operating profitably with a 99 percent repayment rate.

Despite this relentless focus on achieving self-reliance and using market forces to solve social problems, BRAC has recognized since January 2002 that market-based approaches are inadequate to help the "ultra-poor" – the 22 percent of Bangladeshi families who struggle for survival below the food poverty line. Mothers are usually divorced or widows, and generate their meager income by begging or working as a servant in a better-off family. They possess no productive assets and the children have to work and cannot go to school. They are unable to take advantage of the mainstream programs offered by CSOs, such as microcredit.

BRAC's fully grant-based specially targeted ultra poor (STUP) approach provides these usually single-mother households with health services (such as construction of a latrine), assets (such as five goats and ten chickens) and training in husbandry. In 2013, BRAC provided assets to 468,000 ultra-poor women and training to five million of them. The aim of STUP is, over a period of two years, to help these women to "graduate" from this program and get access to the mainstream development programs such as microcredit. A 2011 Randomized Control Trial evaluation demonstrated that participant households increased their income by 46 percent (against 16 percent for the control group) and "reduced their dependency on distress occupations like housemaid and begging." But this is not a black-and-white debate. While people living in absolute poverty below $1.25 PPP per day (in 2005) cannot pay a cent even for essential goods, people slightly better off (as in living on between $1.25 and $2 PPP 2005) can generally pay something, but not the full amount of the good or service. Thus, philanthropy and business should not be opposed but need to actually complement each other through cross-subsidy schemes. Clients will gain choice and dignity from being treated as clients, not as beneficiaries, while accessing a service otherwise too expensive for them.

Cross-subsidy schemes are a variant of a widespread business marketing ploy: multi-tiered pricing. The principle of multi-tiered pricing is to propose the same service at different prices depending on what different customers are willing to pay, to capture the "consumer surplus" of people who can pay more for the service than what it costs. This is what airline yield management does: a consumer buying the ticket in advance will often pay less than the one who chooses to buy at the last minute. As more customers (in particular less wealthy ones) can now fly through this system, airlines invest in larger planes and lower their operating cost per passenger, allowing them to further lower the average price of flights and grow the market.

Cross-subsidies work in the same way: profit made on "regular customers" is reinvested to compensate for the lower price paid by poorer customers. It is common that water or electricity utilities are granted a local monopoly through a concession to have the obligation to connect poorer neighborhoods and to offer them a "social tariff."

For example, the concession that Manila Water won in 1997 required the company to extend its network to achieve universal water coverage in the part of Manila where it was awarded. Manila Water set up the program "Tubig Para sa Barangay" (TPSB, literally "Water for the Community") in 1998 to connect low-income communities. Today, Manila Water effectively serves 99 percent of the population within its concession area, including 340,000 households (or around 1.7 million people) through TPSB. A progressive pricing scheme gives a price of $0.18 per cubic meter to households who consume less than 10 cubic meters per month, while people consuming 20 cubic meters pay on average around $0.27 per cubic meter and people consuming 40 cubic meters will pay $0.51 per cubic meter. Additionally, since 2007, Manila Water waives the initial connection fee for poor households, as designated by the municipality.

Whereas the multi-tiered pricing of the airline industry is predicated on a different quality of services for different classes, Manila Water offers the same quality of water and standard of service across the board. This scheme is designed to reach low-income areas based on a clear business case: under-served, low-income households demonstrate a willingness to pay for safe, reliable water and connecting these communities means reaching new markets while reducing costs from inefficiencies and illegal connections for the company. The "Water for the Community" program also introduced flexible financing options and affordable water rates through staggered connection fees, cost sharing among residents and average water rates for bulk connections, among other alternatives. Beyond the subsidies, the community is given a strong sense of ownership of the project. Beneficiaries play key roles in water-meter monitoring, payment collection and maintenance of their connections. Manila Water also provides livelihood opportunities to the community to enable them to sustainably pay for their monthly bills and to keep the connections going.

The health-care industry has similar cross-subsidy schemes for surgeries, be it for cataract at Aravind or for cardiac care at the Narayana Health (NH), both in India. A world-class quality of care at lower costs than in the developed world (NH charges one-tenth of the cost of US heart surgery!) attracts wealthy patients from richer countries, who pay a higher price than lower-income patients. Importantly, the medical treatment is strictly identical (surgeons don't know who is paying what), with the only difference being the comfort of the patient's hospital room. Treating a large number of patients through these cross-subsidized schemes allows the overall cost of care to be lowered, by maximizing utilization of the operations room and surgeons' time as well as buying medical supplies in larger quantities.

These cross-subsidy strategies apply to any industry characterized with high investment and fixed costs. In these situations, charging poorer clients below full cost can actually be profitable, as long as marginal contributions remain positive.

Charging poorer clients below full cost can actually be profitable

Elusive returns on investment

There are other less obvious, more pervasive reasons that explain why the poor, who could afford to buy the products and services they would greatly benefit from, actually don't.

Poor people are reluctant to invest in a new product or service when the expected benefits are too far into the future and uncertain. For example, providing micro-nutrients to children to help their physical and intellectual development has been declared in 2012 the "smartest investment for Policy-makers and Philanthropists" by the Copenhagen Consensus Center, an independent think tank of leading development economists that includes four Nobel Prize laureates.[102] Providing micronutrients during the critical first two years of a child's life would cost less than $5. However, the economic return of an improved nutrition will only be seen when these children reach working age. Moreover, the actual impact of this "investment" is also dependent on access to clean water, health care, education and so on. In other words, micronutrients are a necessary condition but are not sufficient to guarantee a future adult with better income. The Global Alliance for Improved Nutrition implements large-scale fortification programs (such as adding iodate in salt to prevent goiter) that are sustainable but require a government intervention to make fortification mandatory and enforce its application. As we will see in Chapter 12, despite the remarkable success of Britannia in selling fortified biscuits, a significant impact on reducing malnutrition among Indian children will be best achieved by fortifying the 150 million daily meals distributed for free in Indian schools, not by selling micronutrients to the poor.

The deferred and uncertain return of fighting child malnutrition with micronutrients stands in sharp contrast to the immediate and certain return of enabling working-age adults to recover the use of vision through surgery or lenses, as has been demonstrated by a number of players such as Aravind hospitals in India, Visionspring in Bangladesh or Asembis (see box) in Costa Rica. Indeed, bringing back vision (an instant benefit brought by simple reading glasses!) has found a large willing-to-pay market among the BoP.

A S E M B I S

Founded and led by Rebeca Villalobos in Costa Rica, Asembis has successfully developed a sustainable and scalable business model offering access to high-technology vision care for the BoP.

Asembis has achieved a market share of 60 percent of the sales of corrective glasses and is the only player in many rural areas. This coverage is achieved through a two-tiered pricing that ensures that the wealthier customers actually pay for the poorest.

It also provides full eye care. Contrary to many popular eye-care CSOs, Asembis is not limited to selling cheap "readers," it organizes detection campaigns and sophisticated eye surgery.

It is sustainable and profitable. Asembis has generated $100,000 in profits in 2010 out of $5.7 million in sales. A new clinic achieves break-even within about a year.

And it is scalable: Asembis has redesigned the eye-care process to maximize the utilization of the scarcest resource: the optometrist. In its clinics, optometrists routinely visit an impressive 70 patients per day.

Not surprisingly, many philanthropists have long focused on improving the lives of children, and on investing in causes such as primary education that – like the fight against malnutrition – provide critical yet deferred and uncertain social returns. These are areas where philanthropic and government money is probably needed the most to reach the poorest.

Tragedy of common goods

Some market-based approaches are only possible if a whole community embraces them, such as relocating a slum in a new area or having it purchase property rights from the legitimate owner of the land (see the Terra Nova example in Chapter 6). The deal can only take place if the whole community agrees to it – and the process of convincing every member of a 500-person community can take a long time.

Even more complex are cases where each household can decide to buy a good or service on his or her own, but will derive full benefits from it only if all of his or her neighbors adopt it as well. This is the case for sanitation: individual users will derive convenience benefits from constructing a toilet in their home, yet the ultimate objective of keeping neighboring water sources free of bacterial disease requires all inhabitants to stop defecating in the open. In order to overcome this obstacle, BRAC has set up a partly subsidized approach (part of the Water, Sanitation and Hygiene – WASH – initiative). They first raise awareness on the importance of sanitation and its link to health, then set up village committees to monitor and publicize the status of sanitation adoption in the village. To make sanitation possible for all, WASH offers technical assistance to those who can afford toilets, and loans or subsidies to the poorer who cannot. By this smart alliance of market-based mechanisms and targeted subsidies, and with the help of social pressure, WASH manages to get full sanitation coverage in villages, thus ensuring that maximum health benefits are achieved for all.

Regulation needed!

Not only can market-based solutions be irrelevant, they can – dangerously – give the illusion that they can solve problems on their own.

Let's take the example of higher education in the US. In the academic year 2008–09, 3.2 million students enrolled in US for-profit colleges, 13 percent of the total number of students and 23 percent more than the year before. For-profit colleges have rapidly grown over the last two decades to fill the market gap left by rigid public institutions. Today it is a $29 billion industry comprising listed companies such as the *Washington Post* that owns Kaplan (110,000 students) or Appolo Education Group that owns the University of Phoenix (450,000 students).

This seems like a remarkable example of a market-based solution to a pressing social need. But it is also an example of what can go wrong with unbridled business approaches: in August 2010, the US Government Accountability Office (GAO) published a report stating: "undercover testing finds colleges encouraged fraud and engaged in deceptive and questionable marketing practices."[103] In February 2011, the US Department of Education issued data showing that for-profit colleges leave 25 percent of their graduates unable to pay back their loans, compared with 11 percent at public institutions and 8 percent at private nonprofit institutions.

While for-profit colleges are quick to point out that these higher default rates are – at least in part – due to the fact that their students come from less privileged backgrounds than their public counterparts, there is a wide recognition that aggressive marketing practices have resulted in students paying excessively high prices for courses that do not provide them with the employment opportunities they hoped for.

Some corporations have taken intriguing initiatives to attempt to change the rules that govern an industry and drive behavior of corporations. Skepticism is in order when a corporation pretends to "change the world." As Adam Smith stated in *The Wealth of Nations* (1776): "the interest of the dealers… in any

L U M N I

Felipe Vergara, a Colombian, has identified what is fundamentally wrong with the model of financing higher education through loans: loans mean it is the students who bear the full risk of deciding to invest in their education, and in a particular course. Instead of giving loans, Lumni, the organization Felipe co-founded, invests in equity: each student commits to pay a fixed percentage of income for a fixed number of months after graduation. "When the student does well, so do the investors. When the student fails, the investors share the risk," says Felipe.

particular branch of trade or manufactures, is always in some respects different from, and even opposite to, that of the public... The proposal of any new law or regulation of commerce which comes from this order, ought always to be listened to with great precaution, and ought never be adopted till after having been long and carefully examined, not only with the most scrupulous, but with the most suspicious attention."[104]

Are corporations claiming to do good, acting indeed against their self-interest (charitable CEOs acting as idealist do-gooders who slander away the wealth of their shareholders for their own satisfaction or prestige) – or are they just paying tribute to virtue and whitewashing (or greenwashing) their products? Or have these enlightened corporations found ways to align their interest with society's?

In many cases the jury is still out, but it may be worth describing three types of strategies that corporations have been using.

The entrepreneur activists – Trojan horses?

The Body Shop was created in 1976 in England by Anita Roddick and focused on "natural" products that are good for the skin and for the health. The young company initially committed to "no animal testing" then progressively extended its concept to "real beauty" for "real women," "safe environment," "sustainability" and, ultimately, "fair trade." Each shift addressed consumers' sensitivity to these questions before these concerns became mainstream. Hardly ten years after its founding, the chain was listed on the London Stock Exchange where the stock was given the nickname "the shares that defy gravity" as its price increased by more than 500 percent.[105] This financial prowess was as talked about as the controversies that arose from the gap between the lofty values and the founder's decision in 2006 to sell the company for £652 million to L'Oréal, the world's largest cosmetics producer that had not then abandoned animal testing. Campaigners against animal testing called for a boycott. Anita Roddick was accused of abandoning her principles and vowed to give away the £130 million she had personally made from the sale.

Like Anita Roddick, other entrepreneur activists who have been smart or lucky enough to pick on a societal trend have seen their early niche turn into a major market segment, and have become very wealthy as many of them have cashed in by selling to the large companies that were their archenemies: Ben & Jerry's to Unilever, Stonyfield to Danone, and so on.

Anita Roddick declared after selling her company to L'Oréal that she saw herself as a "Trojan horse" that would change the practices of a large company.[106]

Critics will argue that these entrepreneur activists have just sold out to large corporations and lost their soul in the process, demonstrating that activism is highly soluble in capitalism. Nevertheless, these successful entrepreneurs appear to have had an effect on their industries and forced their competitors to emulate their attitudes. The Body Shop helped to change the EU regulations on animal testing in 2004.[107]

The leader strategists

The vision written in Walmart Sustainable Agriculture Fact Sheet is that agriculture and food industry should be local. Greenpeace activists would not say it better. The company focuses on three broad areas and defines the goals to achieve by the end of 2015: (1) support farmers and their communities; (2) produce more food with less waste and fewer resources; (3) source key agriculture products that meet sustainability requirements. The program will be implemented in each market served by Walmart according to the specificity of each region.

Up to one in seven of the truckloads of perishables delivered to a store will be thrown out, due to bad logistics.[108] So when Walmart announces it will reduce in-store food waste by 15 percent in its emerging markets and 10 percent in all other markets, this means solid money for the company.

Simultaneously creating value for shareholders and society is not restricted to start-ups. Industry leaders can act strategically to strengthen their competitive advantage by voluntarily deciding to adopt business practices that may somewhat increase their cost, but much less than the costs of their smaller or less able competitors who will find themselves forced to comply with these new standards by consumers or regulators. These industry leaders accept a tactical loss for a strategic victory.

Industry labels

In June 2003, a group of banks led by Citigroup, ABN AMRO, Barclays and WestLB agreed on the Equator Principles that have become the de facto standard for banks and investors on how to assess major development projects around the world. The Equator Principles were based on standards of the World Bank and the International Finance Corporation. Similar standards have been set in a number of industries: mining, forestry, fisheries and so on.

Those organizations leverage consumer awareness on environmental issues. They "sell" eco labels to companies that integrate demanding standards and behaviors in their processes (that is, "responsible" fisheries practicing fishing in an environmentally responsible way so as not to aggravate the global problem of overfishing). Those companies get a "competitive advantage" from the label, which allows them to enhance reputation, to gain market shares or to raise their prices. To be effective and legitimate, these labels eventually need to become independent from the players that started them.

And what about the planet?

By enabling people to get out of poverty and onto the path of economic development, are we contributing to global warming and over-consumption of the world's resources?

It is quite remarkable that all the innovations we have mentioned so far actually have a *positive* impact on the environment and particularly on global warming: solar lanterns and systems substitute for kerosene; cookstoves reduce burning of biomass; water plants avoid boiling water; and better-built homes save building materials and last longer. We don't seem to have to choose between helping the poor and the environment, probably because extremely cost-efficient solutions have to be extremely frugal in the use of resources.

In the longer term – that is, if these initiatives are successful and indeed enable the poor to climb up the economic ladder – the question will arise. After all, China's economic growth helped to lift more than 700 million people out of poverty but it also made China the world's greatest contributor to CO_2 emissions (29 percent of the world's 34.5 billion tonnes in 2012 against 11 percent in 1990).[109] To put things in perspective, if Africa was to follow the same path as China – that is, to reach 7.4 tonnes of CO_2 emissions per capita – this would increase the total global emissions by 20 percent.

Whether this will accelerate global warming and environmental issues depends on three factors:

- How quickly will socio-economic development in emerging markets lead to declines in birth rates? United Nations forecasts point to the world population reaching 9.6 billion by 2050, assuming a reduction in fertility rates in the 48 least developed countries from 4.53 today to 2.87 by 2050. If this reduction did not happen, the world population would reach 11.1 billion people in 2050.[110]

• Will emerging markets innovate and invent more frugal, less resource-intensive development models? As a reminder, rich countries differ remarkably, ranging from less than 6 tonnes of CO_2 per capita in France to over 16 tonnes in the USA. Urban planning decisions being made in Africa and Asia will determine the boundary conditions for our future.

• Will richer countries addicted to resources consumption be able to change their models, adopting innovations developed in emerging markets?

Economists will debate the answer to these questions for years. Importantly, given the focus of this book, these issues are not specific to market-based approaches.

* * *

As we have seen, market-based approaches are no panacea. They have limitations, they need regulation in many cases and won't solve the environmental issues on their own.

Yet the preceding chapters have amply demonstrated that market-based approaches can make a big difference to the life of poor populations. Each of the solutions we have described in the previous chapters have proven to be economically sustainable, while affordable by the BoP.

Table 5 illustrates which strata of the pyramid these solutions target as customers.

With both the magnitude of the potential and of the limitations of market-based approaches in mind, it is time to turn to the reasons why these solutions

TABLE 5 Segments of the BoP targeted by each solution

BoP segment	% of world population	Improved cookstoves	Solar lanterns	SHS	Water from kiosks	Water from utility	Home improvement (PH)	New homes (HFA)	Financial services	Farmers' improved income initiatives
Upper segments	35%	X	X	X	X	X	X	X	X	X
Moderate poor	18%	X	X	X	X	X	X		X	X
Extreme poor	22%	X	X						X	X

are so rarely scaling up and replicating beyond the scope of local programs run by social entrepreneurs.

This will take us through a wide review of the systemic obstacles standing in the way of these solutions and, most importantly, the possible strategies to overcome them. This is what Part 2 of this book is about.

Part **2**

Obstacles to scale

The path to scale

We have seen in Part 1 of this book many examples of businesses that managed to bring essential goods and services to the poorest in a commercially sustainable way. We have also seen that they were still far from answering the immensity of the needs, and required in most cases a lot of additional effort to be extended to the too many who do not yet benefit from their work.

Part 2 of this book will analyze the systemic obstacles that prevent these solutions from scaling up. We start by analyzing the obstacles faced by the lead players in this field, social entrepreneurs and corporations:

- As illustrated in the cases of Toyola or SELCO, social entrepreneurs themselves believe that grass-root approaches are essential. In Chapter 11 we will see how *social entrepreneurs*, the natural owners of most of the ideas and initiatives that successfully serve the poor, could increase their impact by seeking to achieve a maximum influence on their ecosystem as an alternative to scaling their own organization.
- Patrimonio Hoy and Codensa, while producing tangible business benefits, have not been scaled up by their respective corporations. In Chapter 12, we will turn to *corporations*, which are so good at adapting and replicating globally successful business models, in order to understand why and how they can and should engage in scaling up social innovations.

We then turn to some new business approaches that these players need to design and implement:

- Initiatives such as Housing for All demand collaboration between social, business and public sectors. After looking at what the social and business sectors can each do on their own, Chapter 13 takes us through new possible collaborations between these traditionally opposed sectors: *hybrid value chains*.

- Our previous chapters have shown that engineers have done their part of the work (in that affordable, effective products do exist) yet marketers are struggling. Marketing innovative products such as solar lanterns or improved cookstoves to BoP families is about *"turning needs into wants,"* the focus of Chapter 14.

- Chapter 15 explores in depth a particularly critical missing link of the value chain to the BoP – the *last mile distribution* – to see how the existing gap is actually a business opportunity.

We will end this review of obstacles to and strategies for scale by analyzing how funders – financiers and philanthropists – are often part of the problem but can be part of the solution:

- Making all these changes happen will require finance. Chapter 16 discusses how *financiers* avoid a looming bubble from exploding and, more proactively, accelerate the geographic replication of proven social business models.

- All social entrepreneurs will complain about how well-intended philanthropy-funded giveaway programs create their worst enemy: "expectation of free help." Chapter 17 looks at how *philanthropy* has a critical role to play in catalyzing market-based approaches.

chapter 11

Social entrepreneurs –
size or influence?

The social entrepreneurs at the origin of the innovations we have seen in the previous chapters understand better than anyone their market and the possibilities of their solutions. They have immense creativity, leadership and determination. Yet so many fail to achieve the scale of impact they were envisioning that helping to "scale up" innovations has become a new buzzword in the philanthropic community.

We have observed three main strategies for social entrepreneurs to achieve large-scale impact:

- **Size**: they grow their organization to reach more beneficiaries.
- **Influence**: they keep their own organization small but focus on influencing other, bigger organizations.
- **Serial entrepreneurship**: they just move on to the next big idea.

As we will see in this chapter, all paths can lead to success but are paved with their specific set of challenges.

Size

As in the business world, the size of organizations is driven by their geographic scope (some businesses are global in nature, some are local) and whether they are single or multi-business groups (see Table 6).

Let's illustrate this diversity with three cases of social entrepreneurs who have driven their organizations to relatively large scale: Bill Drayton of Ashoka, Sir Fazle Abed of BRAC and Jean-Marc Borello of Groupe SOS.

TABLE 6   Six types of social businesses

	Single business	Multi-business with operational synergies	Multi-business with few synergies, but sharing support resources (finance, accounting, legal assistance, HR, marketing, etc.)
Global (*network, standards, etc. that by essence must be global to have value*)	Global standard organizations (e.g. Transparency International)	Ashoka: Creating a unique global community	
Multilocal (*start in one country and then replicate elsewhere with some adjustments*)	CDI: Franchising the model wherever there is demand	BRAC: Growing organically, country after country	Groupe SOS: Integrating new entities that can benefit from centralized support

Bill Drayton – Ashoka, a global community of social entrepreneurs

Ashoka was "born global." This CSO is designed to promote social entrepreneurship by setting global standards and helping spread best practices; it must be global or it will not last. Today Ashoka is the largest global community of social entrepreneurs, with 3000 Ashoka Fellows in 86 countries and employing 250 staff in 30 offices worldwide. In recent years, Ashoka redefined its mission as "Everyone a Changemaker" and has launched a series of new programs designed to enable changemaking at universities, schools, corporations and society at large. These programs are now the building blocks – together with the selection of Ashoka Fellows – of a strategy focused on mindset change and collaborative entrepreneurship at scale.

Critical to the mission of Ashoka is ensuring that the Ashoka Fellows it elects hold the same high standards across the world, despite differences in language, culture and sectors. Bill Drayton recalls the first days of Ashoka in India in 1981: "One of the central questions we asked ourselves during the travel and interviews in India, Indonesia and Venezuela during the late 1970s was: Can we develop a system that will reliably identify the world's best social entrepreneurs – before they are famous? Selections cannot rely on the intuition of one or even multiple people. There needs to be very clear criteria and then a reliably tough selection process. Since the first Fellow we elected, we asked ourselves the question of how to streamline this process of selection, so that it could be done by other people as thoroughly as any of us had done it. It had to be scalable from day one." After over 30 years of existence, Ashoka has relentlessly focused on improving its rigorous search and selection process and ensuring that Fellows that join its community have an idea with high-impact potential and are committed to changing the pattern in his/her field and nationally within five years.

As Ashoka replicated its model across the world, Bill Drayton implemented a "decentralized yet integrated organization." Country representatives are chosen through a very rigorous process yet they enjoy a high level of independence to manage their office and country – as long as they follow the head-office policy in terms of Fellows' election and other standardized procedures.

In addition to its own success, Ashoka has inspired the creation of more than 80 organizations that seek to support social entrepreneurs, including the Skoll Fellowship, Lemelson Fellows, Schwab Fellows and more recently Schwab's Social Entrepreneur of the Year, echoing Green Fellows and Avina Leaders. Ashoka is delighted with these followers that have helped to achieve its goal of promoting social entrepreneurship in the world.

Sir Fazle Hasan Abed – BRAC, an integrated group of social enterprises

Sir Fazle Hasan Abed is the founder and managing director of the largest CSO in the world, impacting in 2013 more than 135 million people in 12 countries. BRAC has an annual budget of $728 million and a staff of more than 120,000 employees.[111]

BRAC diversified its operations in order to achieve full impact. As Rumee Ali, BRAC's former MD for Enterprises says: "Our businesses started as interventions to solve a problem, then we figured out how to make them sustainable. For example our dairy operations started because we had to buy the milk from the farmers who had bought cows with the loans of our microcredit program."[112] The organization built on a first success in Bangladesh before replicating in new geographies, going deep before going wide.

An early feature of BRAC has been its focus on measuring results. The walls of BRAC village branches are covered with charts that track progress against key performance indicators (KPIs). Abed also set up an audit team independent from the rest of the organization, reporting directly to him. This allowed him to understand what worked to further build the organization, ensuring that BRAC could correct mistakes rapidly and progress constantly.

Thinking about scale from the start, Abed insisted on creating very simple business models, which could be replicated in thousands of villages. For instance, BRAC offers only two types of reading glasses (black or gold) at 115 taka (around $1.5), while Aravind offers a rich product range starting at 180 taka ($2).

When we suggested in a conversation in 2009 with Abed the possibility of enlarging his product range, he declined: "I understand that we could probably earn more money from this broader product range but our 97,000 semi-illiterate Shashthya shebikas (community health promotors) would not be able to deal with this complexity."

Jean-Marc Borello – Groupe SOS, a national conglomerate of social businesses

An educator by training who started working at age 18, Jean-Marc Borello was a civil servant working for the "inter-ministerial mission for the fight against drug addiction." He then held various positions in government offices before leaving the civil service in 1987 to chair a business group of communication activities, restaurants and hotels. In 1997 he decided to focus full time on Groupe SOS, a nonprofit organization he had co-created in 1984. The structure, a CSO that hosted drug addicts in safe environments to help them quit drugs progressively, started with ten volunteers, including Jean-Marc who was managing it in his free time. Since then, the group has grown into a €650 million, 11,000 employee conglomerate of diversified social businesses: health care and housing, education and child protection, social inclusion, international solidarity and impact investing.

SOS grows through innovation but also through an unconventional method in the social sector: strengthened by its know-how and the management tools that it has developed, Groupe SOS has acquired numerous organizations over the years. They have all developed synergies, professionalized their activities and pooled their expenses.

SOS backs innovative social entrepreneurs who lack resources and skills. They also take over large, struggling organizations and turn them around. Groupe SOS is somehow becoming a General Electric of social businesses, adding value to existing social businesses by providing access to shared resources and instilling management skills.

Jean-Marc insists on the need for "institutionalization": "When you are an organization with 30 people the reporting is done automatically, informally, through the dinners you have with your team or through the morning coffee break. But once you find yourself running a 1000-employee organization, it's a different story. What was done through totally spontaneous human behaviors needs to be institutionalized via management tools so that the structure maintains its values and quality standards throughout the organization. It took us time and external consultants to do it but if we hadn't, we would never have become what we are now. Plus, all these quality insurance processes are the guarantee that even if I disappear, the structure could still go on without me. Institutionalizing processes is the only way to both grow while maintaining quality, and make the structure sustainable in the long term."

Institutionalizing processes is the only way to both grow while maintaining quality, and make the structure sustainable

* * *

Unfortunately, so far, the examples above remain exceptions because of lack of skills, the founder syndrome and the "small is beautiful" mindset. Let us analyze each of these obstacles further.

As in the business sphere, few social entrepreneurs possess the *skills* required to bring organizations to scale. Jean-Marc recognizes this for himself: "I hate to work on details and the logistics of growing something that works. What I am passionate about is solving a given issue, trying something new… once we have cracked a model I leave it to my teams, and the organizations within Groupe SOS take it forward." Arnaud Mourot, director of Ashoka France, summarizes: "Some people are born inventors while others are developers. As in business, most social entrepreneurs do not have both innovator's and manager's skills, but for them, recognizing this is made even more complex by the fact that they are inextricably, emotionally tied to their organizations, way more so than business leaders."[113]

Interestingly, in spite of their differences, the three organizations we analyzed share one characteristic: in order to grow, they institutionalized their management processes so that they could maintain excellent quality without the need for direct control by the head of the organization. In short, their founders "accepted to let go." Rodrigo Baggio, the founder of CDI, a Brazilian CSO that uses ICT to fight poverty, explains: "People become social entrepreneurs because they have inspiration or a trauma or something that they really have at heart; this makes social entrepreneurs cling to their current structure and not let go of their original idea. Founders see their organization as their baby, and can become 'control freaks'. They become a bottleneck for every new step and slow down expansion." Additionally, they often get caught into an emotional "fame syndrome": social entrepreneurship is one of the few (if not the only) business area where running a $100,000 money-losing organization is enough to get invited to speak at prestigious global conferences.

The social sector believes that "small is beautiful, and that everything should be tailor-made, carefully crafted for the individual situations of each beneficiary," as Jean-Marc says, rather than planned and rationalized, or even industrialized, for growth. Social entrepreneurs hearts and heads disagree in the scale debate, seeing it as a choice between quality and quantity. As Jeroo Billimoria, the founder of Child Helpline International, puts it: "Social entrepreneurs often think small is beautiful and scale is not necessary. With scale you can't have the 100 percent perfect program. Whatever happens does not go as perfectly as you wished, and you may lose quality or at least end up with a program different from what you had in mind. So scale is something many social entrepreneurs don't want." Jean-Marc adds, "social entrepreneurs will be reluctant to try to 'industrialize' their work, feeling that their organization would then lose its soul. They are also afraid of this professionalization process because they do not know how to do it, and they fear that they will lose control."

Influence

The vision of New Profit, an organization supporting social entrepreneurs, "began with a question – what prevents social entrepreneurs from scaling their innovations at the same pace and quality as Coca-Cola?"[114] But what if this was not the *right* question? Konstanze Frischen of Ashoka explains: "Social entrepreneurs should distinguish between growing the size of their organization and growing the impact they want to have. Contrary to what all business management books will say, maximum impact for a social entrepreneur may mean not growing his organization, but influencing others to take on what he or she has invented – by making their idea the new standard in the field, through new protocols, smart networks or alliances, lobbying, open source or other means."[115]

THE (INACCURATE) ROLE MODEL OF THE BUSINESS ENTREPRENEURS

The social entrepreneurship movement has looked up to the business entrepreneurs for funding, obviously, but also for inspiration. They see the likes of Steve Jobs and Bill Gates, who started doing electronics in their garage and ended up CEO of the organizations they had created worth billions of dollars – as role models.

However, the buzz of Initial Public Offerings (IPOs) and their charismatic CEOs is hiding a forest: the overwhelming majority of business innovations brought successfully to scale grew *after* they were acquired by large corporations, and not by themselves. Ivy grows fast because it grows on trees, leveraging the years of efforts required to grow trunks and branches. Similarly business innovators often leverage the assets of existing corporations in order to reach scale quickly. The visibility of the Microsoft, Apple and other eBays of this world overshadows the role of Unilever or General Electric in multiplying, scaling up and replicating innovations.

Hystra has analyzed the exit strategies of venture capital (VC) funds in the USA between 2004 and 2010.[116] These statistics show that out of the 2401 exits recorded by the National Venture Capital Association (NVCA) since 2004, less than 13 percent of them were IPOs while the remaining 87 percent were merger and acquisitions (M&A) deals. Seen in this light, IPOs are the exception rather than the rule: only when a start-up cannot find an existing corporation able to accelerate its development does it have to go to the stock market.

International lobbying: Arnaud Mourot uses the role of Professor Yunus as an example for Ashoka Fellows about how to scale impact: "Professor Yunus's main achievement is more his great evangelization job about microfinance, which popularized the concept and inspired many others to start microfinance organizations, than the Grameen Bank itself." Though the bank is indeed a scaled social business with 8.6 million clients, the movement has now grown to serve 195 million people. This was made possible because Professor Yunus separated from the start the role of chairman from that of CEO, evangelization from operations – because he let someone else (Dipal Barua for many years) run the organization while he was away on roadshows.

Publicized proof of concept: 50 percent of Ashoka Fellows claim to have changed national policy. Lobby for changes in regulations is the most frequently mentioned approach to scale impact. Bringing proof of concept of the proposed initiatives strengthens the lobbying efforts. Jean-Marc Borello discusses his ideas with relevant authorities before doing a pilot on the funds of his association. His teams set up the pilot, including an evaluation of savings realized for the public sector compared to the status quo. Armed with these numbers, Jean-Marc can convince politicians to change regulations or even to obtain funds for his organizations to scale up directly.

Open source: if an idea is good and applies to a large number of people, why not share the idea so that several players can take it forward? As Konstanze Frischen explains: "If you are focused on growing impact rather than your own organization, then why not invite the world to help your idea reach scale? Especially internet-based models lend themselves to such an approach – look at how Wikipedia has grown. But technology can also leverage 'offline' ideas, as Darrell Hammond's KaBOOM! illustrates." KaBOOM! is an organization that aims to create a "great place to play within walking distance of every child," and mainly builds playgrounds in low-income communities in the USA. The year they open-sourced their playground model, 1600 playgrounds were self-built by local communities, almost as many as KaBOOM! had managed to build directly in its 14 previous years of existence. The ratio is now one playground built by KaBOOM! for every ten built as do-it-yourself.[117]

Changing the competitive landscape: new attractive business propositions are likely to be picked up and replicated by competitors. In 1992 in India, David Green created Aurolab, the first low-cost eye-lens manufacturing company, to supply the Aravind hospital that was (and still is) providing low-cost eye care and surgery to clientele mainly composed of BoP clients. Aurolab started selling at $10 per lens when prices were at $300. David recalls how this revolutionized the eye-care industry:

> *When the system got known, it stimulated new entrants to come into the field. They competed our prices down to $2 (our cheapest product today). The effect that this had was enormous. Aravind surgeries went up dramatically and that growth was mirrored in the Indian marketplace where you started to see start-ups competing with Aurolab. From 1992 to the early 2000s India's surgical volume increased from 800,000 cataract surgeries per year to five million, and much of this was driven by a price-competitive ophthalmic industry. With Aurolab we were able to change the competitive landscape, with pricing as the weapon. Aurolab in 2007 sold one million lenses and had a turnover of $5 million. A major multinational competitor sold seven million lenses and had revenues of $920 million – with that same volume of seven million lenses Aurolab would have had only $35 million in revenue. Aurolab sculpts its costs and margins throughout its supply chain to ensure affordability to low-income people, while achieving profitability. It chooses to maximize distribution while being profitable, versus solely maximizing return on investment.[118]*

Serial entrepreneurship

Some social entrepreneurs, instead of scaling their organization or the influence of that organization on others, initiate a multiplicity of ventures and then let others run the show (through *scale* or through *influence*, depending on each venture) while they move to their next idea. We describe here two remarkable examples of this rare species, Michael Young and Jeroo Billimoria.

Michael Young, Lord Young of Dartington (1915–2002), has been described as "Britain's most brilliant social entrepreneur of the 20th century. The organisations he has directly launched are numbered in dozens. The people he has helped runs into millions."[119] His Open University, offering distant teaching, has had more than 250,000 students so far, while the British model of the University of the Third Age (U3A) celebrated 30 years of existence in 2012.[120] The Consumers' Association created in 1957, rebranded *Which?* in 2004, is now Europe's largest consumer rights organization, with over 700,000 members.[121]

How could one person achieve such an impact from so many and such diverse organizations in only one lifetime?

Like most social entrepreneurs, he was full of "intellectual restlessness and extraordinary energy"[122] and "fizzing, almost literally, with ideas."[123] He created the College of Health, for example, after he was hospitalized with cancer. He would not let go of his ideas until they had been tried. "When Michael Young believes in something he campaigns for it, fights to make it happen, badgers people, bores people, irritates people and goads them into action," wrote Tessa Blackstone, who worked with him when he was president of Birkbeck College.[124]

What set him apart was his willingness to hand his ideas to others, as Kay Andrews, former director of Education Extra, one of Michael Young's ventures, explains: "he knew he could not develop all these ideas on his own so he called on people like me to create the institutions."[125]

Finally, his greatest strength was probably his acceptance to let go, not of the cause he was fighting for but of organizations: "Michael normally moves on once his latest design is up and running, satisfied the people he has picked up are fully competent to run the show."[126] Kay Andrews explains this capacity to move on: "As soon as an organization became very successful Michael would be gone, because then he was not interested in it anymore. He was bored when there were no more issues to solve. And because he had had recognition and influence from his youngest age, he was not interested in the formal idea of power or in getting recognition of the paternity of his ideas. Rather, his goal was to bring the maximum number of his ideas to life!" And so he did.

Jeroo Billimoria, born in 1965 in Mumbai, studied as a social worker. Her first enterprise – Unnati, a center for the rehabilitation of street children – did not work out, but in 1991, at 26, she created MelJol to work with children from private and municipal schools toward breaking stereotypes related to class, gender and ethnicity. MelJol now works in 5,300 schools with over 750,000 children, mostly in Maharashtra.

In 1995, Jeroo created Childline to provide support to street children with a 24-hour emergency telephone service, manned by children themselves, combined with follow-up support. Three years later, she was elected as an Ashoka Fellow. Today, in 291 cities and districts of India, every year, over two million children call "1098" and hear a friendly voice ready to help. In 2003, to leverage this experience and achieve greater scale, Jeroo founded and became the executive director of Child Helpline International, a helpdesk for existing child helplines around the world, and grew its reach to 141 countries. She remembers how difficult it was to convince donors to fund that new idea, because it was about funding means for *influence* rather than funding a concrete new organization:

> It would have been easier to fundraise to replicate Childline India in a new country, than to fundraise for Childline International, the network, the overhead that would support the concept and leave local organizations to do the rest. People did not understand that this was going to be more impactful. I could probably have raised more money going from one country to the next, as opposed to marketing a concept, but I knew the concept would be more effective and powerful. And indeed now thanks to the support of Childline International, other people and organizations are doing these Childlines in multiple countries.[127]

Since 2001, Jeroo was experimenting with MelJol on how to radically transform the lives of these children, helping them break free from the cycle of poverty and crime, and helping to alleviate their sufferings. She also wanted to leave Child Helpline International, feeling that her continued presence was stifling the organization.

That's how she created Aflatoun in 2005, a nonprofit organization whose mission is to "inspire children to socially and economically empower themselves to be agents of change in their own lives and for a more equitable world." As of 2012, Alflatoun had already provided social and financial education to over two million children in 102 countries across the world. As Jeroo has done with Childline, she leveraged the Aflatoun success to create Child and Youth Finance International with the objective to "provide financial access and education to 100 million children and youth in 100 countries by 2015."

Jeroo's drive and willingness to challenge herself constantly is truly extraordinary and her impact amazing. And Jeroo is less than 50 years old…

So, in summary, what are the key characteristics of a serial social entrepreneur? Like any social entrepreneur, a permanent concern for social justice and never-ending persistence; and, rarer, a continuous flow of good ideas to fill society's gaps, a capacity to find and convince people (both funders and to-be managers) to take these ideas to reality, and, finally, the rare ability to entrust the newly created organizations to others – to let go and look to the future issues to be solved without seeking personal recognition for past achievements.

While business entrepreneurs can easily sell off their company when they wish to do something else – or close it if it is not successful enough – a social entrepreneur is morally and emotionally tied to the "great cause" he or she is defending. Caroline Casey, another Ashoka Fellow, took a back seat two years ago, retiring from the role of CEO of her organization, Kanchi. She acknowledges the hard choice:

> *Retiring and letting go was a hard decision, because myself and many other social entrepreneurs are workaholics, super committed to our cause and organization, and we need this recognition, this personal sense of worth from being leaders of our organizations. The problem of social organizations is that they can become "too much of the founder," whereas the business should stand on its feet without its founder. Today I feel really proud of having left my CEO role at Kanchi, because it clearly goes on without me. And I can actually focus on our next strategic move: scaling internationally and building the Ability Awards franchise.*[128]

And the ties are not only emotional, but also financial, as Arnaud Mourot explains:

> *Often social entrepreneurs know nothing else than their organization; they live only for it and only through it, in financial terms as well as it is their only source of revenue. There is no money in the social space for founders who change business... On occasions where the business world would compensate financially an inventor by buying his company or offering him money to move to his next invention – and leave his existing business in the hands of others to grow – social entrepreneurs have no such motivation. Instead, their only recognition is their current power position at the head of their innovative organization. Without any compensation, it is hard to tell them to let go to start all over again a different business.*

Jeroo experienced that difficulty: "I would have made ten times more money staying in my previous organization. It is not even easier to fundraise the second time, however good your track record might be, because donors or investors do not understand why you change and why you do not continue on your successful path."

Jean-Marc Borello adds: "After years spent on only one issue, it can become impossible to move on to something else. It is not the researcher who found a revolutionary molecule who will know how to make a medicine with it and market it globally. However, in the social entrepreneur space, not only you but also the external world expects you to do both. The world instead should encourage you to find your next molecule."

One social entrepreneur once jokingly referred to the $5 million prize that Mo Ibrahim offers to leaders in African countries as an incentive to leave their dictatorial position, so as to avoid being tempted to cling on to power for monetary reasons,[129] concluding: "we might need a similar program for founders of social organizations!"

Which path to choose?

Social entrepreneurs should therefore ask themselves two tough questions:

1. Would their idea grow faster if it was in the hands of another existing organization (or organizations)? If so, what is their strategy to make this transfer of ownership happen? What are the key assets (reputation, brands, technology, access to customers, distributors and so on) that are critical to scaling up? Who controls these assets and what could be their incentives in leveraging these assets to promote social change?
2. If indeed their organization is best placed to take this idea to scale, are they the best individuals to take it to scale? If not, how will they find the right person to lead the organization to the next stage of growth? Bill Gates exited the role of CEO of his company Microsoft in 2000 to leave it in the hands of the person he thought would be better equipped for it...

The only way for social entrepreneurs to address these questions with the objectivity required is to already be thinking about their next big idea. So maybe the most important question that a social entrepreneur should ask him or herself is: "What's my next big idea?"

It helps to be a serial social entrepreneur like Lord Michael Young, who once said: "I can't stop thinking of what appear to be worthwhile ideas. They seem so obvious to me."

12

Corporations – the
incumbent dilemma

Multinational corporations (MNCs) have a key role to play in accelerating the scaling up of social innovations, by leveraging their networks, brands and capabilities. They can also benefit from this involvement, tap into growth opportunities, stimulate their innovation and provide meaning to their employees and customers.

However, large corporations tend to be inflexible. Some are so focused on their traditional ways that they are simply unaware of opportunities; others are unable to overcome internal organizational resistance or are unwilling to do so by fear of jeopardizing the financial performance of their core businesses. Their size and scope are their strength but also their weakness. Facing the dilemma of the incumbent, they run the risk of being outmaneuvered by weaker but more nimble players.

Some pioneering companies have resolved this dilemma. Though each journey is different, they seem to provide six lessons: (a) they set themselves the mission to tackle a specific social problem; (b) they recognize their ignorance; (c) they progress by trial and error and act as entrepreneurs; (d) they nurture intrapreneurs; (e) they create an internal organizational space to protect the experimentation; (f) they find ways to involve the entire organization.

Are the successes of pioneering corporations due to their unique tradition, ownership or industry? We don't believe so: it is the vision and determination of their leadership that constitutes the critical factor.

The ivy and the tree

The story of Vinita Bali, CEO of Britannia Industries until 2014, shows the formidable potential that lies in leveraging existing corporations' assets to bring social innovations to scale quickly.

VINITA BALI – BRITANNIA INDUSTRIES LTD, MD/CEO, 2005–14 [130]

ILLUSTRATION 13 / Vinita Bali

I grew up in a middle-class family in New Delhi. Education was the way to succeed in life. I studied Economics and Business at Delhi, Bombay and Michigan State Universities. I then worked overseas for 16 years with Cadbury Schweppes and with the Coca-Cola Company. During these years, I was focused on growing the business and must admit that I paid limited attention to social and environmental concerns.

In 2005, I decided to return to India and was offered the exciting opportunity of becoming the CEO of Britannia Industries Ltd, the third largest Indian food company, which had started as a small biscuit shop over 100 years ago.

Our journey started almost accidentally, when I was new to Britannia: on one of my visits to our factory I saw boxes of biscuits with the WFP acronym. On asking, I learnt that Britannia was one of the certified suppliers for the World Food Program, and that we manufactured calorie- and nutrition-dense biscuits for relief programs.

At around the same time, I met people from GAIN (the Global Alliance for Improved Nutrition) who were visiting India and I was fascinated with how biscuits and bread could be the 'carrier' for micronutrients. The magnitude of the malnutrition problem, which is almost a silent emergency in India, also hit me very hard. Despite India's celebrated economic progress, around 50 percent of its children under five are still malnourished and 70 percent suffer from anemia.

Like most Indians, I thought that poverty was the primary reason for nutritional deficiencies and that therefore these were beyond what a food company such as Britannia could address. What I realized was that it was not just access to food, but also access to micronutrients that was at stake, and that we had the ability to contribute to solving a problem that is hurting many lives and limiting India's growth and development. There were enough successful examples of food fortification from other countries, including emerging nations. In India too, we have been successful in iodizing salt and today hardly anyone mentions words like goiter!

We started by "removing the bad" (transfats) and then "added the good," i.e. fortified our products with micronutrients. It was a welcome challenge for our enthusiastic R&D team. We conducted 16 product trials over six months to come up with a recipe that would be fortified and taste good! Our marketing team insisted that we would supply these biscuits at cost – instead of giving them away – to ensure our involvement would be sustained. We wanted and still want to be part of the solution, not part of the problem.

The success of this initiative led us to realize the potential impact we could have on malnutrition if we were able to fortify the more than six billion packs of biscuits we sell annually to 300 million households through 3.6 million stores in urban and rural India.

We put together a focused team comprising the head of R&D, a category marketing director, a production manager and a commercial manager to work out a sustainable model that would become part

Continued

Continued

> *of our business model. We made very quick progress. The fortified "Tiger" biscuits led to fortification of several of our other brands. Every day, we sell ten million packs of these fortified products, some of which are at price points accessible to the vast majority of people.*
>
> *It is certain that the overall image of our company has benefited from these initiatives, making us the most trusted food brand in India (Britannia has been rated the #1 most trusted food brand in India and voted among the Top 10 Most Trusted Brands across all categories in India for a continuous period of ten years, according to independent studies by AC Nielsen and the Economic Times). Other manufacturers are also following our lead and fortifying their products."*

As we have already said, ivy grows fast because it grows on trees, leveraging the years of effort required to grow trunks and branches. Similarly, multinational corporations possess critical assets (brands, networks, capabilities and so on) needed to accelerate the scale-up of social innovations.

Consumer goods companies such as Britannia are not the only ones that can leverage their brands. When Total decided to leverage its 3,700 gas stations in Africa to distribute d.light, Greenlight Planet and Sundaya solar lanterns it made a very strong and credible statement that it endorsed their quality, reassuring African customers who were wary of purchasing an innovative product. Similarly, Unilever has made an exception to their long-standing rule not to associate their corporate name with product brands. They put the credibility of the Unilever brand behind a "social innovation": Pureit, a water purification system targeting poor communities. As Unilever's website claims: "The Unilever brand gives low income people the confidence to know that the product will deliver on its promise, so their money will be well spent...."

Codensa, the electric utility in Bogotá, Colombia mentioned in Chapter 8, is leveraging its existing customer database, invoicing and payment collection infrastructure to provide its half a million customers with financial services and loans. The program was initially started to enable households to purchase electrical appliances on credit and pay back over time with amounts included in their electricity bill.[131]

Large corporations can also leverage their technological capabilities mentioned in Chapter 8. In Danone's joint venture with Grameen Bank, the company mobilized its R&D teams to develop a yogurt that would taste good while containing the significant amount of micronutrients needed to reduce the nutrition deficiencies of Bangladeshi children. Schneider Electric was able to develop its low cost InDya solar lantern by leveraging its position as the largest buyer of lithium batteries, due to its global leadership position in the UPS business. As Jean-Pascal Tricoire, Schneider Electric's CEO, told us eloquently: "A corporation is not just a profit and loss statement, it is a community with a mission, an unmatched collection of skills that correspond to society needs, that meet a purpose."[132]

Motivations

Not only do MNCs have a key role to play in scaling up innovations, but they can greatly benefit from doing so.

External pressures are mounting. Corporations are perceived to be more powerful than governments, and they often are. But they are also at risk of losing their license to operate if they are not seen to do all that is in their power to tackle societal issues.

However, the primary motivations for corporations to engage in this space are not defensive. It is not pure profit either: in the last five years working with a dozen large MNCs, we have found out that the sole profitability argument is not sufficient because each of the individual markets is small, because these markets require designing new and complex businesses (mustering skills that corporations are uncomfortable with), and because there is a perceived reputational risk for MNCs to be seen as taking advantage of the poor.

The reasons MNCs engage in this market are probably best described by a metaphor of a three-legged stool comprising growth, innovation and meaning. The importance of each of the three legs varies over time and depending on whom you speak to within the corporation, but they need to co-exist to ensure the stable and lasting commitment of the company.

Growth: these initiatives enable MNCs to explore the only untapped large growth opportunity markets of the future.

Innovation: they also enable them to innovate, learning new marketing skills, building new alliances, testing new technologies. General Electric is famously using "reverse innovation" developed in emerging markets to "disrupt" itself.[133]

Meaning: a growing number of CEOs also realize that after years of exclusive focus on quarterly financial results, and wave after wave of cost-cutting programs, the social fabric of their organizations has worn thin, and their corporate mission sounds hollow to the ears of the generation of upcoming leaders. Today's talent aspires to have a job with a meaning. Emmanuel Faber explains that "when Danoners realize what is at stake in the solutions they propose and when we let them align themselves to what emerges from their personal conscience, we obtain levels of energy and commitment that cannot be compared to what you get from obtaining 0.1 point of trade margin from Carrefour!"[134] The importance of meaning is not limited to the confines of the organization: customers and civil society are also critical. In Vinita Bali's story, for example, she acknowledged the positive impact their initiative had on the overall image of her company.

Family-owned businesses are particularly aware that their continued existence is dependent on how useful society at large considers them to be. In 2014, the Ayala Corporation celebrated in Manila its 180th anniversary as one of the largest and most revered conglomerates in the Philippines with a "Sustainability Summit." Its leaders and main shareholders, Jaime and Fernando Zobel de Ayala, feel a deep responsibility to ensure that this family business will endure for another 180 years, and for that to happen, they know they need to be perceived by the Filipino people as adding significant value to their society. Their foundation is one of the largest in the Philippines, distributing about $7 million per year. However, as Jaime and Fernando put it, "as an institution, we believe that we need to be relevant to the needs of our communities, and that we have a role to play in addressing the tremendous socio-economic gaps that exist… While we do a lot of work through our foundation, we have integrated over time a much more inclusive approach into our business models, developing a broader set of products and services that cater to the needs of underserved communities." They believe that the most effective and sustainable approach is for their businesses to provide services to the poorest. Manila Water, their water treatment and distribution company, provides water to 6.2 million residents in Metro Manila, including 1.7 million previously unconnected poor. Their Tubig Para Sa Barangay (TPSB) / "Water for the Poor" program to connect the poorest communities was set up after Manila Water won the East Manila water concession in 1997. TPSB partners with community leaders and involves communities in decisions about infrastructure, notably in the type of connections they need – collective or individual. Manila Water successfully lobbied to waive the obligation of households to have a formal land title in order to get a connection. Connection cost has been lowered to $74, which is affordable for most households (revenues $110–$150 per month). Most of the work is done by locals: before-the-meter by a subcontractor possibly hiring locals, after-the-meter totally by locals with technical assistance from Manila Water.

This three-legged stool of growth, innovation and meaning is what motivates the leaders of corporations. In short, if it was only business, they would not do it. If it was only philanthropy, they would not do it either.

growth, innovation and meaning is what motivates the leaders of corporations

Multinationals: unaware, unable or unwilling?

Despite the critical role that MNCs can play and the benefits they can derive from it, too few MNCs are actually engaging in this field. In our experience, the key reason is that, as already stated, large corporations tend to be inflexible. This can be because they are simply unaware of opportunities, unable to overcome organizational resistance, or unwilling to do so for fear of jeopardizing their core businesses.

Unaware

Ed Jardine, the former head of Proctor and Gamble for the Andean region recalls: "In the '90s, Ebel, a small Peruvian company, reached a 12 percent market share in the Colombian shampoo market without us realizing it. How did this happen despite our multimillion-dollar market research budgets? The answer is surprisingly simple: Ebel used a door-to-door distribution model, reaching consumers without going through retailers, which are the source of the Nielsen data that our marketing teams analyzed in such excruciating detail."[135]

Similarly, Western manufacturers of solar home systems (SHS), as well as foundations engaged in multimillion-dollar rural electrification programs in Africa, were convinced that the cheapest SHS "needed" to cost $1000 and as a result could not possibly be sold on a commercial basis to the poorest. Conventional wisdom, still dominant in some development circles, is that "rural electrification schemes require subsidies." The debate then hovers around how to dispense these subsidies – in case you're wondering, the preferred option is to subsidize capital expenditure and let the poor pay for the maintenance cost. This thinking simply ignores the fact that social entrepreneurs such as SELCO and Grameen Shakti have sold over one million SHSs to poor families in India and Bangladesh by redesigning traditional products and business models to sell them at $300, with a profit (see Chapter 5 on lighting for more detail).

These innovations challenge common business wisdom, which explains why they are usually generated by social entrepreneurs or local businesses. For the incumbents, they seem based on counterintuitive customer insights. For example, one of the most resilient ideas is that price is the sole barrier preventing access to low-income people. Contrary to what is generally thought, ability to pay is not the primary bottleneck that prevents the poor from buying. As we will see in Chapter 14, the primary reasons are unavailability of financing options, worries about the quality of the products, the availability of after-sale services, concerns about the status products provide and so on.

Unable

Even when corporations see the opportunity and decide to act, they face implementation challenges that have to do with both the unusual nature of the goals and the modus operandi of these social businesses.

It took many years of trial and error for Cemex to design their now celebrated Patrimonio Hoy program described in Chapter 6 on housing. What made Cemex successful was their leadership's determination to find a solution after the first pilots proved unsuccessful.

When your name is Cemex (Cementos Mexicanos) – or Manila Water! – you cannot just leave the country and go somewhere else. This stands in sharp contrast with the three to five years of "tours of duty" in local subsidiaries given to expats in most multinationals. By the time the new general manager has addressed the company's most pressing business issues, discovered the social issues that plague the country, designed a new program, found local partners and launched an experimental pilot, he or she is packing and waiting for the movers, bound for their next job. This makes it particularly hard for these multinationals to develop lasting social businesses.

Unwilling

Large corporations, as opposed to innovative entrepreneurs, have much to lose and are often unwilling to take the risks associated with capturing new opportunities at the BoP.

Most large corporations are active in mature industries where market growth is slow and technology innovation minimal. As technologies mature, products become "engineered commodities," which consumers buy primarily based on prices. Anyone familiar with these industries knows how much effort and creativity is put into avoiding the feared "commoditization" of products. For example: pharmaceutical companies spend 30 percent of their revenues on sales and marketing (more than on R&D) peddling drugs to doctors; engineers add unnecessary features to products (think of software updates!) to prolong a competitive advantage; marketers design sophisticated customer loyalty programs solely designed to increase switching costs; and so on.

The outcomes of these strategies are high-priced, overengineered products with very high gross margins but also with very costly selling, general and administrative expenses. Capturing a large BoP market with a radically simpler, lower-cost solution might be tempting but the fear of cannibalizing one's core business is paralyzing.

Contrast this with BRAC's philosophy. In 2009, we visited BRAC and observed its community health promoters (*shashthya shebikas*), semi-illiterate women selling a core set of drugs and eye glasses. As discussed in the previous chapter, they carried only black or gold reading glasses at 115 taka (the term "reading" glasses is a misnomer as the women are mostly illiterate and the test used to ensure the correction is adequate is based on a thread and a needle). Watching these elegant women with colorful saris and golden bracelets wear the same clumsy glasses made us sad. We wondered whether BRAC could not capture profitable opportunities by segmenting customers and differentiating products/services and prices. Such multi-tier pricing would enable cross-subsidies between income groups. When we suggested this idea to Sir Fazle Abed, he said: "I see the value in product differentiation, but by moving from eight references of glasses (four strengths of correction and two colors) to 20 or 30 we are creating a complexity in our operations that I fear will be outgrowing the capabilities of our 100,000 Shashthya shebikas." It was clear we were not the first ones to suggest ideas to "improve" BRAC programs by making them more complex. Abed's relentless focus on keeping operations simple ensures that millions of poor people can receive affordable products and services daily in tens of thousands of villages of Bangladesh.

Large corporations could face a major threat by inaction. Ignoring the BoP markets is strategically risky. Left unaddressed, these opportunities might become the launch pad of local players that multinational companies are currently treating with disdain or candidly disregarding. This is a pattern reminiscent of the low-cost airlines or generic drugs. We know how these stories ended…

Six lessons learned from pioneers

Describing how large corporations are "unaware, unable and unwilling" may help us to understand why many are not taking action – but should in no way serve as an excuse. Indeed, some pioneers have been able to overcome these obstacles. Our experience shows that they share six features:

1) They set themselves the mission to tackle a specific social problem.
2) They recognize their ignorance.
3) They progress by trial and error and act as entrepreneurs.
4) They nurture intrapreneurs.
5) They create an internal organizational space to protect the experimentation…
6) … but find ways to involve the entire organization.

The consistency of these six features is paramount.

Focusing on a specific problem

Compare two groups of corporate mission statements:

- "Defeat diabetes by finding better methods of diabetes prevention, detection and treatment" (Novonordisk); "Save money. Live better" (Walmart); and "Bringing health through food to as many people as possible" (Danone).
- "Lead in the invention, development and manufacture of the industry's most advanced information technologies" (IBM); "Committed to being the world's premier petroleum and petrochemical company" (ExxonMobil).

The first group is focused on problems to be solved and is implicitly opened to others joining in the effort, while the second group is self-centered and competitive, seeming to pay more attention to their competitors than to their customer. Many corporation founders were indeed focused on problems but, as they mature, companies seem to lose track of their original intent. They need to go back to their roots and redefine their *raison d'être*: solving an important problem for their customers.

Selecting the right problem to focus on will entail a "triangulation" between three criteria: (1) an important problem for society; (2) an existing set of innovations (for example, promoted by social entrepreneurs) that suggest that the problem can actually be solved; (3) a clear value added by the corporation. Whatever the approach followed, a good test is that employees and external observers should think that: "only corporation X could have done it."

Recognizing ignorance

Corporations don't know the BoP, even in their home countries.

As we described in Chapter 6, after the 1994 Tequila crisis, Cemex had realized that the housing market of the poor had not been as affected as the rest of the market. Because non-cyclical market segments are of great economic value in such high fixed-cost industries as cement manufacturing, Cemex decided to investigate how to grow its presence in this market segment it had never focused on. In 1998, with support from the consultant Fernando Flores, the company stated its famous "Declaracion de Ignorancia," and launched a "garden project," an anthropological study with managers living within the BoP for months in order to understand the market of slums. In 1999, Patrimonio Hoy was launched in Guadalajara. When the CEO visited the project after a year of experimentation there were few results to show, but he nevertheless reiterated his commitment to the learning process. The project continued undergoing significant changes in its business model. It was only in 2002 that Patrimonio Hoy was first featured in the press, four years after inception.

Acting as entrepreneurs

For many corporations, the first step after a strategic opportunity is identified is to prepare a business plan for approval by the executive committee. This is often a 6- to 12-month affair involving literally hundreds of meetings and often hundreds of thousands of dollars in consulting fees. Respecting such corporate rituals is often necessary, but always frustrating as most business plans do not stand up to the test of reality.

One of the most successful projects tackling the issue of toxic fumes produced by cooking with traditional biomass is First Energy (originally BP Oorja), described in Chapter 4 on cooking, Roberto Bocca, who set up the BP team, tells the story: "For five months, we had a team of ten people doing nothing else but understanding consumers' needs. We quickly found out that the most urgent problem to solve was the use of raw biomass for cooking by millions of poor people. Originally we thought that selling gas to these people could have been the best answer. This solution would have been a perfect avenue for BP: promoting gas stoves in rural India enabled BP to develop one of its key businesses and to dramatically change people's lives. We started looking for an LPG stove and met people from the Indian Institute of Science. They insisted that we tried another solution that they had already started developing in their research center: an enhanced cookstove still using biomass, but 50 percent more energy efficient and significantly reducing toxic smoke emissions."

The team came out with a two-burner prototype, one powered by LPG and the other by biomass. They gave it for trial to several households from rural areas: "The truth is that we put all our expectations in the LPG one. Yet after the trial period, all the households said: 'This biomass stove is terrific. But we don't understand why you put a gas burner next to it, it is completely useless.'"

Despite its efforts, the BP team had come across one of the most common pitfalls of top-down approaches: neglecting cultural habits and customer preferences. As Marc Gosselin, then VP Africa/Middle East Dairy division and BOP/Social Business of Danone, says: "To invent new solutions and get rid of our old habits, we need to get out of our comfort zone, put ourselves in extreme, stretched situations such as deciding to set up a very small plant in Bogra, not a large one in Dhaka (for our Grameen Danone project). This eventually led us to equip the Bogra plant with a second-hand cold room compressor bought in Chittatong's shipbreaking yard for $3000, a fraction of the price of the cheapest Chinese machines." Marc continues: "We learn by trial and error, not by planning. To know where the wall really is, you need to bang your head against it."

Nurturing the right intrapreneurs

Regardless of how insightful the strategy is and how committed the corporate leaders are, progress will eventually be limited by the number of people in corporations who are able to bridge the gap between public- and citizen-sector partners: what has been coined "social intrapreneurs." Marc confirms: "Selecting the right individuals is key. They will succeed because they are fully committed and are true entrepreneurs. Their track record and personal credibility makes them immune to hierarchical pressures."

EMMANUEL LÉGER – AN INTRAPRENEUR IN A GLOBAL OIL COMPANY

ILLUSTRATION 14 / Emmanuel Léger

Being brought up in a family of medical doctors instilled in me the sense of responsibility to listen to others and led me to travel to India. There, I learnt that good intentions are not sufficient and that business-like efficiency is needed to ensure long-term social impact.

As the head of TATE (Total Access to Energy) until 2014 I had to ensure that our pilot projects were successful, managing a team of eight people in our headquarters and close to 30 in the field. This entailed solving issues as operational as rerouting a container of solar lamps from Senegal to Burkina Faso in time for an unplanned marketing opportunity. A very significant amount of my time was spent explaining to all internal stakeholders why it makes sense for Total to create a social business.

Since its inception in January 2009, the project has gone through four main phases:

1) *Opportunity identification: for nine months the corporate sustainable development team worked with BoP consultants (Hystra) to explore innovations carried out by social entre-preneurs in the field of access to energy, and identified the opportunity for Total to play a catalytic role in distributing solar lanterns by leveraging our network of 3,700 gas stations in Africa and the credibility of our brand with customers.*

2) *Business plan: it then took us over a year of efforts of a cross-functional team to develop a business plan that was successfully presented in December 2010 to our executive committee. This phase was absolutely critical in turning a "headquarter initiative" into a project supported by operating managers.*

3) *Pilots: over the next 18 months, we launched three country pilots (Kenya, Cameroon and Indonesia) while identifying and vetting suppliers of solar lanterns. After a successful review of our three pilots with the executive committee of Total in June 2012, the decision was made to set the ambitious target of reaching five million customers by 2015 and to aggressively roll out to ten additional countries in 2012–13.*

4) *Roll out: we learnt that while some lessons can be transferred, the model still needs to be adjusted to each local context. We created our own brand of distribution of solar lanterns and associated*

Continued

Continued

> services "Awango by Total" that was launched in November
> 2012. As of January 2014, 500,000 solar lanterns had been sold
> in 12 countries. The next objectives are to sell one million by the
> end of 2014 and ten million by 2020.

What advice would I offer to recently appointed project leaders?

- *The first is not really a piece of advice: but you need to be an insider, to know the aspirations and hot buttons of the company.*
- *You just cannot overcommunicate. You need to have the patience to spend countless hours listening and convincing.*
- *You need to seek and manage high-level supporters. We founded a formal board that proved very useful, and benefited tremendously from the coaching of a recently retired senior executive.*
- *You need to be ready to take risks. Until TATE, I'd had a very successful but uneventful career joining the Finance Department from a first-rate school. My good analytical skills and sense of diplomacy had helped me progress fast. This role was different: for the first time in my career, despite all my efforts, I ended up frustrating some people!*
- *You need to be extremely driven and committed (I never worked so hard) but you should avoid becoming too emotional and defensive.*

Creating an internal space in the organization

Creating such a space within the organization resembles the process of building a house. You need to secure land, set the pillars and prepare the foundations.

The CEO first needs to secure land, that is, to get support from the shareholders. Not doing so will lead company insiders to doubt the long-term commitment to the initiative, and will lead outsiders to criticize the CEO's attempt to get personal glory for charity by using the shareholders' wallet. Franck Riboud asked its general assembly to approve the creation of Danone's ecosystem fund and obtained a 98 percent supportive vote, one of the strongest endorsements they ever got. Similarly, Gérard Mestrallet, chairman of GDF Suez, the French energy operator, got the general shareholders meeting to vote for the creation of "Rassembleurs d'Energie" – their social impact fund. Interestingly, these votes came from shareholders that include pension funds, often labeled as financial vultures by the press.

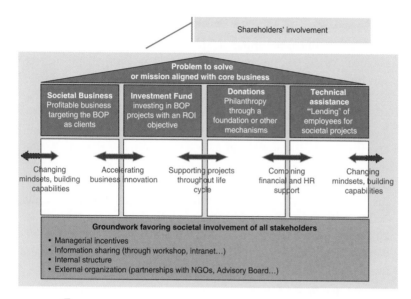

FIGURE 5 A strategy to address a societal problem can be based on four pillars with potential synergies

Second, the CEO needs to build strong pillars, that is, to create dedicated entities (BoP business unit, foundation, investment fund, technical assistance programs) that reinforce each other and all contribute to solving the problem selected (see box). The challenge is to create a space where this initiative can be protected from business-as-usual rules while ensuring a constant flow of ideas and people with your core business. Marc Gosselin says: "We need to protect our teams from the rest of the organization, especially at the beginning. danone.communities and the BoP CBU (Country Business Unit) operate in an organizational area of freedom. To some extent, we are 'outlaws'. The challenge is to reconcile outlaws and 'inlaws,' to nurture projects that are sufficiently independent (in funding and governance) but at the same time integrated and, somehow, complementary."

Transforming the culture of the entire organization

These initiatives are taken to heart by people in organizations, sometimes unleashing surprising passions. We have seen financial experts volunteer their help on projects that did not involve their units in any remote way. Conversely, we also saw senior managers passionately arguing that it was immoral to "make money on the back of the poor."

While BoP experiments need to be protected from the rest of the organization, a strong effort needs to be made to avoid their becoming marginalized.

T H E   F O U R   P I L L A R S

Societal businesses units: as Marc Gosselin says: "in 'social business', there is the word 'business'." The profitability targets can be slightly lower than for "normal businesses" (for example, 5–10 percent return on sales versus 15 percent) on account of the experimental nature of these new businesses, this being acceptable given the small absolute size of these businesses. Led by Jochen Ebert, a 20-year Danone veteran line manager, Danone's BoP unit is a Country Business Unit (CBU), the building block of the Danone organization and therefore has a five-people leadership team, all full time: finance, marketing, industry, R&D and HR. Since July 2009, the BoP CBU has been focused on the Indian market, with a 20-people team based in India. The BoP CBU reports to the head of dairy products for Africa, the Middle East and India, a senior executive with a strong track record of running profitable businesses.

Social investment funds: Emmanuel Marchant, a 12-year Danoner was the first leader of danone.communities. He had a team and an annual budget of around €5 million with which to identify, invest and support projects in Bangladesh, Senegal, Cambodia, India and France. By creating an independent unit (danone.communities is a mutual fund, a French SICAV), with its distinct ownership and governance model, Danone exonerated it from the short-term aggressive financial KPIs of the rest of the organization. It aims for "no losses," with 2–4 percent ROS. danone.communities is the "advanced lab" for innovation, taking on riskier challenges, primarily investing in projects led by non-Danone entrepreneurs.

Philanthropic structures: philanthropic money, governance and structures are often required to conduct activities that are in the long-term interest of the corporation but that require collaboration with socially minded partners. The Ecosyteme fund was created in 2009 by Danone to support businesses in Danone's "ecosystem." Danone has invested €100 million (+1 percent annual profit) in this *"fonds de dotation"* (grant fund) to finance projects chosen by subsidiaries linked to the Danone value chain.

Technical assistance: identifying employees willing to use their skills to support social businesses is generally easy but it requires some simple management rules to ensure their hierarchy is supportive. Danone is compensating the departments that bear the cost of these employees with an internal price transfer system by which employee time is paid "at cost."

Marc Gosselin takes it even further: "the ultimate objective is to transform all Danone employees into entrepreneurs. We believe that serving the BoP is a learning experience for the entire organization. We have 'soldiers' (focused mainly on business objectives) and 'monks' (focused mainly on social objectives): we need to have 'soldier-monks'."

* * *

Do the six lessons we have outlined apply to any company?

Fisk Johnson is the owner and CEO of SCJohnson, a fifth-generation family company that makes leading global household brands. When asked during a conference at Cornell University whether other corporations could be as bold as SCJohnson in adopting green practices, Fisk stated that only a privately owned corporation could. Similarly, Franck Riboud mentions the importance of Danone's historical social and humanistic values, as shaped by his late father Antoine.

Undoubtedly the legacy of a visionary founder or being privately owned might make it easier for a company to build inclusive businesses – yet we believe that the critical ingredient is management will: a leader's willingness to put his or her career at risk in order to manage the company in a way he or she deems responsible.

When Franck Riboud became CEO of Danone in 1996, he remained remarkably quiet for many years about the social values inherited from his father. Instead, his first six years were about radical business portfolio restructuring – relentless focus on financial performance that reached a climax with the restructuring of the LU biscuit plants in 2001. The public opinion crisis that resulted from that was a wake-up call for Franck and his team. The Danone social fabric and reputation were so eroded they could have snapped with no hope of repair.

It was then that Danone initiated a number of initiatives: the "Danone Way," the famous 2005 Riboud–Yunus handshake initiating the Grameen–Danone collaboration, a new corporate mission "bringing health through food to the greatest number", the acquisition of Numico baby foods, the creation of danone.communities, the Ecosysteme Fund, the Nature Fund, the BoP business unit, and so on. As Franck Riboud, stated: "The aim is to move from a dual social and economic project, very much Franco-French, to a dual social and economic project serving the needs of Danone's global approach."

Despite Danone's rewriting of its corporate history, the key lesson to be learnt is that – while the company undoubtedly had a social tradition – it was Franck's *decision* to transform Danone that was critical.

chapter 13

Bridging the business–citizen sector divide through hybrid value chains

As we have seen in Part 1, there are vast opportunities for social businesses, both corporation-led and social enterprise-led.

The "for profit" and "not for profit" sectors differ in their aims: maximizing profit or maximizing impact. However, what should be a fine borderline has become a wide "no man's land" often plagued by mistrust and misunderstanding.

This chapter will show that through collaboration the business and citizen sectors could accelerate the emergence of businesses able to generate profits while tackling social problems, at scale. It will also illustrate through examples how commercial business/social alliances – that go beyond CSR – need a new type of operating framework to ensure that the hybrid value they create together speaks to both wealth creation as well as social impact goals. The solution is to harness the power of market forces and social capital in hybrid value chains that combine corporations and CSOs.

But first let's look at why business and social collaboration makes sense.

Why the innovations and core assets of social entrepreneurs and CSOs are relevant to mainstream businesses

The 1980s saw an explosion in the number of CSOs around the world and with that the emergence of increased competition. In Brazil, the number of CSOs rose from about 100,000 in 1990 to nearly a million today.[136] In the

USA their numbers have grown by more than 300 percent since 1982.[137] According to Crutchfield & McLeod, the USA today has 1.5 million nonprofits, which account for more than $1 trillion in revenues annually of the nation's economy.[138] This explosive growth has led to new roles for CSOs, competition and, as a result, increasing levels of professionalization of the – until then – so-called "third sector."

As a consequence of this growth, in the last two decades partnerships among corporate and CSOs are becoming increasingly common. However, the vast majority are still centered on philanthropic goals, corporate social responsibility and/or reinforcing the brand identity of major companies.

As the citizen sector expands at an accelerated rate around the world, powerful social innovations are emerging. Many of them are relevant for business as they explore new markets for growth or more effective ways to source the inputs they need to expand their operations. Citizen-sector organizations have for decades been serving the informal sector – by definition outside the mainstream economy – and in doing so have developed solutions that work where traditional business models fail to provide access to markets for small producers, access to financing and other products that are essential to sustain livelihoods.

In 2001, the late C. K. Prahalad and his co-author Stuart Hart captured our collective imagination with the notion that the next frontier after globalization was serving the underserved markets in emerging economies.[139] The part of Prahalad's insights that is rarely told is that many of the business models featured in his book were examples of disruptive innovations that found their inspirations directly or indirectly in the citizen sector. For example, the concept behind Cemex/Patrimonio Hoy described in Chapter 6 emerged in part as a result of the design team learning about the Grameen microlending model and using it as the starting point of an integrated offering to improve progressive home building. ICICI, the leading private-sector bank in India, started its exploration in the microfinance world through a series of partnerships with citizen-sector organizations that had access to local networks and potential end clients. Today, ICICI/FINO – a model described in Chapter 8 – is one of the world's leading banking services models. In both cases, however, the model that was brought to scale was fundamentally different from the original inspiration, group lending for Patrimonio Hoy and microfinance for FINO.

In the footsteps of these pioneers, many corporations are partnering with CSOs to accelerate their learning, and together they are co-creating new value propositions and building inclusive supply and distribution chains. Just as corporate teams are embracing the notion of inclusive businesses, many CSOs are understanding that the solution to large-scale problems will not be solved purely on the basis of limited philanthropic resources or by advocating for better public policies when most governments around the world are facing severe financial constraints.

Businesses offer scale, expertise in manufacturing and operations, and financing. In return, social entrepreneurs and their organizations contribute lower costs, strong (and trust-based) social networks, complementary services and deep insights into customers and their communities. Together, they have the potential to solve large-scale problems that neither group has been able to solve on its own.

Examples of a new type of business/social alliance

The two cases briefly discussed below constitute a new type of business/social alliance where social entrepreneurs and companies collaborate to develop a new business model based in part on the insights, innovations and knowledge of social entrepreneurs and their organizations. Because these are profitable models that are consistent with the core business strategies of the companies involved, it is the private sector company that is the one taking these models to scale. Together they redefine value and shape the roles required to succeed.

The $90-billion microinsurance market: a new frontier for the insurance industry?

Estimating that the four billion people living on less than $2 per day represented an annual market for insurance services of more than $90 billion, Zurich Financial Services, the fourth largest insurance company globally, decided to set up a Zurich group-wide business unit focused on this potential market. Today, this unit provides microinsurance to low-income households in 11 countries across four continents. In 2009, policies reached 1.5 million microinsurance customers, with annual growth rates above 50 percent. Central to their growth has been getting access to existing local distribution channels and consumer knowledge, and in many cases social entrepreneurs are best equipped to provide that.

One case in point is Zurich's partnership with AMUCSS to provide micro life insurance in rural communities in Mexico. AMUCSS, led by Ashoka social entrepreneur Isabel Cruz, is a network of close to 100 microfinance institutions serving over 350,000 clients in marginalized communities in more than half of

Mexico's territory. Had it not been for AMUCSS's extensive distribution channel, the costs of Zurich building up distribution from scratch might well have been so cost prohibitive as to inhibit its entry into the low-income sector altogether.

AMUCSS also had vital information about the needs, income profile and purchase behavior of low-income consumers, which Zurich lacked and which was key to developing a customized and affordable micro life-insurance product. As most low-income clients have not had insurance before, considerable consumer education and trust are required. The early success also rested on AMUCSS's credibility with the local communities, as consumers were superstitious that buying a life-insurance product would be an early sign of death.

In the words of Eduardo Becerril who was director of Mass Markets at Zurich Mexico at the time when this partnership was launched: "for us, the most valuable thing about working with AMUCSS is learning how to develop a good flavor, a good approach, a sense of how to handle this segment and respect its needs. If we do this right, we'll find that we can help a lot of people in Mexico and also find something profitable, some kind of balance between our social responsibility and the responsibility that we have to our shareholders." Since the start of their partnership in 2005, AMUCSS and Zurich have sold policies to over 140,000 low-income consumers.

Zurich's experience is not limited to developing countries. In 2009, Zurich Spain teamed up with BancoSol, the largest Bolivian microfinance institution with presence in Spain, to offer micro life insurance to more than 250,000 Bolivian immigrants in Spain. There are more than 6.4 million immigrants in Spain, a segment large enough to attract the attention of large companies. This effort was built on Zurich's partnership with BancoSol in Bolivia, where they have been offering microinsurance products to BancoSol's 400,000 clients since 2003.

The $90 billion annual microinsurance market has attracted other large players, such as Prudential and Allianz, who are competing to reach low-income customers via partnerships with once-unlikely partners – microfinance institutions, cooperatives, post offices, pharmacies, cab companies, utility companies and others. Ultimately, for the consumer, competition has led to the emergence of a diverse insurance offer, covering burial expenses, survival benefits for spouse and children, accidental death benefit, disability, terminal diseases, repatriation, medical expenses in case of accidents, robbery, educational assistance, health and so on.

One of the most promising product innovations has been in preventive care, where by partnering with social organizations, insurance companies can now bring such services to the home of their clients, improving their health, preventing accidents and reducing medical expenses, while at the same time generating more profit as a result of more premiums and fewer claims. In France, Ashoka social entrepreneur Jean-Michel Ricard is paving the way through its organization SIEL Bleu, which works with over 60,000 elderly people every week on a series of physical and mental exercises to improve their physical and physiological wellbeing, reduce the incidence of hospitalization, and delay the onset of age-related impairment and disease. Such innovations in preventive care are becoming more and more critical due to a growing aging population, which is projected to increase tenfold by 2050 (reaching 22 percent of total population), obviously imposing a tremendous economic burden; in France, €8 billion is spent on care for the elderly every year.[140]

Dairy farmers in Ukraine and beyond

Reflecting Danone's vision that "it is in a company's best interest to take good care of its economic and social environment," in the words of Franck Riboud, CEO and chairman, in 2009 the company created the Ecosystem Fund, which seeks to finance initiatives led by Danone's partners – farmers, suppliers and subcontractors, transport and logistics operators, distributors, territories and local authorities.

One such initiative is the Ukraine Milk Communities co-led with Heifer International, an international CSO founded in 1944 to end hunger by giving people the means to feed themselves through the gift of food- and income-producing animals. The goal of the initiative has been to develop 20 agricultural dairy cooperatives (engaging 1000 small producers) in order to strengthen Danone's local supply chain and improve the living conditions of the small farmers at the same time. This is part of Danone's overall global strategy to "foster the transition from individuals production to services cooperatives production and further to cooperative farms."[141]

Whereas Danone brings to the table the necessary business acumen and dairy knowledge, Heifer has been leveraging its six decades of experience with more than ten million low-income families in 128 countries to launch and develop the cooperative groups. "We complement each other very well indeed: Heifer supplies its knowledge of cooperatives and the local social environment, while we provide technical and managerial expertise," said Viktor Kmytko, outsourcing manager at Danone Ukraine. A similar initiative is being launched in Turkey in partnership with a local organization in order to create 19 central milk parlors (CMPs) engaging more than 1000 farmers – within a CMP system, farmers bring their cows to the milking unit in the village and all the cows are milked in a hygienic way that improves bacteriological quality. The local partner has extensive experience with education and training activities in farming communities in order to increase productivity and quality of production. In this way, Danone and its partners can secure the quality and quantity of supply, while progressively enhancing the livelihood of the farmers – a win for both business and society.

The companies and CSOs involved in these two cases recognize their "blind spots" and defer to the other in the areas where they clearly have stronger competencies. These two cases represent a major departure on multiple levels from traditional business–social collaborations:

- The corporation's motivation is as much about learning as it is about exploring the viability of a business model with a clear potential to become part of its core business strategies. It is definitely not about CSR or a philanthropic investment.
- The CSO is interested in co-developing the product/service and would define success as a function of the scale of the social impact generated for years to come – even beyond its own involvement in direct implementation. The end game for the CSO is about the collaboration becoming an effective way to scale up the impact of its work by influencing the way corporations go about their business. By doing so, the CSO is moving beyond the classical social-enterprise model and is setting its new ambitions for impact well beyond what most CSOs could do on their own.
- Both partners have clearly established a common vision for success, one that speaks as much about wealth creation as it does about social value. Their ultimate measurement for success is about hundreds of thousands, if not millions, of clients being willing to pay for the service.

What are hybrid value chains?

Let's look more closely at the patterns that emerge out of the two examples above and other similar cases that we have studied. As described by Budinich and Drayton, the hybrid value chain (HVC) is a process of collaborative entrepreneurship designed to combine the power of innovation and entrepreneurship of the business and citizen sectors. Essential to this concept of HVC is that this partnership is embedded in a market-based for-profit approach.[142]

As shown in Figure 6, businesses offer expertise in operations and finance at scale. Social entrepreneurs and their organizations offer lower costs, strong social networks and a deeper understanding of customers and communities. As such, HVCs are "disruptive innovations" that ask business and citizen sectors to re-evaluate their traditional ways of relating to each other; to talk

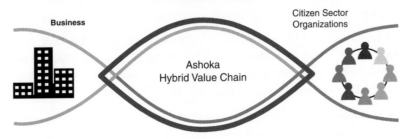

HVCs bring business and citizen stakeholders together to bridge the divide

Gains	Barriers	Gains
• Profitable growth in untapped markets • Push for innovation • More productive supply chains • Creating purpose internally towards employees • Creating purpose externally towards conscious consumers • First-mover advantages	• Lack of communication, knowledge and information about the strengths, assets and needs of each stakeholder • Lack of trust and collaboration across sectors • Inadequate/inappropriate product offerings for new markets • Lack of affordable and integrated solutions for new markets • Limited access to appropriate financing • Inefficient and costly delivery of goods and services • Uneven power-balance	• Improved, appropriate products/services • Lower costs, better distribution channels • Access to new sources of income, sustainability • Financial literacy capacity leading to Full Economic Citizenship (economic and social inclusion)
Assets		**Assets**
• Produces vital goods and services • Ability to operate at scale • Access to capital • Operation and distribution capacity • Infrastructure		• Knowledge of underserved communities and consumers • Trust based relationship with potential clients • Facilitation of alliances, understanding the BoP eco-system • Cost-efficient distribution network to pilot test

FIGURE 6   Hybrid value chain

and work collaboratively together to co-create new value in a market-based environment, in game-changing ways, with each side clearly understanding (and willingly accepting) the risks and rewards.

HVC is built on the equally important (and different) strengths from the private business and citizen sectors. It respects the legitimate goals of business to generate profits, and leverages its access to capital, ability to manufacture and distribute at scale, and specialized talents to invent new products leading to better goods and services available in the market.

HVC respects citizens' value as equal stakeholders in these processes. Their needs and insights into their communities and cultures are essential raw materials to design appropriate products and services; develop affordable quality; produce more accurate and useful market data; and often do a better job of marketing and sales than companies' staffs. When CSOs perform these services for businesses, they are compensated financially for the value they deliver.

HVC is by nature a holistic and iterative process: not based on one-off transactions, short-term gains or individual deals, but an ongoing collaboration based on learning from different perspectives, increased innovation, products and services that reflect manufacturer and consumer and revenues that will transform a sector's development for decades. It is also about creating transparent and competitive markets so that consumers and producers benefit not just from having access, but from better prices, products and services.

HVC is not limited to serving low-income populations. Innovations in sectors often come from the citizen sector's keen awareness of unmet needs: banks, for example, did not develop microfinance institutions or new loan products – even though billions of new customers were ready to sign up. Solutions to the issues of internet privacy are not flowing from major digital companies, but rather from civil society. And the glaringly broken US health-care value chain is not being fixed by the medical profession or private insurance companies. If solutions come, they will most likely involve the insights and ingenuity of multiple stakeholders to get the fix right.

HVC systematically weaves the two parallel, sometimes intertwined and always communicating paths of business and social entrepreneurs – like the double helix of DNA – to sustain a dynamic flow of energy and creativity that produces innovation, economic inclusion *and* wealth creation for all. In sum, HVCs represent a systemic shift in the way that businesses and CSOs interact. They are collaborations that create new value in game-changing ways, with each side clearly understanding (and willingly accepting) the risks and rewards. At the most basic level, HVC applications are about unleashing markets at a scale big enough to transform entire industries while empowering producers and consumers. Over the long term, HVCs are about an irreversible change in the relationship of the two sectors, a system-change designed to achieve significant economic and social impact for all.

Collaborations that create new value in game-changing ways

Lessons learned in building HVCs

Lessons learned in building HVCs fall roughly into two questions: when does it make sense for a corporation and a CSO to partner to create an HVC? What guidance is there for those who want to build HVCs?

When does it make sense for a corporation and a CSO to partner to create an HVC?

Building HVCs takes a significant investment of time and effort – so, unless there are really good incentives to collaborate, the idea is probably not ripe for creating an HVC.

HVCs make sense with "high price-ticket items" that need credit or insurance products to enable a purchase (for example, a house, an irrigation system for the farm) and/or a service that requires significant consumer education and awareness to create real market demand (even if "need" is obvious) to become viable. Take as an example the case of innovative and relatively low-cost drip irrigation systems. Companies manufacturing and selling them seemed to be correct when they concluded that small farmers are not a viable market for their products and services. They were too scattered and remote to find and serve; they had no savings or credit to purchase a new system; and they were not motivated sufficiently to get credit or buy one because their meager productivity meant small orders from local small buyers – so why bother with all that was necessary to get better systems?

But an HVC alliance in Mexico between RASA (an organization providing technical assistance to farmers) and several small farmers' organizations turned around this stalemate. Step one was to show farmers purchase order commitments from bigger buyers if they could improve their productivity and quality. Second, these orders were based on larger quantities than any one farmer could produce, so they were convinced when the citizen organization offered to help them form larger coops and selling groups, aggregating supply to meet the scale needed. Now the farmers became interested in how to fulfill the orders and grow their incomes. They changed their minds, talked with local microfinance companies who offered loans for irrigation systems to the farmers who sold to the big buyers. Local universities and agricultural experts helped with technical assistance on how best to use the systems and other hints for healthier crops – and the HVC resulted in profits to all. Just as in the housing example from India described in Chapter 6, no one company wanted to go through these many steps – they simply sold elsewhere and left potential profits and the farmers in limbo. Now several are vying for this new market segment.

For some large social problems and possible product solutions, HVCs may not be right because the "potential consumers" are the poorest of the poor and hence would not be able to pay for products and services without ongoing subsidies. Subsidies for vulnerable populations are sometimes the only alternative to address their basic needs. If charitable and public support is needed on a recurrent basis, then market-based approaches – and by extension also

HVCs – are not feasible. HVCs and corporations can target the market segments where savings, credit, increased employment opportunities and short-term skill building would transform "beneficiaries" into real consumers able to participate in a market economy to the benefit of all.

There is also a threshold of readiness to become an HVC partner. The corporation should have experience in building alliances in the past (and had beneficial results and practice at growing collaboration with outside or different partners), and a very clear mandate from the CEO and the board of directors that the HVC being built is of potentially central importance for the future of the company.

Finally, for all social entrepreneurs, HVCs only make sense if they believe that by pursuing these commercial approaches in partnership with large corporations they will be able to achieve a significantly larger impact.

What guidance is there for those who want to build HVCs?

Here are several key lessons that emerge from these and other cases:

Invest in the relationship and build mutual trust. It takes a unique blend of management/leadership skills to forge an HVC: empathy and fairness, clarity and humor, finesse to create respect and trust among people who don't move in the same business or social circles in life, and a tolerance for diversity are all required. Ask a respected neutral convener with these skills and multi-stakeholder experience to lead sessions, at least for the first six months, to evolve a diverse group into a working team.

Plan to do several things at the start:

- Choose discrete joint tasks that are low-risk with short-term successes to get them working together and appreciate each other's talents and experience (for example, organize focus groups with intended clients).
- Hold partners' hands warmly and often (as in, build trust).
- Communicate progress of the HVC framework widely – so that it begins to appear/be heard in the news, on radio and TV, at professional events and on blog sites.
- Have sufficient funding to not rush the process at the start (the first phase is, after all, R&D).
- Search for best practices to adapt from pioneers who have forged a successful HVC to fast-track initial steps as much as possible.

Create a shared vision and goals. Articulate them in hybrid language. Help new HVC partners make a U-turn from getting stuck by how different their assets/work/lifestyles are. Remind them often of the reasons why they

showed up: there is a huge social unmet need (which charities and government programs have not been able to solve at scale), which means an equally
huge potential business opportunity (that they have not yet accessed) – and
none of them can do it alone. Remind them often of how valuable each of
their assets, knowledge, experience and strengths are in this venture.

Use language reflecting hybrid values from the beginning. It will help you
to create mindset changes that will make differences easier to discuss and
collaboration easier to envision. Speak with equal emphasis about wealth
creation and social impact through market-based approaches. Some of the
best motivation to get corporations or investors involved in HVCs is to illustrate their recent failed attempts to use traditional business models in new
markets, so why not co-create a new model? Similarly, citizen organizations
are frustrated by not being able to raise enough funding to help all clients who
desperately need their services. Make it clear that these cannot continue to
be mutually exclusive or trade-offs. Clearly confirm that innovative solutions
exist, and they will be found by working together. Remind them that scarcity
is in their minds (cite the new wealth created by the invention of the internet,
for example, solely reusing available resources in new ways). Show how
their competitive edge will emerge from collaboration. Find examples of the
benefits of collaborative entrepreneurship: small projects can get done with
one strong leader and a small team, but big solutions – affecting the whole
community and needing to be sustained over a long time (as with health care or
corporate growth) – cannot be achieved by one perspective, one leader, one
sector, and so on. Collaborative entrepreneurship is the key for reaching scale.

Choose corporate partners carefully. In emerging HVCs, immediate or
short-term benefits are few, or less tangible. Corporations are especially accus-
tomed to quarterly reports demonstrating success. HVCs don't fit this model
at the start. Engage from day one an internal champion with the capacity to
convince corporate buy-in at the top and refuse to get involved unless this
condition is met. This is not about one successful innovative project; this is
about transforming companies from within. Therefore, pick a corporate
partner who understands the value of patient capital, the actual time it takes
to develop an innovation, the means to support the time needed to gel a new
team and the willingness to sell this to the company's board: long-term gains
will trump short-term profits. Choose a company that, despite a strong track
record, feels stuck. They will need less convincing to try something new.

Ditto for citizen sector partners. Select an organization that already feels the
frustration of repeatedly serving client needs and never making a significant

difference in their lives. Build a relationship with a social entrepreneur who is ready to embrace market-based approaches without ideology getting in the way. Look for citizen-sector professionals able to hold their own at the table and to think and act outside the box. Look for the outliers who are already experienced in being part of system-wide solutions that reduce clients' dependency and enable them to grow into full economic citizens. Choose organizations with fairly stable funding, and that have organized projects that require teamwork – both internally and with other organizations – and have the staff level to lead. Many will need capacity building (to communicate without barriers with their corporate partners) and you can help get that for them over time.

Never think you've finished the R in R&D. Running an HVC is like housework. You are never done. Just when you think all the analysis and data about the sector have been gathered, some new obstacle or new opportunity appears, and you do not have at your fingertips the solutions to conquer or seduce it! Invariably, as with any meaningful innovation and entrepreneurial process, at almost every corner new roadblocks will most likely appear. Each will require new learning, more reality testing with multiple stakeholders' perspectives. Yet rather than a setback or a delay (which temporarily they seemed to be) each, ultimately, will add to the depth, resilience, confidence and stature of the HVC team, and open new doors that lead to higher levels of growth and ability to scale.

What is needed for HVCs to reach scale and full global market potential?

While a significant number of HVCs report success and scale, their impact is still minuscule compared to the scale of the market opportunity. Building one HVC at a time, convincing one major corporation at a time or even working in one sector at a time would not see industry-changing and broad social benefits in our lifetime! Therefore, a major lesson is: *it takes an ecosystem to make HVC changes in business frameworks, values and skills ubiquitous.*

For HVC to take hold, it needs a handful of leading corporations, management consulting firms and business schools embracing this vision and translating into major impact affecting millions of people, producing billions of new revenues in order for the momentum to reach a tipping point and accelerate change. If the metaphor for a single HVC is the DNA double helix, the metaphor for an HVC ecosystem is the interrelated synapses of the brain – an enormously complex constantly communicating system with multiple functions, diverse styles and complementary strengths.

The HVC ecosystem has the same diversity of stakeholders as does an individual HVC – but more join at higher levels of responsibility and impact. At some point in an HVC's growth, regulations or laws, roads or tax incentives, public sewage systems and municipal services, significant amounts of capital investment or capacity-building will be needed. To mainstream HVCs it will require building awareness, consolidating and sharing the value, and building relationships with those who will champion HVC in larger institutions: universities with MBA and executive education programs or cutting-edge, interdisciplinary global innovation labs; management consultants who will translate concept into solid management practices across the for-profit and citizen sectors; business media to share HVC stories and lessons widely; and building a supportive global community who continue to nurture each other in dynamic ways to find solutions to scale. Ecosystems are functional, but they also create the environment that allows the bigger story of human and business transformation to grow.

HVCs now spend necessary but long work convincing essential players to join: the more conservative or risk-averse, the harder to get them on board. But imagine if bankers, CEOs, policymakers, top economic consultants, management experts, government leaders, MBA professors and the most respected business and public thought leaders all were writing and blogging not about HVC as innovation, but about tangible HVC benefits emerging in sector after sector, region after region. About the excitement of a movement toppling silos and gaining adherents everywhere. Then the questions are not if investing in an HVC is right, but how can we build them better, cheaper, faster? What's my role in this? What can I do? How will making HVCs more powerful enhance my own success? Those who lead HVCs need to have one eye on their daily tasks, while the other sees far ahead to build commitments well into the future and at levels that no one HVC alone can achieve.

Innovative management consultants are key to spreading HVC practice into standard operating procedure

The current conventional corporate wisdom of "shareholder as king" was once only an idea promulgated by management consultants, who then developed the practices enabling thousands of CEOs and hundreds of thousands of line or function managers to implement them. Just as that sea change about corporations' purpose happened 40 years ago, now is the time for them to play an important enabling role to make a new 21st-century vision, framework and set of practices viable for corporations, as well as become new revenue streams for themselves.

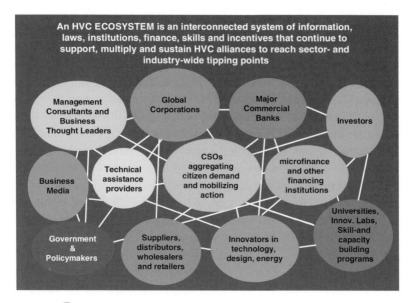

FIGURE 7 / Hybrid value chain ecosystem

Building HVC entrepreneurship and practitioner capacity is essential

If we could wave a magic wand and tomorrow create 1000 HVCs in a dozen major sectors, we would not find 1000 CEOs, 6000 corporate line managers and 3000 citizen-sector organizations to lead 30,000 local community groups to be strong partners in them. Nor would banks know how to process and serve millions of new customers ready to enter a formal economy. At all levels, capacity-building must be addressed.

This is a huge opportunity for universities, private and public technical schools. Business academic leaders in MBA and executive education programs and interdisciplinary innovation labs are a cutting-edge source of skill building for current and emerging business and social leaders. Why not offer courses in HVC frameworks, metrics and hands-on HVC innovation or application internships? CEO boot camps for industry leaders have been career and life changing, to quote Harvard alumni. Why not develop HVC executive boot camps to match the CEO vision and match HVC leadership qualities? Or help develop HVC skill-building courses offered through networks of private and government-funded technical institutes, just as they do when more contractors or engineers versed in LEED (Leadership in Energy and Environmental Design) or green building standards are needed?

Multiple messengers are needed to raise awareness, document progress and champion HVC work

Social entrepreneurship and frameworks such as HVC need serious business media to cover them with the same gravitas as they do the stock market or mergers and acquisitions. Corporate HVC first-movers need to share their vision broadly with their boards, their company as a whole and their colleagues – who will respect and "hear" their messages more clearly from a respected peer. There is a clear need to establish tools for the global HVC community of practitioners (or those who want to become them) to get information openly, share best practices, get assistance when needed, meet online potential talent or partners for their own HVC to grow. This needs to be done collaboratively, making the platform interactive – both a source as well as a magnet for new information, innovative solutions, places to find resources or offers, where deals can be sparked, mentors identified. Organizing this global community of HVC entre-preneurs, practitioners, resources, knowledge and talent will parallel our work to build ecosystems, capacity and momentum for HVC to meet the challenges of scale.

Ultimately, creating ecosystems that will be strong and flexible enough to multiply disruptive innovations in the service of reinvigorating capitalism through HVCs and values that speak about both social impact and wealth creation requires holding the vision of a better possible future, great respect for the strengths others offer to the whole and great willingness to move among teams of teams – leading some, being a supportive member in others. It takes all of them truly believing their collaborative path is more effective than the old models of the past (even if messier at the start). What gets all this to continue are the win–win–win set of goals and the hybrid value chain frame-work as the engine.

In order to realize the full potential of these markets, all actors involved – from builders and materials corporations, to bankers and investors, to citizen organizations working in local communities linking potential consumers to the formal market – need to see themselves as change-makers, who by joining their assets and strengths together are making possible the global transformation of industry for sustained wealth creation and social impact. And that is the most hopeful vision for long-term robust and inclusive capitalism.

chapter 14

Marketing – from needs to wants

The chapters of the first part of this book have shown that a number of affordable products exist that can improve the lives of the families living at the BoP. While existing products can and need to be improved, they are already "good and affordable enough": improved cookstoves could limit the toxic fumes that still kill four million people per year.[143] Similarly, costing between $20 and $40, water purifiers could prevent the deaths of 3.4 million people per year as a result of waterborne diseases.[144] Yet too many BoP families still do not buy these products.

Why is that so? The answer is straightforward: engineers have done their job but marketers have not. There are fortunately exceptions that we can learn from: across the world a few social entrepreneurs have developed effective marketing approaches that often challenge what business schools teach.

In this chapter we highlight five characteristics of these successful marketers for the BoP, grounded on our own experience and research:[145]

1. Focus on wants of BoP families, not their needs.
2. Reduce perception of risk, not price.
3. When financing is needed, offer in-house financing solutions, rather than relying on microfinance institutions (MFIs).
4. Rely on word of mouth, not advertising.
5. Achieve sustainability with high gross margins, not large volumes.

Focus on wants of BoP families, not their needs

Successful marketers have designed simple, compelling value propositions for their products that stress how customers will benefit from their product.

Some marketers have it easier than others. These are the ones selling products that actually save money for the consumer. Toyola's (see Chapter 4) slogans for their cookstoves – *don't burn your money* – is a powerful illustration of this key principle. Indeed, buying such a cookstove is particularly attractive to families spending precious cash buying charcoal or wood. Similarly, families who boil their water to make it safe to drink see water purifiers such as the Pureit range sold by Hindustan Unilever in India as a source of savings. In these cases, the internal rate of return of these investments is quite extraordinary: up to 5000 percent for cookstoves and 400 percent for water purifiers.

Making the case for buying products that do not guarantee immediate savings is more challenging. Successful marketers find simple yet effective ways of making benefits tangible: d.light or Greenlight Planet sell their solar lanterns at night in markets to show how much brighter solar lanterns are compared to kerosene lamps; handwashing programs use special gels or powders that make germs "glow" in the dark.

The slogan for Toyola's cookstoves is "don't burn your money"

When benefits cannot be demonstrated tangibly and immediately – as is the case, for example, for fortified food – smart marketers get around the problem by focusing on different attributes such as taste and convenience. In Madagascar, Nutri'zaza, a social business selling fortified porridges for infants, has successfully built their Koba Aina brand via sales ladies delivering warm, ready-to-eat porridges at the doorstep of poor families every morning at

WHAT ABOUT CELL PHONES?

Cell phones have had a viral spread, with the proportion of cell phone subscribers in developing countries rising from 23 percent in 2005 to 90 percent in 2014, that is, 6.8 billion people.[146] Many BoP customers spend 20–30 percent of their disposable income on mobile communications.[147] Why has cell phone penetration been so fast compared to, for example, solar lanterns or cookstoves that cost about the same price ($20)?

Cell phones do not replace an existing technology, they provide a new and unprecedented channel for information and communications in remote areas. Most crucially, cell phones were initially marketed for the urban rich with huge marketing and advertising investments in billboards, radio and TV, making them aspirational items for lower income populations.

breakfast time. Not only does this save mothers precious time but, in addition, children love it: they chant "Koba Aina! Koba Aina!" when the salespeople show up in the streets where they live.

Reduce perception of risk, not price

Needless to say, products need to be affordable in order that the poor can purchase them. But this does not mean that poor people will always choose the cheapest product. Actually, quite the opposite happens when they are given a choice. For example, a social business selling two water purifiers of identical functional properties, but differentiated by their looks, has seen 90 percent of poor families buy the more expensive product when given the possibility to purchase on credit.

For customers to decide to buy an expensive, innovative product, they need to be certain that their investment will bring them the expected benefits. Grameen Shakti's customers rightly feel that a $300 investment on a SHS supposed to last 15 years bears substantial risk. Grameen Shakti's CFO also probably feels it is very risky to make a three-year loan to a poor farmer. Both risks have been drastically reduced by having the maintenance technician collect the payments when they make their monthly visits, thus reassuring the customer that the technician will indeed come every month.

Other marketers use strong consumer brands to reassure their customers. These cases are few but quite encouraging. As we have already mentioned in Chapter 12, the Hindustan Unilever brand of the Pureit water purifier is seen as quality insurance by Indian clients. Similarly, Total is leveraging its well-known brand and network of gas stations in Africa to sell quality solar lanterns (with a one-year guarantee).

In the case of beneficial consumer goods such as soap or fortified complementary food for infants, the type of risk is different. These are not a risky one-time investment, as they are bought in small quantities over time. However, it is still ethically key to ensure that customers get the benefits of the products over time in order to justify their high price. For example, fortified porridges for infants typically represent five to eight times the price of staple foods otherwise fed to infants (a minimum for the companies selling them to hope to recoup their costs)![148] Successful marketers of such products have shown that parents are ready to pay such an amount, as they want to provide their children with the best they can afford. Hence, the challenge is not so much

DIPAL BARUA, FOUNDER AND CHAIRMAN OF BRIGHT GREEN ENERGY FOUNDATION

ILLUSTRATION 15 / Dipal Barua

Dipal Chandra Barua, founder and chairman of Bright Green Energy Foundation (BGEF), is a pioneer of solar energy in Bangladesh. Mr Barua was co-founder of Grameen Bank and dedicated the next 35 years till December 2009 as the bank's deputy managing director. Dipal was the first award-winner of the prestigious Zayed Future Energy Prize 2009 for his efforts and achievements in lighting rural Bangladesh.

I was born in 1954 in Jobra, a small village in Chittagong where my father was a farmer. My village had no electricity, just like 85 percent of people in Bangladesh. Everyone used kerosene lamps, and so did my family. I led Grameen Shakti since its beginning in 1996 to promote alternative energy in Bangladesh. We did not spend money on billboards or advertisements on radio. When we started a new branch in a village, we equipped the school with a Solar Home System (SHS) and then patiently waited for villagers to see for themselves that our devices and services were reliable. Then, customers just came to us on their own: first the least risk-averse,

> *then the others over time. By being patient and ensuring our existing customers were delighted with our devices and services, we could minimize our marketing costs and achieve high penetration.*
>
> *Since my work with Grameen ended in 2009, I set up Bright Green Energy Foundation to help make Bangladesh one of the first "solar nations" in the world in January 2010. This dream is what keeps me going every day.*
>
> *As of May 2014, Bright Green Energy Foundation has 350 branches covering 52 out of 64 districts of Bangladesh. Our 1700 employees have installed more than 100,000 solar home systems. We have also installed 63 biogas plants and 15,000 improved cookstoves in rural areas of Bangladesh.[149]*

to lower the price (there is limited opportunity to do so, given the cost of manufacturing and distributing these products), but to ensure compliance over time. This means ensuring that children get fed a sufficient quantity of these foods to get the full health benefits. Only this will make this investment in their child's future worth the extra expense.

When financing is needed, offer in-house financing solutions, rather than relying on MFIs

While customers may be convinced of the benefits of the product, they may not have the required cash at hand. Interestingly, even when they do, they would rather not pay cash immediately in order to be sure that the product does work before paying off the supplier. As seen in various market studies, when BoP customers say "I don't have the cash," they may actually mean "I don't believe in the product benefits."

In-house financing is a way of providing customers with a guarantee that their product will work, as they know they can stop paying if the product does not deliver. As we have seen in Chapter 4, Toyola salespersons encourage their customers to deposit in the "Toyola box" (a small recycled metal can used as a piggy bank) the money they save on charcoal. As a stove pays for itself in a couple of months, the Toyola salesperson comes back to open the box with their customer (and invited neighbors) and collect the money. Toyola customers could get a 10 percent discount if they paid cash immediately, but they are ready to forego this discount in order to be absolutely sure their stove works as well as the one used by the salesperson during the demonstration.

As described above, Grameen Shakti uses a similar system to reassure clients: when they purchase a $300 solar home system on credit, it is a technician who goes to their home and collects their monthly payments – called "service charge," also checking that the SHS is working well. In spite of the interest rates built into this "service charge," 97 percent of clients choose to buy the system on credit.

In addition, providing in-house financing can be a lucrative activity. Patrimonio Hoy (see Chapter 6) offers its clients to pay for their $1000 project over 70 weeks, through a "membership fee" that includes their financing cost, adding a 26 percent premium over the price of materials. To access this credit, clients only need to show their official ID and to pay in advance for five weeks, proving they can abide by the weekly payment. At the end of the first five weeks, they get ten weeks' worth of material, in effect getting five weeks' worth of credit. These cycles of savings and credit evolve over the 70 weeks of the program, so that the last cycle asks for only two advance payments to get 16 weeks of credit. Repeat clients get even better credit conditions. This, and high penalties in case of delays in any weekly payment, ensures that customers adhere to their plan and fully pay the material package for their housing project. Providing this financing in-house results in very low default rates and a cash-positive business for Patrimonio Hoy: a large proportion of clients request to receive the material in one bulk at the end of the program (as they do not have the cash to start paying a mason while they pay for the materials), and in effect pay Patrimonio Hoy fully in advance.

One of the key success factors of these in-house credit schemes is that they match the cashflows of their target households. The Toyola scheme allows clients to save on their daily charcoal expense. Grameen Shakti computed its credit scheme so that its monthly installments with a three-year loan for a $300 SHS correspond to the average $8 monthly typical spend of families on kerosene and candles. Patrimonio Hoy requests weekly payments in Mexico, where employees are often paid weekly or every other week.

Many distributors are reluctant to handle the risks and complexity of providing credit to their customers and have tried to build partnerships with microfinance institutions (MFIs), who have existing privileged access to poor clients, know them well, are well trusted and can provide finance as necessary. Indeed, some

MFIs have been very successful in using their monthly meetings of their members in order to promote products together with a loan. The Self Employed Women's Association (SEWA) in India is providing additional services to its 1.9 million members by selling them solar lanterns and marketing new homes. Hindustan Unilever Ltd (HUL) has reached over 55 million people through Pureit,[150] its line of water-purifying devices, through partnerships with MFIs or CSOs organizing self-help groups. However, not all MFIs have the desire or capabilities to transform themselves into marketing channels. One leading manufacturer tried close to 20 partnerships but so far only two have worked effectively. In any case, the greatest limitation of working through MFIs is that, unfortunately, their penetration still remains very limited (about 18 percent of the unbanked in 2013).[151] It is thus necessary to look at methods that go beyond those MFI clients if we are to serve the remaining 90 percent of people who also need these products.

Rely on reputation and word of mouth, not advertising

Despite the many advantages (intensity of light, safety, convenience) of solar lanterns, only 15 percent of Ethiopians mention them as their preferred type of light (excluding mains-powered light bulbs), while 44 percent of them prefer traditional solutions: paraffin lamps or candles.[152]

Too often, the response to this annoying situation has been to invest in social marketing or consumer education campaigns to "explain" to the "uninformed" consumers why they should buy these products. Judging the effectiveness of such "above the line marketing" (TV, radio, posters or leaflets) on actual sales is notoriously difficult. We interviewed a dozen leading distributors of such products,[153] and most mentioned that social marketing campaigns helped to build awareness; yet, *none* of them were willing to spend *any* of their own resources in such activities, preferring to invest in "below the line" marketing, that is, demonstrations in villages.

A field force can also ensure that customers are highly satisfied with their purchase, which is critical to "word of mouth" marketing. Successful marketers are not content with maximizing short-term sales, with the risk that customers may have been convinced to purchase a product but cease to use it. Patrimonio Hoy (see Chapter 6) is actually implementing "Net Promoter Score" surveys of its customers to measure whether they will proactively recommend the products to friends and neighbors. Relying on word of mouth is the most cost-efficient marketing strategy and ensures social impact but requires marketers to be patient, which is often at odds with expectations of donors financing the early stages of these ventures, and who want quick results.

Several marketers leverage the social capital of their sales force. Greenlight Planet, selling solar lamps in rural India, chooses its salespersons from well-regarded people in each village (such as teachers). The BRAC WASH program has been successful at having hundreds of thousands of families pay for latrines – by village WASH committees drawing a map of the village to indicate which households have adequate latrines and which ones are lagging behind. Those who cannot afford the full amount of the toilets but want to participate are given subsidies. As the WASH committee insists on the need to have the whole village equipped in order to avoid water contamination, laggers quickly find themselves in a difficult position in their community. Through this system BRAC has successfully equipped 40,000 entire villages (more than 70 percent penetration) today.

Word of mouth is the most cost-efficient marketing strategy and ensures social impact

JACK SIM, FOUNDER OF THE WORLD TOILET ORGANIZATION

ILLUSTRATION 16 / Jack Sim

I was born in Singapore in 1957. Singapore was a very poor country back then, poorer than Cambodia, Myanmar and the Philippines.

My father helped do deliveries in a shop, earning such a meager salary that my mother had to become an entrepreneur. That's how I went to business school . . . with my mother, when I was five years old. She started by volunteering for a make-up demonstration at the beauty counter of a shopping center, and after that one session she bought a set of cosmetics, tested her skills with my sister and declared herself a beautician for weddings. She trained women beauticians, sold the cosmetics, and so on. Little by little she became a one-stop wedding planner, taking commissions on every new line of business: wedding cards, dinners, ribbons – everything. She helped more than 3000 couples get married!

I started my first business at 24, and added one more business every year, so when I was 40 I had 16 businesses, in building material, trading, brick manufacturing, etc. I was happily married with a wonderful wife and four lovely kids. But I was unfulfilled as I realized that I only had another 40 years to live before I would die!

One day I was reading the newspaper and my prime minister was saying that we should measure our graciousness as a society based on the cleanliness of our public toilets. The journalist was blaming the state of the public toilets on all Singaporeans, whereas the problem was that the design was poor and the cleaners untrained and badly paid. So I created the Restroom Association of Singapore in 1998 to clean up our country's public toilets. I explained to shopping malls that they were losing customers if the toilets were not clean, because customers would leave their building once they needed to use the toilet. And so malls started to clean their toilets. Then I discovered there were 15 toilet associations around the world. We came together and they told me "if you want to create the headquarters, we will join you." So I started the World Toilet Organization on 19 November 2001.

To break the taboo on toilets, I made a media stunt by calling ourselves the World Toilet Organization, or WTO, playing the pun on the World Trade Organization. People said "if you call yourself 'toilet' no one will take you seriously and people will laugh." I answered

Continued

Continued

that *"if you make people laugh then you have their attention to listen to what you say"! And it worked: we became an influential advocacy group on sanitation. I was invited to the World Economic Forum in Davos; I was elected an Ashoka Fellow; endorsed by the Clinton Global Initiative; got named Time Magazine Hero of the Environment 2008 and Reader's Digest Asian of the Year. Yet in 2013, I achieved my greatest PR success when the UN General Assembly announced the creation of the UN World Toilet Day on 19 November, the founding day of our little organization!*

In the last five years I've developed SaniShop, a social business: we train people to source and sell toilets locally. As of 2012, we sold 23,000 toilets so far in Cambodia, and now we've also started SaniShop in India and Mozambique. Before that, we tried giving people toilets, but then people were not using the toilets, instead making them into a kitchen or a storeroom . . . plus it was not scalable because it needed more philanthropic money.

Our salespeople are village women who work part-time, earning a commission each time they sell a toilet. We trained the women to adapt their sales pitch to each customer. We realized that while toilets provide health and hygiene, people would buy more if it was sold as a status symbol and object of desire. Sometimes they would buy it for filial piety to show their aged parents they care. Whatever their reasons for purchasing, they always justify their reasons as health and hygiene, privacy and convenience. Seldom do they mention it was to keep up with their neighbors, although that is a major reason for their purchase. We also paint the wall of the toilet, so everybody has a different picture and people talk about it; those who don't have toilets have nothing to talk about. Word of mouth energizes the demand through jealousy and envy. Plus it is a visible marketing strategy because people see it from the outside. We want to make toilets a status symbol and an object of desire: we want to make toilets sexy. The lesson we learn here is that emotions are neither good nor bad. They are useful for behavioral change.

FMCG distributors again face different challenges. As they aim at repeat purchase of their products, they need to make them available close to home at any point in time, which is what traditional "mom and pop shops" offer. But selling via small retailers requires convincing the distribution chain (wholesalers and retailers) to take the product into their space, which often requires a minimum amount of mass-media marketing. Successful actors in selling infant porridge testify, however, that just one TV campaign per year is sufficient for this, and that local marketing and word of mouth does the rest of the trick to convince consumers to buy.

Achieve sustainability with high gross margins, not large volumes

Some BoP observers seem to believe that the recipe for distributing to the BoP is "low margins, high volume." This is not what the experience of the most successful BoP marketers seems to indicate.

First of all while the BoP market is large, it is extraordinarily fragmented. Each country, or state in large countries, is a different market, with its specific set of distributors, language and regulations.

Our research shows that marketers of beneficial durable goods (solar lanterns, water purifiers, latrines and so on) would need gross margins in the range of 25–50 percent in order to hope to be profitable when they reach full scale.[154] This is at least comparable to the gross margins in the global retail industry for consumer electronics (BestBuy: 25 percent; Kesa Electricals: 32 percent) or building materials (Home Depot: 34 percent). This is not surprising given the difficulty of reaching the BoP consumers and the range of services they require.

The numbers are similar for fast-moving consumer goods (FMCG): our research shows that existing companies selling affordable fortified complementary foods for infants require gross margins of above 50 percent at this early market stage, as they need to bear the high marketing costs of building the market, still offset by relatively small volumes (these companies typically sell around 10,000 meals per day).[155] As a comparison point, large companies selling typical FMCG products (such as soap, snacks, and so on) in developing countries only need gross margins of around 25 percent to pay for their marketing, distribution and overhead costs. Even though new beneficial FMCG require an extra layer of marketing, with time and scale, organizations selling branded affordable complementary foods and other beneficial FMCG should be able to lower the share of their revenues spent on marketing and sales to below 45 percent, because they will:

- Reduce their marketing costs needed today to convince distributors to take on their products, once these are better known.
- Improve their sales force productivity by professionalizing their sales process and gaining experience.
- Automatically see their marketing costs as share of sales decrease as the constant marketing costs (in absolute value) will be progressively offset by larger revenues.

For both FMCG and durable goods, building sustainably high sales volumes takes a long time, as companies need to wait for word of mouth to kick in and sustain sales for the long term in each of the communities where they operate (the alternative being to spend a lot of money on mass media, to see sales spike and drop again as soon as the campaign ends). Hence, this business needs to be a (relatively) low-volume, high-margin one before it turns into a high-volume, high-margin one and serves sustainably all those who need and want these beneficial goods and services.

chapter 15

Sales and distribution – the longest mile (or, fortune at the end of the road?)

The previous chapter has described lessons drawn from successful marketers of innovative products for the BoP. Here we turn to the less glamorous but vital task of actually getting the products into the hands of their intended beneficiaries.

Have you ever wondered how Coca-Cola manages to put bottles of their famous fizzy drink within your reach in the most remote places on Earth? The so-called "last-mile" challenge (that is, the difficulty many marketers face in reaching BoP consumers, especially in rural areas) doesn't seem to trouble them much. Why is that?

Hundreds of millions of BoP families purchase food and daily necessities at local shops (*sari-sari* in the Philippines, *kirana* in India) that still account for over 90 percent of total retail sales in India,[156] or 64 percent in Brazil.[157] This highly fragmented channel delivers quite cost-efficiently the products that consumers know about and desire. Thus, the last-mile challenge is not really about physically delivering products, it is first and foremost about promoting, explaining, financing and servicing innovative products that BoP consumers are unaware of or whose benefits they are skeptical about. Once the products are known and requested by end users, retailers will want to stock and sell them. One day, solar lanterns that currently require active promotion by direct sales forces will be as widely available in retail stores as the kerosene lamps they intend to replace.

Have you ever wondered how Coca-Cola puts its bottles within reach in the most remote places on Earth?

We start this chapter by drawing lessons from pioneering manufacturers that have succeeded in building direct sales forces to promote and sell their products. We differentiate the strategies followed by: (1) distributors of products that are "one-off" purchases such as solar lanterns or cookstoves; (2) the ones who sell consumer goods that are purchased weekly or even daily; (3) We then turn to the strategies that are currently deployed to improve the efficiency of existing networks of small, informal retailers that will eventually end up carrying the products initially promoted by the direct sales forces described above.

Direct sales forces for innovative devices ("one-off" purchases)

We have observed four types of distribution approaches for innovative devices corresponding to four different ways of maximizing revenues (see the equation below), which are represented in Figure 8 (based on data collected from 15 leading BoP distributors):[158]

Number of household clients per salesperson x sales per household = revenue per salesperson

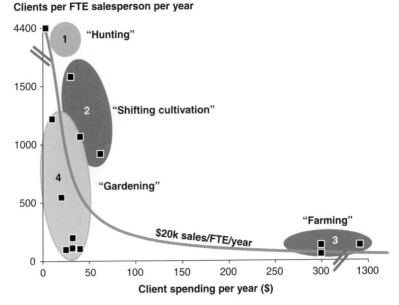

FIGURE 8 / **Distribution approaches for innovative devices**

Note: FTE means full-time equivalent. If companies employ a full-time sales force, the sales per salesperson FTE equals the sales per salesperson.

As a rule of thumb, distributors need to achieve sales of at least $20,000 per year per full-time equivalent (FTE) in order to hope to be profitable.[159] This is what the curve on the graph indicates.

To achieve this $20,000 goal, *Hunters* such as Toyola (see Chapter 4) recognize that sales per household will be limited to $5 per year (assuming they purchase a $15 cookstove every three years), and thus try to maximize the number of households served by each salesperson, giving each of them a vast "reserved territory" to cover. Hunters typically sell products below a $20 price point that do not require financing and thus speed up the selling cycle. They use intermediaries paid on commission to aggregate demand: for example, Toyola's "evangelists" get a 5–10 percent commission on each cookstove they help sell (or a free cookstove for each order of ten cookstoves). They deploy their sales force to maximize its efficiency, riding the natural product penetration cycle, spending time in a village only once demand has been generated. Toyola's reps leave the first products in a village for one month and then come back to collect money and make new sales, waiting to be called by the evangelist for the following ones. Hunters also relentlessly weed out activities that do not add value to their clients. For example, Toyola does not do any paperwork for the credit it offers, trusting customers to pay for the cookstove on time (they have had a 0 percent default rate, partly thanks to the remoteness of the places where they sell cookstoves: people would have nowhere to run or hide if they did not repay).

An alternative strategy is to maximize penetration in a given area before heading to the next. We have called this approach "*shifting cultivation.*" HUL sells their water purifiers, Pureit, in India, via a specialized sales force, sent in teams to a region to conduct repeat demonstrations until they reach over 50 percent penetration, before moving to the next, leaving behind only a few sales people to do the maintenance and the replacement sales (new water filters for the purifiers). This approach allows them to provide slightly longer credit than the "hunting model", as the sales team stays locally available to collect payment for a certain time (generally one to two years to saturate their area), hence products sold via this mechanism can be slightly more expensive than those sold by hunters, while the number of clients per salesperson will typically be slightly lower. However, one should keep in mind that setting up a financing scheme and organizing payment collection can be expensive, and hard to justify economically for loan amounts below $100.

Maximize penetration in a given area before heading to the next

At the other end of the spectrum, some organizations have chosen to maximize the amount of sales per client, serving a limited number of households (typically 300 per FTE salesperson) with a comprehensive offer. We have called this model *"farming"* as these models are typically organized around a branch (the "farm") and "cultivate" a limited territory of potential clients around this branch with long-term services.

"Farming" marketers such as Grameen Shakti, SELCO (see Chapter 5) or Cemex Patrimonio Hoy (see Chapter 6), sell their clients goods worth over $100, a very significant share of these families' non-food expenses. They build trust-based relationships with their customers over time, selling not just one product but a comprehensive package answering their clients' needs: Patrimonio Hoy sells the complete range of building materials needed for a room, not just Cemex products, along with technical assistance on how to build that room, as well as options for deferred deliveries to avoid any issue with stocking materials. SELCO and Grameen Shakti, selling Solar Home Systems (SHSs), similarly provide installation and maintenance services in addition to the systems themselves.

"Farming" marketers typically require financing in order to serve their clients, and provide them the product and service they need for a monthly fee they can afford. Most also realize that financing is too important to be trusted to external financiers (see Chapter 14 on marketing). By providing in-house financial services (whenever legally possible), "farming" marketers can instead benefit from (often) lucrative financial schemes: Grameen Shakti gets concessional refinancing rates from World Bank-financed IDCOL to promote the uptake of solar in Bangladesh, while Patrimonio Hoy finances its credit to customers by the savings deposited by other customers.

Finally, some organizations have opted for a different way to increase their sales per client: offering a basket of goods via their sales people. They hire local people as salespersons who in effect act as local providers of these various goods for their neighbors, as a part-time activity. We have called this model *"gardening."* So far, this model has struggled to take off as the sales people were little qualified to sell a complex range of products. Also, as they quickly saturated their area with their best-selling product, many lost interest in doing a job with too little financial reward over time. Though, in theory, having local sales people earning extra income by selling beneficial products may sound very appealing, we are yet to see a model become commercially profitable.

In terms of products, those above $100 (sold via the farming model, with financing mechanisms) or below $20–25 (or an equivalent local "psychological" amount not requiring financing, such as 1000 rupees in India, 20 cedis in Ghana and so on) are the ones that have found the most economically sustainable models. Products sold above $20 and for less than $100 require too complex business models (including end-user financing) to reach out to sufficient potential customers and do not have a sufficiently rich offering to live off a small number of customers. They can move to the "farming" model, broadening their product range with related products (such as adding a shelter to a latrine), or adding maintenance services that increase revenue per client and make cash flow more regular. They can also attempt to move to the "hunting" model, avoiding the complexities of financing by designing a less expensive product to kick-start a market without microfinance (Geres selling a low-cost cookstove; or Greenlight Planet selling an entry solar lamp at $17, after which people sometimes come back to buy the more expensive lamp equipped with a phone charger when they have the cash at harvest) or reducing its price with output-based subsidies (as Envirofit is doing with carbon credits) to get below the $20 psychological threshold. Yet these efforts, if successful, might be short-lived, since when penetration rises and competition arises, products worth less than $20 are likely to become mainstream and be carried by retail – making a direct sales force unnecessary for such products.

Extensive marketers have jumped on new communication technology to further streamline their operations: Toyola and Pureit marketers report every day via phone (SMS and voice) to their managers, without the need for face-to-face interaction that takes a lot of time in rural areas.

Direct ("door-to-door") sales force for consumer goods

Consumer goods companies generally focus on promoting their products through advertising, and leverage their wholesalers and retailers to get their products into the hands of their consumers.

In 2000, Hindustan Unilever Ltd (HUL) realized that this was not sufficient if they wanted to increase their penetration of rural markets dominated by local brands. HUL, India's largest FMCG company, covers a broad product portfolio from household and personal care products to food and beverages. Through Project Shakti, HUL selects women entrepreneurs belonging to microcredit self-help groups (SHG) and CSOs to set up an enterprise to distribute HUL's range of products. After three months of training from HUL, with an initial start-up loan from their respective SHG, each woman, called *"shakti amma"* starts selling HUL sachet-size products in six to ten villages, covering a population of 1000 to 2000 people. Supplied in products at their doorstep by HUL rural distributors, the shakti ammas are responsible for the supply of villagers and of the village retailer. The Project Shakti program initially doubled the household income. The program received a much-needed boost – actually more than doubling the number of salesmen – when HUL decided to provide each of them with a bicycle that would enable a man in their family (generally the husband or son, called shaktimaan) to deliver products to shops in neighboring villages. By the end of 2013 the Project Shakti network comprised 65,000 shakti ammas (and 50,000 shakti maans) covering more than 160,000 villages across India and reaching over four million households.

Since its inception in 1974, Natura, a Brazilian cosmetics producer, has decided to rely exclusively on a direct sales force of 1.2 million "consultants" able to counsel its customers in ways that no retailer would. Natura has built a successful and profitable $3.1 billion cosmetics business, with a 12 percent market share in Brazil, ahead of all the global leaders – P&G, Avon and Unilever – and a 60 percent penetration of Brazilian households.[160] These consultants are women who have a distributor agreement with Natura, buying products at an average 30 percent discount off the consumer price. Most sales are driven through the personal relationships of the consultants, starting with themselves and their families. A typical active consultant would sell to a network of 100 households who would probably buy products three to five times per year. The average Natura consultant generates an annual income of approximately €1,000, one-third of the minimum wage. Such a handsome compensation for a part-time job explains why sales people turnover is kept below 30 percent, quite an achievement in direct sales channels. This helps keeping training costs relatively low (Natura trained more than half a million consultants in 2011). Natura also uses a "multilevel" model, providing successful consultants with the opportunity to further increase their revenue by becoming sales leaders who help to recruit and manage up to 20 consultants. Sales leaders, in addition to their own commission on their direct sales, earn a percentage of the sales generated by the consultants they have recruited, possibly more than doubling their income. Such performance comes with heavy investments in fixed costs: regional management teams and a network of regional distribution centers able to deliver orders as low as €80 directly to the homes of Natura consultants. As a result, relying exclusively on a direct sales force appears to be well suited to brands with strong leadership positions such as the one Natura enjoys in Brazil.

These two successes may remain exceptions. Both companies enjoy powerful brands and are market leaders. Interestingly, they have not been able to successfully replicate their model in other locations. Indeed, the door-to-door distribution channel is costly to build and to maintain. Hiring and training micro-entrepreneurs is expensive, as is incentivizing those with the most experience to continue working for the company. Broadening the product range to absorb these fixed costs is tempting, but typically generates costly brand confusion and operational complexity.

Improving the efficiency of networks of small retailers

As we have seen, managing a door-to-door sales force is a costly and challenging undertaking that most manufacturers are happy to avoid once retail is ready to take on their products and distribute them. Some interesting initiatives are under way to improve the efficiency of these networks of retailers.

In India, there are nine million kirana stores, typically less than 20 m², often located within or as an extension of the owner's home, for whom this is rarely more than a complementary source of revenue. Low entry barriers explain an extraordinary density, even in rural areas: 57 percent of rural respondents reported having four kirana shops within 1 km.[161] This does not mean choice for consumers, as all kirana stores handle the same 500 to 800 stock-keeping units (SKUs), mostly dry food products because the infrastructure for cold storage is lacking. Shortages are common at retail stores, with an average 10 percent stock-out level of all SKUs due to their limited skills and financing. Consumer goods manufacturers are struggling to promote their products through fragmented distribution channels, involving up to four levels of intermediaries before reaching the consumers (carrying and forwarding agent, distributor, wholesalers/large retailers, small retailers).

A range of approaches have been used to improve the performance of small retailers, from optimizing supply chains (aggregating demand and optimizing logistics) to increasing the productivity of individual stores by adopting modern retail practices (see Table 7).

Bulk purchasing is the first step to streamline rural supply chains in order to increase the bargaining power of small retailers against regional distributors or wholesalers. Drishtee, an Indian social enterprise mentioned in Chapter 2, has built a network of 13,000 rural kirana stores. Under the Drishtee Rural Retail

TABLE 7   Examples of networks of small retailers

		Sourcing	Branding	Real Estate
Drishtee	India 13,000 shops	Supplier contracts and bulk purchasing at district level	No branding	Centrally owned warehouses
Hapinoy	Philippines 350 community stores and 10,000 shops	Supplier contracts at HQ level and bulk purchasing at district level	Microfranchising of community stores (100% of total outlets served)	Warehouses owned by micro-entrepreneurs
Mi Tienda	Mexico 7 warehouses and 7000 shops	Supplier contracts and bulk purchasing at district level	Affiliation program of retail stores (13% of total outlets served)	Centrally owned warehouses
Coca-Cola SABCO	Ethiopia 600 micro-distribution Centers	Bulk purchasing at district level	No branding but high promotion and brand visibility	Warehouses and stores owned by micro-entrepreneurs
Danone OMDA	Egypt In development	Local production	No branding but high promotion and brand visibility	Centrally owned warehouses
Laiterie du Berger	Senegal 8000 retailers	Local production	Branding of the shops	Centrally owned warehouses

Points' (DRRP) program, supplier contracts are negotiated with FMCG companies at headquarters' level. Drishtee also carefully optimizes physical distribution in order to reduce transportation costs and provide weekly delivery to a maximum of retail shops.

Yet improving the performance of small retailers is not limited to adapting modern retail management practices. La Laiterie du Berger, a social enterprise created by Bagoré Bathily in Senegal, has come up with "Pouss-Pouss," a simple yet effective delivery method to small shops (less than €6 in sales per week) located on sandy roads that cannot be used by traditional vans. "Pouss-Pouss" is a two-wheeled cool box that contains up to 150 kg of yogurts and cream, refrigerated just long enough for a one-day delivery. From 30 percent of sales in 2011, the "Pouss-Pouss" delivery channel was expected to reach 50 percent in 2014.

This capacity to innovate is not a specificity of social entrepreneurs. In Ethiopia, Coca-Cola SABCO created a network of independently owned micro-distribution centers (MDCs) run by local entrepreneurs, servicing an area of

1 km in circumference, reaching a maximum of 150 retail outlets. MDCs source products from local distributors, load the products from the central warehouse and deliver them manually – mostly by pushcarts – to local retailers. This model, which offers retailers constant access to products (12 hours per day/ six or seven days per week deliveries) generated significant additional revenue and has been replicated in more than 15 countries in Africa and some key Asian markets.

Retailers used to say that there are three key factors of success: location, location and location! However, in the BoP retail market, location is often good, offering a satisfactory catchment area of customers, but it is rarely enough to guarantee success. The ultimate bottleneck is the insufficient store productivity, requiring investments to upgrade the stores' infrastructure, to retain its customers and to fund its working capital.

High entry barriers mean significant competitive advantage of first movers and eventually large profits over time

Mi Tienda – operating in rural areas of Mexico and founded in 1999 by José Ignacio Avalos, one of the founders of Banco Compartamos – supplies stores with small quantities or even a single unit of products, reducing cash outlays for shop owners, improving management of inventories and merchandise mix for the stores. In addition, Mi Tienda offers a second level of support to selected stores, called "affiliates." Mi Tienda helps them to improve their productivity, with a full suite of services: in-depth diagnostic, new logo and change of colors, physical layout, financing of working capital and modernization investments. Modernized stores have experienced an average 35 percent increase in sales.

* * *

The characteristics that we have enumerated – small individual transactions, risk adverse and geographically dispersed customers – are operational challenges that can become formidable sources of competitive advantage. While building a last-mile distribution for the BoP requires patience and upfront investments, we know that high entry barriers mean significant competitive advantage of first movers and eventually large profits over time.

So far, with the exception of a few distributors like Mi Tienda, the only players we have seen attempting to capture this opportunity have been manufacturers. This is not surprising as the development of the retail industry in Western markets shows that distributors have lagged behind manufacturers in the race to globalization: P&G and Unilever became global companies long before Walmart or Carrefour.

Yet we also know that powerful distributors have managed to build strong bargaining positions and extract a substantial share of the value created by the consumer goods industry. Similarly, we believe that local players – able to build distribution organizations that are able to actively distribute innovative products to the BoP – stand a good chance of securing strong sustainable competitive positions. Once a strong local position is built, they will have the opportunity to expand into neighboring regions or countries.

In the meantime, we trust that an industry platform is needed to help distributors address common challenges:

- Source products and suppliers, evaluate technologies, conduct due diligence, guarantee quality of products and negotiate best prices by aggregating orders.
- Share best practices through workshops and training modules on social marketing, recruitment, impact measurement capabilities and so on.
- Facilitate access to finance.

Selling life-changing products to the BoP is not about helping to scale up one organization, it is about accelerating the development of a new industry. An industry-wide coalition of players must come together, centered on the pioneering distributors who have learned their lessons the hard way but supported by philanthropists and industry players who have the financial and technical capabilities required. The collaborative ethos that graces the social business field is a key reason to be hopeful that such initiatives can succeed.

The "last mile" is an opportunity for distributors able to adapt to the specificities of the BoP market. The last mile might be the longest, but – paraphrasing C. K. Prahalad – there might be a fortune at the end of that road.

chapter 16

Financing social businesses

The social sector has been thrilled at the sight of the global financial community bringing its formidable resources and capabilities to its rescue. Financiers were also thrilled to redeem themselves by using their skills to solve our world's problems.

With so much excitement on all sides, could there be a bit of a "bubble" in the process, with too much money chasing too few deals?

As Serge Raicher, the former chair of the EVPA,[162] puts it: "The danger is that unreasonable promises made by the promoters of some social finance products could lead to an imbalance, with too many assets chasing too few bona fide programs, creating a pool of investors disappointed to find that their investment resulted in little societal impact. In such a social finance "bubble," excess funds could end up piling into investments, from microlending to private equity in emerging markets."[163]

To answer this question, we discuss the following points:

- How big the need for financing is, and for what kind of money.
- How much has already been raised to fulfill this need.
- How many actual investment opportunities exist.
- How attractive these opportunities are.

How big is the need, and for what kind of money?

In terms of *needs for social finance*, some optimistic estimates were put forward over the recent years.[164] Our own work, for instance in the capital-intensive housing industry, suggests that providing financing to half of the 200 million urban families that are in need of a better home would require $180 billion in mortgage loans portfolio after ten years and around $60–70 billion in investment in businesses.

Maybe more important than the size of the needs is the nature of the financing required: less than 30 percent of funds will be needed to provide equity and loan financing to innovative and fast-growing social businesses. The average tickets will be quite small, given that these are new, riskier markets, where the few existing pioneering companies are still comparatively small, and where the fewer bigger players will invest cautiously and progressively. The bulk of the other 70 percent will be needed to refinance MFIs or housing finance institutions.

How much has been raised to fulfill this need?

Frustrated with purely nonprofit approaches, investors are attracted by the promise of "doing good while doing well." Social finance is all the rage… but still with much confusion about what it includes or not. In this chapter, we only consider those actors who directly invest in social businesses or microfinance institutions (MFIs), excluding the socially responsible investment players that apply socially minded selection methods to otherwise standard portfolios of corporations. Figure 9 attempts to lay out the landscape of social financiers that invest in social businesses, plotting funds along two axis: the financial return expectations they have from their investees, and the returns (social, financial or a combination of both) they have promised to their own investors. The area of each circle gives a rough idea of the relative amount of capital that each player represents.

Starting from the bottom left corner of the chart, *public donors and private foundations* have been the traditional providers of grants to the social sector, and by far the largest source of social finance (over $2.7 trillion cumulated over the period 2001–11). Some of the most innovative ones such as the Shell Foundation or the Bill and Melinda Gates Foundation have started moving toward the middle of the chart.

At the top right corner of the chart, *private equity* players operating in developing countries (having fundraised more than $290 billion over the period 2001–11) may claim to have an indirect social impact by creating jobs and economic development. These include players such as Aureos, originally

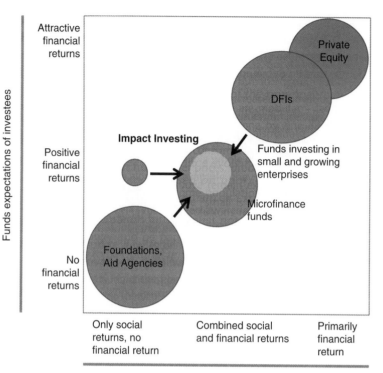

FIGURE 9 / The social finance landscape

Source: OECD (2014) Development: Key Tables, http://www.oecd-ilibrary.org/development/development-aid-total-official-and-private-flows_20743866-table5; Aspen Institute (2011) Impact Report, http://www.aspeninstitute.org/sites/default/files/content/docs/ande/ANDE-2011-Impact-Report-Final.pdf.

Notes: Bubble size for DFIs: estimates from Hystra, based on desk research and reports from DFID and ODI. Bubble size for impact investing: estimates from Hystra, based on amounts fundraised by the most representative funds in the impact investment field (e.g., GBF, Root Capital, Bamboo Finance, Ignia, E+Co Acumen Fund, Aavishkaar, Omidyar Network, LGT Venture Philanthropy, Gray Ghost Ventures and a handful of corporate funds).

founded by the UK's bilateral development finance institutions (DFIs; see below) as well as small-cap private equity players such as Grofin and Tuninvest – both focusing on Africa.

Lower down come *development finance institutions* (DFIs), which typically allocate part of their investments to the private sector in developing countries (roughly estimated at $260 billion over the same period). The indirect social benefits of creating jobs and supporting economic development is deemed sufficient by the investors (often governments and aid agencies) that back them. Some of them are, however, moving toward the middle of the chart as their investors are increasingly demanding a more explicit focus on social and development impact. This is the case, for instance, for FMO, which manages several funds for the Dutch government in order to support higher risk projects promising greater development impact. One of these, the MASSIF fund, provides financial institutions with resources to aid the development of micro, small and medium-sized enterprises in developing countries.

Funds investing in *microfinance institutions* (MFIs) have continued to expand and professionalize their operations, to reach a total gross loan portfolio of almost $70 billion in 2010. Through their focus on the creation and growth of microenterprises, they create jobs and improve the livelihoods of many of their beneficiaries. One of the most renowned (and replicated) of these funds is BlueOrchard Finance, which has successfully provided funding to MFIs since 2001, and has been instrumental in establishing microfinance as an alternative asset class for mainstream capital (including pension funds and high net-worth individuals). Their investment model consisted in providing loans to established MFIs, as well as equity. They also developed the first microfinance bond, which had a three-tranche structure: the riskiest tranche was subscribed by development finance institutions, while the least risky tranche was subscribed by large mainstream commercial banks.

For years, pioneers (identified as *impact investing* in Figure 9) such as Endeavor, Acumen Fund and E+Co have scouted the world for "social, inclusive businesses." Interestingly, while looking for combined social and economic returns, many of them were not promising any returns to their own "investors," or only because their own operating costs were covered by grants.[165] Indeed, while the individual investments were producing positive returns, they were way too small to pay for the important operating costs of these organizations. These pioneers have been followed by dozens of players such as Grassroot Business Fund, Bamboo Finance, LGT VP, Bonventure, Alphamundi and others. Corporations such as Danone and GDF Suez have also entered the fray, leveraging their CSR budgets and employee volunteering programs to cover the large operating budgets.[166] Taking solely into account what is defined above as "impact investing" we estimate that about $1 billion has been raised by the pioneering impact investing community. Their ability to grow is limited, however, because of their reliance on philanthropic resources to finance their own operations. Hence, some of these players are raising new funds that do offer financial returns to their investors, and are moving toward the right of the chart. For instance, Grassroots Business Fund has raised over $40 million investment capital since late 2011 for its new for-profit fund.[167]

Lastly, funds investing in *small and growing enterprises* operating in "social" sectors such as agriculture, education, health and so on. This pocket of financing is already larger than impact investing, given its broader mandate (an estimated $20 billion over the period 2001–11). The largest and most successful player in this area is SEAF (Small Enterprise Assistance Funds), which has set up over 20 funds investing into local, smaller size companies with tickets averaging $1 million.

How many actual investment opportunities exist, in light of the billions raised?

It is important to distinguish between the financing needs of the social sector and the size of investable opportunities. The difference between the two lies in the existence of entrepreneurs able to put together investable projects. Today, our work shows that while financing needs are measured in hundreds of billions of dollars, investable opportunities range in hundreds of millions:[168] there are still very few investable targets in the field of "impact investing," or at least very few that are investable through traditional investment schemes.

Let us take our affordable housing example: in India, there were only an estimated 25 developers who were building or planning to build affordable housing homes (as of mid-2010), putting on the market 25,000–50,000 new homes that year in a country where 25 million households live in substandard housing.[169]

The same picture emerges in other sectors. Over the last six years, we screened close to 1000 promising projects in the fields of access to energy, water, agriculture, education, health and financial services, and found that about 70 of them delivered social impact at some scale while aiming at achieving financial sustainability.[170] Yet only a few of these 70 social businesses are "blockbusters," truly profitable and growing rapidly. All the other projects require (sometimes significant) adjustments to their business models (and oftentimes to their organization and governance) to actually become investable. Let us take the example of water kiosks. As we discussed in Chapter 7, none of the half a dozen promising players have achieved profitability and they all struggle to scale up further (at least without grants and subsidies). To understand how to keep improving on the existing models requires developing insights on how the sector could be restructured and what type of players and resources would be needed. In the case of water kiosks, it is key to understand how the expansion of this type of infrastructure could be better modeled: should water kiosks be operated as fully integrated operations, as networks of local franchisees, or by independent village-level entrepreneurs?

As a result of this lack of investable pipeline, the actual amounts invested are significantly less than the amount raised, and many impact investors would privately recognize that they are struggling to invest the money they have raised because of the scarcity of the deals, their complexity and their limited size (often in hundreds of thousands of dollars rather than in the millions needed to keep the ratio of "transaction costs/amount invested" at reasonable levels). Based on the JPMorgan and GIIN surveys,[171] 50 of the largest impact investors have invested – in equity or loans – approximately $600 million in roughly 900 businesses (excluding microfinance) "intended to benefit low-income populations," meaning an average ticket size of $700,000.

How attractive are these opportunities?

While investable organizations that truly deliver social value are few and far between, expectations for financial returns are also unlikely to be met, for a variety of reasons.

First and foremost, there is as yet no track record of successful exit strategies for such type of investments. As any investor in a venture capital (VC) or private equity (PE) fund knows, as long as exit strategies have not been realized, any discussion on returns is illusory.

Second, most of these investments have only been made possible because the targets benefited from early grants to cover their operating costs, during the time needed to put in place and validate their model.[172]

Third, the costs associated with these complex and diverse investments often represent 20–50 percent of the investment ticket itself, resulting in management fees of 6–10 percent of committed capital. This is three to five times the percentage that VC firms typically get and is prohibitive given the current (very) small deal size. Most impact investors are currently subsidizing origination and operating costs through grants or their own capital. For instance, E+Co spent €5 million to invest €11 million in their first years of operation. Corporate impact investing funds often spend more on their operating expenses than on funding actual projects. The venture capital theory underpinning this disproportionate relationship between investment size and origination and operating costs is that a good percentage of these investments will mature and grow and that original investors will become "serial" investors.

Fourth, social businesses require much more than money in order to grow and succeed. The amounts of technical assistance needed are more important and more complex than for straightforward businesses. Social entrepreneurs also need better access to technology and business networks, and they know it: As Manoj Sinha, the CEO of Husk Power Systems, says: "When choosing an investor it is important for us to know what kind of technical assistance and R&D they can potentially bring us, and what is their long-term goal for investing in companies like us." Interestingly, this is probably one of the distinctive advantages that corporate impact investment funds can bring to their investees: for example, the fund Rassembleurs d'Energies of GDF Suez can provide packages including investments, grants and technical assistance through its programs of corporate volunteering. Similarly, danone.communities focuses on investments that are close to Danone's core businesses and where they can leverage their skills to add value to their investee. These funds are willing to spend significant amounts in technical assistance because of the indirect benefits they also get from employees' involvement in such projects.

Last but not least, experienced social finance practitioners have found out that a major restructuring of the social business is often a precondition to make it investable. Mark Cheng of Chelwood Capital has worked with Fair Finance – an organization providing affordable loans and loan advice. It first identified the business from non-business parts of the organization in order to raise the right kind of finance for each part, and then imagined the links and governance of and between each part.

It is to address these issues that some of the more interesting financial innovation is taking place. This includes, for instance, structures with tiered investment tranches: each tranche is subscribed to by investors with different risk appetites (for example, the riskier tranche is taken by development institutions and acts as a guarantee, while the least risky tranche is subscribed by more traditional investors). Another exciting development is social impact bonds. These aim at addressing the paradox that investing in prevention of social and health problems saves the public sector money, but that it is currently difficult for public bodies to find the funds and incentives to do so. Technically, a social impact bond is a contract with the public sector in which a commitment is made to pay for improved social outcomes that result in public sector savings. The expected public sector savings are used as a basis for raising investment for prevention and early intervention services that improve social outcomes. However, repayment to investors is contingent upon specified social outcomes being achieved. The first social impact bond arranged by the UK-based organization Social Finance in 2010 financed a prisoner rehabilitation program.

INTERVIEW WITH MARK CHENG, EXECUTIVE DIRECTOR AT CHELWOOD CAPITAL, AND FAISEL RAHMAN, FOUNDER AND MANAGING DIRECTOR OF FAIR FINANCE

ILLUSTRATION 17 / Faisel Rahman

ILLUSTRATION 18 / Mark Cheng

Continued

Chelwood Capital is a social investment firm that provides strategic and financial advice to social enterprises and mission-driven businesses looking to access the capital markets.

Fair Finance is a social business that offers a range of financial products (mostly affordable and accessible personal and business loans) designed to meet the needs of people who are financially excluded. Fair Finance also provides loan advice.

Authors: How did your collaboration start?

Faisel Rahman: Fair Finance called in Chelwood Capital in 2008. After a few years of operations, we wanted to understand how we could become more financially sustainable, and have an honest conversation about where the money was. When we started, there were 7–10 million people in the UK at the margin of the financial services industry. In fact, an estimated 50 percent of them turn to loan sharks and predatory lenders for microloans of £500 (on average) – loans for which interest rates start at 400 percent and can go as high as 6000 percent. That is a £2 billion lost opportunity of high-cost exploitation.

Authors: What did you find out?

Mark Cheng: In a nutshell, we realized that some parts of the organization were potentially profitable (and therefore capable of supporting investment requiring a financial return) and some were not. So, we helped them restructure in a way that each activity could be funded with the right type of money. We also had to rethink the whole governance of the management team and the board. As a result, Fair Finance managed to raise £1 million from "angel investors" – that is, high net worth individuals ready to take a risk to fuel the growth of the organization, which in turn unlocked an additional £3.5 million in credit lines from mainstream banks. It was only the advisory activities, capacity-building and R&D that required grant money and subsidies, and comparatively very little of it (£75,000–100,000 per year) – by separating out the business activities in this way, and inviting investors/donors to invest separately in each part according to their risk appetite, we were able to concentrate limited donations and grants on only those portions of the business that really needed it.

Continued

Continued

Authors: What were the main challenges?

MC: We had many. All in all, the whole restructuring process took two to three years. We needed to convince commercial banks that it was possible to fund an MFI in Western Europe, not from the CSR department but from the corporate banking side. We had to strip out all the complexity of what Fair Finance does in order to show what is similar to the type of businesses they know. For instance, Fair Finance has got a historic – hence predictable – default rate. On that basis, you can make a credit risk assessment. By having social investors come in and underwrite all of the operating costs, including expected defaults in Fair Finance's loan portfolio, we made it much easier for commercial banks to come in as a senior creditor and fund the rest. Fair Finance also had to split the non-profit side of the organization (as in, the division in charge of advisory and capacity building) from the corporate entities that do the microlending – to make it totally independent. There is also now a nonprofit "holding company" that holds a dual social and business mission, and overseas all entities.

Authors: What next?

FR: What we really wanted to do is demonstrate that mainstream banking could be involved with an MFI such as ours. We now want to replicate that deal to offer microfinance for small businesses and consumers, requiring anything from £500 to £2000 in consumer finance and £2000 to £20,000 for their business aspirations. This is a very powerful approach and opportunity. We now have access to finance that is 5–20 times bigger than our philanthropic budget alone, and we generate our own income: £600,000 from our own activities last year, rising to £1 million this year. And it is not only about money. Before, I used to spend 90 percent of my time raising money, out of 30 donors, all very different and rather short-term orientated. Now, I can pull money as and when I need it and really focus 90 percent of my time on growing our organization for the long term, while reporting to only a few funders. It is truly transformational.

Authors: What would you recommend to those who want to apply your approach?

MC: A lot of what we have done can be replicated in other situations. I would suggest following a four-step approach: (a) understand all your cash flows to be able to craft a solid forecast; (b) find good lawyers to help you work out the right corporate structure; (c) develop bespoke financial instruments: for instance, Fair Finance uses an instrument between loan and equity, with a capped upside and obligation to return capital to investors only if there are positive profits; (d) find the right set of investors for whom what you propose is a viable proposition and be 100 percent honest about the cash flows, expected returns and financial instruments.

FR: That last point is very important to me: the more honest you can be, the more likely you will get what you need. Often, you have financiers in front of you who try to "force" traditional models onto social entrepreneurs, and that becomes problematic over time.

How to "fast-replicate" and create new investment opportunities

With this in mind, one realizes that there is a significant mismatch between the actual needs, the money at work and the expectations of investors. In fact, it appears that the true challenge is less about raising more funds more quickly, or backing the right entrepreneur and helping them to grow, than about accelerating the creation of entire new industries complete with their ecosystem, either by replicating existing successes, or experimenting in adjusting and improving models with the most potential. Simply waiting for more deals to "come to age" will absorb some of the financing available, but will never allow to tackle the needs at scale.

According to Serge Raicher: "the best growth strategy for the industry is to come up with greater supply – more imaginative programs that blend investment opportunities with government funding for social good."[173]

This has drastic implications for the impact-investing community, as this shift is something that requires much more than money or financial wizardry: it takes long-term, collaborative undertakings of private, public and philanthropic players. For instance, to address half of today's housing deficit over ten years would require training close to seven million masons to build and improve homes, and set up the equivalent of 22 Grameen Banks to extend housing microfinance loans, in addition to thousands of building permits and authorizations, as well as millions of land title regularizations to be issued by the government. For industries that are built up on global supply chains (such as solar home systems provision), such efforts need to be undertaken across geographies.

Hence investors will need to become much more proactive and invest into new capabilities, including developing industry-building strategies and investing with other investors and donors in collaborative ways.

As we have seen, most donors and funds today focus on identifying and supporting local entre-preneurs and projects. Few help them to disseminate their innovations, and if they do so it is with an "export" mindset. By "export" we mean that they take the original idea and team, codify it, and sometimes coach/finance the original team in sharing their success in other geographies. Here, the "export" approach is idea-centric.

We believe that a much more effective alternative would be to adopt an "import" approach, which is "geographic-centric" rather than "idea-centric": one that would focus on the specific needs of a given country, so as to import and adapt business models that have achieved success in other geographies.

The "import" approach requires following a few steps: (1) identifying "social business ideas with the potential for blockbuster inclusive business" that stand out by their prospective scale, impact and sustainability, which are relevant and feasible for a given country; (2) understanding the "DNA" of these blockbusters – that is, the key success factors, governance, partnerships and financials that are behind their success; (3) finding local champions operating in the target country interested in copying the "DNA" of these blockbusters; (4) once the local champions are identified, pilots can be conducted to test local variations of these blockbusters.

The benefits of such an "import" approach (over an "export" modality) are many: (a) cost-effectiveness and speed, given that the original organiza-tion has already worked out the kinks and that many ideas can be tested in each location; (b) adaptability, given that local champions are in the driving seat, making it also easier to build on existing efforts, conditions and craft partnerships.

Such an approach is already a widespread practice in the venture capital industry, where it is called "geo-arbitrage" or "tropicalization." However, much more could be done to spread this approach to the impact investment and development spheres. For instance, the set-up of replication platforms and funds for some targeted geographies could be tackled by both donors and investors; the donors could fund the identification, selection and replication of inclusive businesses and provide catalytic finance to conduct the early pilots. Once a local version of the business model is proven at a small scale, and the company ready to scale up, it would go for a new round of investment with more traditional investors for its additional financing needs.

* * *

In conclusion, the impact-investing space needs to embark on its own reinvention, leaving the safe shores of traditional finance practices and learning how to work more collaboratively, longer-term and with an ecosystem view of entire sectors.

All this amounts to a drastic change of paradigm (see Table 8), but is the price to pay by financiers who hope to contribute to creating the industries in which they could sustainably and profitably invest.

TABLE 8 **Shifting paradigms in the financing of social businesses**

Old paradigm	New paradigm
Help one business grow	Help build a new industry, complete with its ecosystem
Careful evaluation and due diligence of the strategy proposed by a local entrepreneur	Proactive development of an industry-building strategy and selection of entrepreneurs able to play a role in its implementation
Individual investment decisions	Collaboration with other financial, strategic and philanthropic investors

17

The role of philanthropy

As we have mentioned several times in this book, our focus on market-based approaches to social problems does not in any way suggest that straight "giveaway" programs should be disregarded. In the conclusion of Part 1 (when markets fail), in particular, we discussed how they are indispensable to help the "ultra-poor," in emergency situations and to fund programs for which the outcomes are too distant and uncertain.

Yet we have also observed many situations in which "giveaway" programs have unintended negative consequences when they are "competing" with market-based approaches – as we have seen with free distribution of solar lanterns (Chapter 5). As many social entrepreneurs say, their greatest foe is "expectation of free help."

The purpose of this chapter is to advocate for philanthropists keen to address social issues for which market-based solutions do exist to redirect their invest-ments from "giveaway" programs towards catalyzing the development of market-based solutions.

Andrew Carnegie famously said: "It is more difficult to give money away intel-ligently than to earn it in the first place."[174] He certainly did not imply that investing in for-profit businesses is easy. Philanthropists keen to catalyze the solution of social problems through market-based approaches are somehow combining the two difficulties.

We start by describing the catalytic role that foundations and philanthro-pists could play in triggering the emergence of market-based solutions, then analyze why they do not play that role today, and propose ways to shift their approach.

Foundations have a catalytic role to play

Philanthropists are essential to the success of social innovations. Acting as "free agents," they have the capabilities to jump in where government, investors or business may fail to do so.

Some philanthropists, recognizing that they did not have sufficient resources to match the immense scale of needs with "giveaway" programs, decided to undertake catalytic initiatives that in turn triggered much bigger improvements. Such initiatives focused on initiating participation from private sector players, encouraging product and business model innovations, and removing systemic barriers to market development.

A first example is that of PSI, a global CSO active in the field of health care, which has helped to create a local industry for chlorine, a water disinfectant, in Kenya. This is quite an achievement, given that chlorine remains a "CSO product" in most of the world's developing countries, distributed for free whenever there is a sanitary crisis. Chlorine is hardly ever produced and sold in a commercial manner. Indeed, promoting the use of chlorine requires costly marketing campaigns that no private player wants to invest in, as there is no first mover advantage. In addition, private players face "unfair" competition from CSOs that are promoting and distributing their own subsidized products for (quasi) free. Given this situation, PSI Kenya raised philanthropic money for what business was not ready to pay – that is, education campaigns on the importance of safe water and on the solutions available to treat unsafe water. In parallel, it started producing chlorine locally, through a local manufacturer, but for sale (henceforth covering its main operational costs, and not undermining any commercial efforts). In 2012, PSI Kenya sold its chlorine products to about one million people every day. But, more importantly, a number of private players have followed suit, offering similar, affordable products.

Another example is that of Lighting Africa, a joint IFC and World Bank program, which is helping to develop commercial off-grid lighting solutions in sub-Saharan Africa. To do so, it focused on a set of initiatives such as prize competitions for innovative products, quality assurance certification, market intelligence, consumer education, business support and access to finance for entrepreneurs, as well as better-adapted public policies and regulatory frameworks. A few years later, more than 50 lighting technology firms have entered this market.

Similarly, the Bill and Melinda Gates Foundation systematically aims at identifying a specific issue and a "theory of change" to fix it. Once that is done, it takes risks, makes big bets and moves with urgency. For instance, it decided in 2011 to redirect all its efforts away from water and toward sanitation issues – after assessing that this was where both needs and potential were biggest. Within the field of sanitation, it believes that no sustainable technological solution yet exists to equip the millions of slum dwellers with ecological, low-cost, well-maintained toilets. Relying on its technology background, and network within research and academic organizations, it launched a massive program called "Reinventing the Toilet," totaling $42 million in grants, to trigger technological innovation in this field. It has already triggered the development of hundreds of new projects and products as a result.

These cases show a common approach, starting by identifying a market-based solution that works, understanding the obstacles that prevent its scaling up and designing a strategic intervention to remove these obstacles.

What is broken in today's philanthropic market?

While some pioneering philanthropic institutions adopted effective strategies, these examples are few and far between. This is not for lack of generosity. There has been an explosive growth in philanthropic resources: the total assets of the 82,000 US charitable foundations have reached $662 billion in 2011[175] (compared to $476 billion in 2001 and $30 billion in 1975).[176]

This regular (give or take a financial crisis) accumulation in assets is to be expected: each foundation is managed to be "eternal" and each generation of wealthy entrepreneurs contains a certain proportion of philanthropists willing to create their foundation. Though it is understandable, it remains a shocking paradox that the philanthropic world is hoarding resources, refusing to save lives today in order to solve the problems of tomorrow – when they should know that new generations of philanthropists will create their foundations in the meantime. In other words, foundations do not recognize the "time value of good," a wonderful phrase coined by Chuck Feeney, the billionaire who co-created Duty Free Shoppers and sold it to LVMH, deciding to "give while living," when he signed over most of his fortune to Atlantic Philanthropies and committed to spend it all (approximately $9 billion) by 2017. Chuck's determination to achieve tangible impact with his foundation has been relentless, forcing his staff to identify programs that had proven they could make a difference to people's lives – and investing heavily to scale them up. Because the time frame of the foundation was limited and the goals clearly defined, this created a performance ethic throughout the foundation staff and a willingness to make bold commitments.

This stands in sharp contrast to many foundations, which seem to be managed as if "preserving" the foundation itself (that is, to have its funds last for as long as possible). Statistics seem to support this view as US foundations gave away $49 billion, or 7.4 percent of their assets, in 2011, but received $42 billion during the same year.

This risk aversion is combined with fragmentation. Despite the overall growth in philanthropic resources available, the average foundation size remains modest: $8 million in assets and $2 million in annual giving in 2011 in the US. It is difficult to imagine operating an efficient foundation on this scale, if it hopes to tackle global challenges.

More pervasive than the issue of size, decision making in small foundations is affected by the fact that they remain "vertically integrated," in that one donor (often the founder) channels all his or her giving through one professional team that – in turn – gets all its funding from this donor. As a result, we have seen staff in foundations who seem to be more concerned with guessing the donors' preferences than developing an independent point of view on the attractiveness of a given philanthropic investment.

This difficulty in measuring successful investments makes foundation staff more focused on avoiding mistakes, scattering their limited resources in small grants of short duration. They also insist on "restricted funding," that is, funding a specific "project" as opposed to the core costs of the organization. In informal conversations with CSOs, we have routinely found out that "unrestricted" funds are so scarce and valuable that most organizations would be willing to trade $1 of unrestricted funds against $2 of restricted funds. While all this certainly keeps the grant-making machine busy, it is unlikely to produce social impact at scale and it undoubtedly requires CSOs to make a formidable effort to raise the funds they require. The combined cost of raising funds has been estimated to be 22–43 percent of the funds raised, split roughly equally between the costs incurred by CSOs in fund raising and the foundations in administration costs.[177]

Why are competent and well-intentioned people ending up behaving in ways contrary to their goals? At the risk of appearing overly simplistic, we trust that the main root cause for these different problems is that foundations are not held accountable for their actions; as Matthew Bishop states in his book *Philanthrocapitalism*: "The rich need to be accountable for the results of their philanthropy." But if they do not have to raise funds, how can they be accountable? The founders of the foundations are often the sole judges of their performance – while their "doing public good" is rewarded by tax rebates. As a result, very few foundations seek to measure actual impact or compare performance with other actors involved in similar geographies and issues.

In summary, philanthropy is an industry with low barriers to entry, low competition intensity and high barriers to exit. This is not a good prognosis for industry performance.

A new architecture for the philanthropic sector

To change this sorry state of affairs, we need to think about systemic interventions that will trigger a whole restructuring of the sector, so that (financial) resources are allocated to CSOs in a more effective and efficient way. Given what was said above, what could be a vision for a new architecture of the sector?

We believe that philanthropists should embrace competition, learning from how capital markets have become more efficient in allocating financing to companies: over the last 30 years, competition in capital markets has obliged companies to focus on what they are best at (and sell off the rest), and has led investors to finance businesses where they could add more value than other owners. Interestingly, this competition has empowered the best entrepreneurs over the investors, in a particularly visible way since the 1980s. Just as in the social space, great entrepreneurs are the scarcest resource to drive organizations, not money. In capital markets, a fast-growing and remarkably diverse industry of intermediaries has also developed: venture capital and private equity firms, fund managers, hedge funds and so on. All these intermediaries have common characteristics: they are created and led by relatively small teams of highly skilled professionals, have clear strategies, and raise money from investors based on their track record and strategic insights. Interestingly, many of these intermediaries do not provide "measurable performance" in the short term (VC or PE funds require capital to be locked up for five to ten years and their performance can only be judged when they have exited their last investment). Investors are in turn in a position to allocate their investments among these competing teams, based on their views on the market and opportunities for investment, and making sure to align the incentives of the team with the pursued objectives.

Learning from these developments, a possible vision for the philanthropic sector would be a "consolidation" of the foundation space. Foundations would grow into large, specialized entities, which develop very tight relationships with a limited number of CSOs. The relationship between the foundation and the CSO would be one of a shareholder (as opposed to a client): the foundation would "commit" for the long term to the CSO and invest into it so that it becomes a strong implementation partner. Rather than focus solely on funding projects, it would also ensure that the CSO can cover its core costs and develop a strong backbone infrastructure to become the most professional and able organization in a particular field.

In turn, the foundations, in order to reach that size and independence, would need to rethink completely their purpose and functioning. They would have to "disconnect" from their original donor, and become sectorial expert organizations developing a deep understanding and ambitious vision for the resolution of a given social problem. On that basis, they would develop five to ten years of ambitious program proposals, for which they would seek financing from a range of donors. Pitching their expertise and their vision of the problem, their implementation capabilities and their influence network, they would compete for funds in their field.

At the other end, donors would stop being individuals or institutions that take personal glory and satisfaction in having their "own" foundation. Rather, donors should then behave like asset managers, deciding which teams are most likely to achieve impact, and distribute their funds accordingly. In this respect, Warren Buffett's decision to trust his immense wealth to the organization he considers "the best in the business" – the Bill and Melinda Gates Foundation – is to be applauded. Like any asset managers, donors would ask for tangible results, to be ultimately able to judge which team had more impact. Yet, as social work in developing countries is highly uncertain and risky work, their commitment would need to be long term. Results would be judged and compared, across the portfolio, at the completion of the proposed programs.

In addition, the sector would need the development of a diverse industry of professional intermediaries to channel financial resources from donors who do not have the wealth required to set up an effective foundation, or the time and skills to become personally engaged. Today, in the philanthropic space, these intermediaries remain too few (with the exception of historical

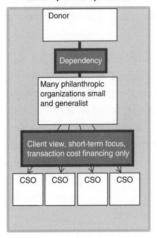

Current philanthropic sector

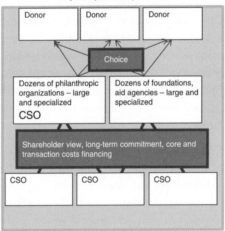

Proposed philanthropic sector

FIGURE 10 / **Overview of current and proposed structure and functioning of philanthropy sector**

players such as Acumen, Ashoka or New Profits, and the emergence of new players such as BonVentures, Impetus or Wise). The challenge is to get these donors to recognize that creating their own foundation might be a short-term satisfaction but that the best way to effectively create social change is to trust professional teams to do so.

Finally, networks of engaged philanthropists would help to reform the system. An attractive feature of what is called today the "new philanthropy" is the increasing numbers of individual donors who are seriously committed to devote their time and use their skills in getting personally engaged. Many of these "hands-on" investors recognize that joining a network of peers enables them to be more effective in identifying the best organizations to engage with, gaining access to state-of-the-art thinking and other like-minded investors. In Europe, the European Venture Philanthropy Association (EVPA) is playing a lead role in building these networks, inspired by some US-based precursors such as Social Venture Partners (SVP) – a network of committed philanthropists. Ashoka – the largest worldwide network for social entrepreneurs – has also created its own support network, the Ashoka Support Network (ASN),[178] now consisting of 400 business people who support Ashoka Fellows financially and with their skills and networks. More needs to be done to encourage and formalize these networks.

* * *

Large foundations kept accountable by competition, networks of engaged philanthropists and a diverse industry of professional intermediaries – these are the three pillars of what could be the new architecture for the philanthropy sector. But what "earthquake" could trigger such enormous changes? CSOs are too fragmented, and generally too under-resourced to influence their funders and send such a shock-wave bottom up.

We believe that change should rather come from the top; as long as foundations and donors do not fundamentally change the rules of the game, actors further down the line will not change their behavior. But what could make philanthropists give up the complacency of today's system?

A possible avenue could be that of regulatory change: by requiring that philanthropic donors spend all their money within five to ten years (for example, by raising to 15 percent the minimum percentage of assets to be given annually) in order to benefit from tax benefits, regulators would force that sufficient money be spent early. This would create urgency, the need for much more ambitious programs, longer-term vision and ambition, and the emergence of more structures able to deliver these programs on a large scale. This would come with higher risk levels, which donors could mitigate by diversifying their "investments" into a portfolio of foundations. As a result, small, conditional grants will hopefully not be possible anymore.

Conclusion – are we reinventing capitalism?

For two thousand years people believed that the sun and all the stars of heaven were circling around them... It has always been taught that the stars are pinned to a crystal vault... Today we have found the courage to let them soar through space without support... Overnight the universe has lost its center, and by morning it has countless ones... Suddenly, there is plenty of room.

The old times are gone, and this is a new age... Everything is in motion... Every day something new is being discovered... In Siena, I saw some masons, after arguing for five minutes, discard an age-old method of moving granite blocks in favor of a new and more practical arrangement of the ropes... A great deal has been discovered, but there is much more to be discovered. Plenty of work for future generations.

Bertolt Brecht[179]

Reading the above lines, one is reminded that change is not a new thing. The words that Brecht puts in Galileo's mouth bring to life the Copernican revolution but also echo so many of the words of social entrepreneurs across the world. For decades people believed that the sole purpose of business was to create value for its shareholders. Indeed it takes courage to challenge this dogma – but now, as Brecht movingly said, there is "plenty of room."

We share in the excitement that Brecht's Galileo experiences at the dawn of a "new age" of society: we believe we are standing on the verge of a renewal in the way that social problems are addressed.

We do not expect change to happen overnight, as old habits die hard. But so many changes are at work: much like the masons of Siena, entrepreneurs, farmers, vendors and bankers in the villages of remote India, in the favelas of São Paulo, in the Kenyan bush, are indeed discarding their age-old ways to innovate and make the world a better place.

Although the road lies long ahead, let us pause and reflect on what we have discovered so far, so that this learning may guide us in our endeavor. What have we learnt in our exploration of this hybrid territory where entrepreneurs of all breeds are laboring to invent new ways of solving society's travails, while making a living for themselves and their colleagues, and satisfying the return expectations of their investors?

In Part 1, we discovered the countless ways in which market-based approaches can contribute to solving our world's problems, as well as their limitations. In Part 2 we looked into the reasons that prevent them reaching scale, and pointed at promising ways to overcome them. Throughout the book we have made the acquaintance of fascinating entrepreneurs whose lives touch us.

But, beyond all this, three simple lessons emerge – lessons that may be simplistic to the brain but that ring true in our hearts:

1. Not all profit is bad... or good.
2. We need more change-makers.
3. Be the change you want to see in the world.

Not all profit is bad... or good

The first lesson is that not all profit is bad. And that not all profit is good, either.

As illustrated by our Chapter 3 story of a large building-materials company wanting to contribute to closing the global housing deficit, philanthropic resources are simply not enough, given the scale of the problem. This initiative needed to be a profitable business to have any chance to achieve a meaningful scale. Any grant-based CSO or foundation knows that its ability to do good is restricted by the amount of money it can raise and that it is therefore forced to make the choice of selecting which poor people to help, which lives to save. Is there a good way to make such a choice? How can one explain to a child that there was not sufficient money to save all of them and that he was just unlucky not to be selected?

Dwelling on such unsettling dilemmas is not gratuitous cruelty by the authors of this book. It tries to convey why we feel that we have the moral obligation to constantly push the envelope of what market-based approaches can do, even if these carry their own set of moral dilemmas – such as those our building-materials clients were struggling with.

Profit is good because it frees us from begging for grants and enables us to hope to save all those in need.

Though we wholeheartedly agree with Liam Black (see box) that profit is not necessarily bad, we know by experience that any profit is not necessarily good, contrary to what Milton Friedman seemed to say when he claimed that: "the social responsibility of business is to increase its profits."[180]

ILLUSTRATION 19 / Liam Black

Liam Black is a well-known figure in the UK social entrepreneur-ship movement, having created and led some dozen social businesses, including Jamie Oliver's Fifteen. Today he runs the global network Wavelength (www.thesamewavelength.com).

In the old days – the late 1980s/early 1990s – the idea of merging social change and business was not only unheard of but actively

Continued

Continued

> *resisted. I was booed at numerous events when I would ask people to stand, take a breath and repeat after me: "PROFIT IS GOOD!" At one gig in north-east England, I had a shoe thrown at me – it missed!*
>
> *Today it is accepted that for some social ventures profitable trading is the way to financial viability, freedom from the tyranny of fundraising and the way to achieve velocity in terms of scale and impact.*
>
> *The emerging field of impact investing is the next frontier. It is messy, contested, there are no shared metrics, and there are too many talkers not doers – but this is inevitable at the beginning of profound change.*
>
> *Optimism is a choice. The world is confronted with many challenges, some of which seem insurmountable. Inequality worsens around the world. But I – like many social entrepreneurs – choose to believe that we can make a big difference and find new ways of creating wealth and opportunity. For me that's what social enterprise is about.*

It is society that decides which profit-making businesses and business practices are good or bad – that is, legal or illegal. Selling drugs is illegal; selling alcohol to children is illegal. Price cartels are illegal; polluting water is illegal. The views of society about what is legal and what isn't differ across countries or states and vary over time, eliminating any hope that this is a clear-cut situation.

Interestingly, some large businesses seem to be attracted to the "wrong" kind of profit, the illegal kind. Indeed, every year, some of the world's largest and most prestigious companies are requested to pay billions of US dollars in fines, actually over $3 billion per year, by the combined US Department of Justice and the European Antitrust Commission.[181]

But what is driving otherwise probably law-abiding citizens to revert to such illegal and dangerous behaviors?

As we saw in Chapter 12, large corporations are most often active in mature industries in which opportunities to create value for society are limited to constantly improving efficiency of operations and transferring these gains to society in the form of price reductions as a result of competition between companies. This ever-shrinking outlook is not very pleasant for managers, and the temptation to avoid brutal direct price competition by excessively extending pay off of R&D investments by using a barrage of patents or questionable marketing and pricing practices is understandable, as is trying to avoid destructive "price wars" by costly customer loyalty programs (legal) or cartels (illegal).

What has been identified and fined as illegal practices is only the tip of the iceberg of business practices designed to protect the profits of corporations that have reached a stage of maturity. These practices, though usually legal, are mostly driven by the will to serve shareholders in the short term, rather than society at large.

So, when are shareholder's and society's interests best aligned? As we saw in Chapter 12, it is in the early, creative phase of the life cycle of industries; when a corporation mission is not to sell products but to solve a problem for society.

It is the role of a leader to steer his or her company into the fastest-flowing streams in the river, where value can be created for all. As Jean-Pascal Tricoire, CEO at Schneider Electric, explains: "Each time we align the interests of society and business, we achieve the best possible results. For example, when we redefined our mission from electrification to helping our clients save energy, we multiplied our rate of growth."

It is the role of a leader to steer his or her company into the fastest-flowing streams

We may be overestimating the dramatic nature of these changes. The "shareholder value" activists have managed to persuade us that the golden boys of Wall Street define capitalism. We know that this type of faceless capitalism is limited in time, geography and proportions. Utopian capitalists have existed in the past. Didn't Henry Ford say: "A business that makes nothing but money is a poor business"? When Olivier Kayser started working with McKinsey in 1985, he remembered French CEOs being very uncomfortable with the idea that shareholder value creation should be the sole determinant of their performance. They were distrustful of the vagaries of the stock market, but just as importantly concerned with the excessive say given to shareholders at the expense of their "other" stakeholders: employees, communities, customers, suppliers and so on. Jean-Paul Bailly, formerly CEO of La Poste, criticizes the excess of the 1980s and forcefully shares his conviction that: "Growth and long-term value creation rely on building of trust and trust relies on the balanced taking into account of all stakeholders."

At McKinsey itself, in the 1980s there were promoters of stakeholder value analysis as an integral part of business strategy. The fact that this analysis was cumbersome and produced debatable results was probably a key factor for choosing the simplest methodology: shareholder value. This is another version of the story of the man looking for his keys under the streetlight – not because that's where he lost them, but because that's where the light is.

We need more change-makers

The second lesson is that the ultimate bottleneck for enabling social innovations is the scarcity of "change-makers" in most of our societies.

When Anand Shah, founder and former CEO of Sarvajal, is asked about the barriers he faced in scaling up Sarvajal (see Chapter 7), he says: "There is a shortage of talent. People… are extremely motivated by solving a problem… but lack the skills and drive to replicate what has already been found. Scaling up means doing the same thing over and over again. It is hard to find talents that are truly motivated by working on scaling up."

Our own work with corporate clients shows that individuals able to bridge the citizen and business sectors are scarce. The temptation to recruit "social experts" from the CSO world is great but very often we have seen them being marginalized because they don't have the informal networks so critical to make change happen in a large organization. Looking for internal candidates makes sense because their track record gives them credibility but they just lack the package of "social entrepreneurship skills": ability to work without any resource, empathy with the poor as well as people working in social organizations… And when they are really good, they are hard to retain in this "innovative and risky" position as they are offered other career opportunities.

Hence, we need to invest in building these capabilities, which is what pioneering companies do by seconding high-potential employees to social organizations or training programs. In our experience, enabling these executives to join a community of like-minded individuals in other corporations is a great strategy to build their capabilities and keep their spirits high. We need a community of change-makers able to bridge gaps between sectors, countries and social classes.

The scarcity of change-makers does not only affect corporations. They are as badly needed in other institutions, such
as governments and social organizations. This is the
vision of Bill Drayton, Ashoka's founder, who claims
that there should be a lot more change-makers,
trusting that a high proportion of change-makers
will be the key source of competitive advantage
in future for all institutions, be it corporations, social
organizations, nations, cities and so on.

A high proportion of change-makers will be the key source of competitive advantage in future

While social entrepreneurship is now a global movement, garnering momentum, we cannot rely solely on the leadership of a few to solve the problems of
the world. The complexity and the magnitude of the change required render
futile any effort to set a clear vision and build a plan to achieve it. Instead, we
should grow the capacity of our societies to adapt by broadening our collective understanding of the issues we face and of the diversity of point of views
that our societies have. Hence, a key part of the solution will be to promote
"everyone as a change-maker" in society.

Be the change you want to see in the world

This vision for society resonates with a motto attributed to Gandhi: "Be the
change you want to see in the world."

But to do so, each of us needs to chart his or her own course, and decide what
is good and what is bad. We cannot continue dividing the task, with some of
us focusing on making the economy work efficiently while others are trying to
keep society working using the taxes paid by the former.

But this is not easy. Things are not clear-cut anymore, neither for the CSO
members who believed that their "not-for-profit" status was a proof of their
moral superiority, nor for the business executives who trusted that the pursuit
of any (legal) profit was justified. Each of us has to recognize that we are
unlikely to have all the answers: listen to others but ultimately figure out what
we believe is right and just do it.

Jean-Paul Bailly explains: "I am constantly arguing with managers who complain that they cannot reconcile contradictory priorities! But it is the essence
of their job to reconcile the interest of stakeholders (customers, suppliers,
local politicians, trade union representatives and so on) that are by their sheer
nature, contradictory."

Each of us needs to chart his or her own course, decide what is good and what is bad, and what risks to take. Do not listen to the crowds that surround us, whether they chant the supremacy of shareholder value or the glory of not-for-profit. We all have full individual responsibility in our life choices – whether we are citizens, consumers, employees or investors. Hiding behind the authority of a boss or an obligation to shareholders is no excuse: we all know how soldiers blindly following orders have caused some of the darkest hours in human history.

PARVEZ SUFI
CEO OF PHARMAGEN

After high school, my father advised me to train as an accountant, which I did. In 1977, I returned from London to Karachi, eventually creating my own auditing firm. While my firm was successful, I was always looking for something more worthwhile.

At the age of 37, I became the CEO of the first production plant of Active Pharmaceutical Ingredients in Pakistan, supplying international and local pharmaceutical companies. I eventually

ILLUSTRATION 20 / Parvez Sufi

became the majority shareholder of a successful $40 million business.

My family has strong rural roots in Kot Ishaq, a small village in Punjab. Many of my family members still live in this village. My father went to a public college in Lahore. He succeeded in the competitive exam to get into the prestigious Indian Civil Service – this was before the partition. He went to Cambridge University and came back to a brilliant career as a civil servant, including serving as Cabinet Secretary in two governments. He was a tremendous individual of the highest integrity. He has been my role model because not only did he serve his country, but he also was a very considerate human being who made anyone he was talking to, from any social stratum, feel they were important. His humility and ability to relate to the poor was such that while he passed away in 1987, to this day the community in our village remembers him fondly. For me this is the test of being a good human being: how you are remembered when you are gone.

In 1995, after my father and mother passed away, I wanted to continue in my father's footsteps and contribute to improving the lives of rural communities.

I decided to fund the building of a school in Kot Ishaq. We hired four young female graduates from the village and sent them for a one-year training to Lahore to learn the methodologies of active learning, as opposed to the rote-learning practices prevalent in Pakistani schools. The parents of our first class were so amazed with our results that we have had remarkable success ever since. We now have over 4500 students up to high school in thirteen schools. Our vision is to have 25 schools going up to high school with 1200 students each. This will allow us to have 30,000 students, 15 percent of the children in this region. We trust this will be a critical mass that will tip the system, forcing all other schools to adopt our approach.

Our family is providing the initial capital investment for building these schools, together with the support of donors. The parents are paying 1300 Pakistan rupees per month (US $13), a fee that is enough to cover the operating expenses of the school and finds its

Continued

Continued

> *justification in the excellent results we achieve; 10–15 percent of the children receive scholarships when their parents cannot afford to pay the full fee.*
>
> *In 2007, we decided to diversify Pharmagen's activities and to focus on addressing the health issues of urban and rural communities by setting up a network of 16 Watershops in Lahore's low-income areas, providing the surrounding communities with reverse osmosis (RO) processed, clean drinking water and creating a chain of state-of-the-art pharmacies staffed with trained pharmacists, selling only high-quality drugs from reputable suppliers, equipped with cold chain for vaccines in rural areas. The latter operation we have had to discontinue as it was financially unsustainable, while our water business is currently reaching around 80,000 consumers.*
>
> *You can do good in any profession: a successful doctor can visit patients in need. But to achieve impact at scale, you need to professionalize your approach – to institutionalize it.*
>
> *My father never gave me any advice, he led by example. The choice was mine. I hope my own children will make similar choices.*
>
> *Life is very short but there is a lot that we can do. We need to set our vision and goals as high as possible and try our best. An individual can only do his or her best, sincere efforts.*

To steer us through these difficult choices, we all have rich personal stories to draw from. As we undertake this journey, our individual decisions will be grounded in our own life story, as is the case for each of the dozens of entrepreneurs we have worked with or interviewed for this book.

* * *

Five years ago, when we started writing this book, we were hopeful to draw a "road map for entrepreneurs in a changing world." The process of writing has made us more humble, or at least more aware of all that we don't know.

The magnitude of the unknown would make us lose courage if we did not feel the energy, warmth and camaraderie of the thousands of entrepreneurs who are at work to make this world a better place for our children and our children's children.

Valeria loves to repeat a phrase of Fernando Flores, a philosopher and her long-time friend and mentor: "Ideas are not in our mind, they exist in the spaces created by our conversations." Thank you for entering into this conversation. We look forward to continuing it.

References

1. This research was conducted by Satyan Mishra of Drishtee, on behalf of Hystra.
2. Exchange rate in June 2014: US$ 1 = INR 60.
3. World Bank – Poverty and Inequality Analysis.
4. A. Sen (1992) "Inequality reexamined," explained by Erik Thorbecke (Cornell University), in "Multi-dimensional Poverty: Conceptual and Measurement Issues" (2005).
5. P. Townsend, *Poverty in the United Kingdom* (London, 1979).
6. Research for this section was conducted by Terra Nova on behalf of Hystra.
7. Exchange rate in June 2014: 1 USD = 2.2 BRL (R$).
8. World Bank (2009) PovCalNet, iresearch.worldbank.org/PovCalNet/povcalSvy. html.
9. Average P&L – all non-monthly expenses or income have been computed annually, then divided by 12.
10. UNICEF (2011) Global Inequality: Beyond the Bottom Billion.
11. The World Bank website.
12. C. K. *Prahalad, The Fortune at the Bottom of the Pyramid* (Philadelphia, PA: Wharton School Publishing, 2004).
13. This research was conducted by KickStart on behalf of Hystra.
14. Exchange rate in June 2014: 1USD = 87 Kenyan shillings (KES).
15. A. Hammond, "The Next Four Billion", World Resource Institute and the International Finance Corporation, 2005, http://www.wri.org/publication/next-4-billion.
16. B. Drayton and V. Budinich "A New Alliance for Global Change," *Harvard Business Review*, September, 2010, pages 56 to 64
17. Bureau of Labor (2010) Consumer Expenditures.
18. Utility tariff is US $0.12 per cubic meter while people pay up to US $7.5 per cubic meter. Hystra (2011) Access to Safe Water for the BoP, http://hystra.com/ safe-water/ (PALYJA Water for All Case Study).
19. Upper-scale water purifiers are as effective as boiling water and cost about US $40 to own on a yearly basis, while people in rural Cambodia spend $70–180 per year on fuel to boil water.
20. Hystra (2011) Access to Safe Water for the BoP, http://hystra.com/safe-water/.

21. World Energy Outlook (2011) Energy Access Database, http://www.worldenergy outlook.org/resources/energydevelopment/energyaccessdatabase.

22. Business Insider (2013) The Unbanked Population of the World, http://www. businessinsider.com/the-unbanked-population-of-the-world-2013-1.

23. See Chapter 8 for more details.

24. GLTN Secretariat by UN-Habitat (2010) Tackling Tenure Security in Slums through Participatory Enumerations, Global Land Tool Network Brief I, March 2010, http://www.gltn.net/jdownloads/GLTN%20Documents/2992_alt.pdf.

25. S. Mishra (2011) interview.

26. For more details, see Chapter 6 on housing.

27. A. Albuquerque (2011), interview.

28. R. Layton (2012), interview.

29. D. Moyo, *L'aide Fatale* (Paris: Jean-Claude Lattes, 2009), p. 5.

30. M. Bishop and M. Green, *Philantrocapitalism: How the Rich Can Save the World* (New York: Bloomsbury Press, 2008).

31. Next Billion (2011) Housing for All Series: Sizing Up the Affordable Housing Deficit, www.nextbillion.net/blog/2011/10/13/sizing-up-he-affordable-housing-deficit.

32. V. Akula, *A Fistful of Rice* (Cambridge, MA: Harvard Business Review Press, 2010).

33. Hystra (2011) Access to Safe Water for the BoP, http://hystra.com/safe-water/.

34. www.hystra.com: Access to Energy for the BoP (2009), Leveraging ICT for the BoP (notably in the field of financial services, 2011), Access to Safe Water for the BoP (2011), Access to Housing for the BoP (2012).

35. Expenditure of Low-Income Households on Energy, Evidence from Africa and Asia, Extractive Industries for Development Series, 16 June 2010, available at http:// siteresources.worldbank.org.

36. In 2012, malaria killed over 600,000 people (World Health Organization (2014) Malaria, http://www.who.int/mediacentre/factsheets/fs094/en/), while toxic fumes from biomass were responsible for 4.3 million deaths. (World Health Organization (2014) Household Air Pollution and Health, http://www.who.int/ mediacentre/factsheets/fs292/en/).

37. R. Bocca (2012), interview.

38. A. Roy (2012), interview.

39. Envirofit (2014) http://www.envirofit.org.

40. According to Suraj Wahab, co-founder of Toyola.

41. Now Persistent Energy Partners.

42. S. Deshpande and N. R. Lee, *Social Marketing In India* (SAGE Response, 2014).

43. Clean Cookstoves (2014) http://cleancookstoves.org.

44. GIZ (2011) "Carbon Markets for Improved Cooking Stoves," *A Giz Guide for Project Operators*, p. 6.

45. J. Smith (2011) "Protecting Health and the Planet With Clean Cookstoves," *National Geographic*.

46. K. Newcombe (2012), interview.

47. International Energy Agency (2013) Electricity, www.iea.org.

48. International Energy Agency (2003) World Energy Outlook. This amount was computed to connect the 1.4 billion people who lacked electricity in 2003, which has not changed much since then.

49. French economists talk about the *"petit équilibre"* when revenues cover running costs and *"grand équilibre"* when they also cover capital charges.

50. P. Roy and K. Nightingale (2010) "Financing Solar Power for the Poor," *Science and Development Network*; D. Miller (2009) *Selling Solar: The Diffusion of Renewable Energy in Emerging Markets* - IFC (2007) *Selling Solar – Lessons from More Than a Decade of IFC's Experience.*

51. P. LaRocco (2009), interview.

52. Grameen Shakti, in zones of Bangladesh with population density of 1000 inhabitants per km², has one center for each zone of 25 km radius. SELCO, with density of "only" 300 inhabitants per km², has one center with a maintenance team of five full-time equivalent (FTE) staff for zones of 100 km radius, effectively serving 1500–2000 families per center.

53. Ned Tozun (2012), interview: www.dlightdesign.com.

54. M. Adema (2010), interview.

55. G. Pande (2011), interview.

56. HPS operations (2011), field visit.

57. GLTN Secretariat by UN-Habitat (2010) Tackling Tenure Security in Slums through Participatory Enumerations, Global Land Tool Network Brief I, March 2010, http://www.gltn.net/jdownloads/GLTN%20Documents/2992_alt.pdf.

58. "Privately Build Low-Income Housing in India: Opportunity, Challenges and potential interventions. Report by Deloitte Consulting LLP (July 2013). http://mhupa.gov.in/W_new/14_Vikram%20Jain_AH%20scenario%20in%20India.pdf

59. Price in purchasing power parity (PPP): see box in Chapter 1, p. 13.

60. B. Drayton and V. Budinich, "A New Alliance for Global Change," *Harvard Business Review*, September 2010.

61. Inter-American Development Bank, Many Paths to a Home: Emerging Business Models for Latin America and the Caribbean's Based of the Pyramid, 2014, http://publications.iadb.org/handle/11319/ 66?locale-attribute=en.

62. Interview with Israel Moreno, former CEO of Patrimonio Hoy.

63. I. Moreno (2011), interview.

64. Privately Build Low-Income Housing in India: Opportunity, Challenges and potential interventions: Report by Deloitte Consulting LLP (July 2013). http://mhupa.gov.in/W_new/14_Vikram%20Jain_AH%20scenario%20in% 20India.pdf.

65. V. Swaminathan (2011), interview.

66. See blogs by V. Swaminathan and M. Wengle. Both blogs are available in: The Next Billion (2012) *The Big Idea: Global Spread of Affordable Housing,* an ebook published by Next Billion in partnership with Ashoka, Hystra and other practitioners in this field. https://www.ashoka.org/sites/ashoka/files/The-Big-IDEA-ebook-FINAL.pdf.

67. Next Billion (2011) Housing for All Series: Sizing Up the Affordable Housing Deficit, www.nextbillion.net/blog/2011/10/13/sizing-up-the-affordable-housing-deficit.

68. H. De Soto, *The Mystery of Capital: Why Capitalism Triumphs in the West and Fails Everywhere Else* (New York: Basic Books, 2000).

69. Terra Nova estimates, Interview with André Alburquerque.

70. Next Billion (2011) Housing for All Series: Sizing Up the Affordable Housing Deficit, www.nextbillion.net/blog/2011/10/13/sizing-up-the-affordable-housing-deficit.

71. Unless otherwise specified, all data, graphs and analyses in this chapter are taken from Hystra (2011) Access to Safe Water for the BoP, http://hystra.com/safe-water/.

72. World Health Organization (2013) Diarrhoeal Disease, http://www.who.int/mediacentre/factsheets/fs330/en/.

73. United Nations (2011) World Urbanization Prospects, http://www.slideshare.net.undesa/wup2011-highlights.

74. A. Shah (2011), interview.

75. L. Kawa (2013) "Here's Why 2.5 Billion People Still Don't Have A Bank Account," Business Insider, http://www.businessinsider.com/the-unbanked-population-of-the-world-2013-1.

76. FINO shop in Dharavi, India (2011), interview.

77. A. Gonzales (2011) "Defining Responsible Financial Performance: Understanding Efficiency," Microfinance Information Exchange, http://www.themix.org/publications/microbanking-bulletin/2011/05/microfinance-efficiency.

78. Microcredit Summit Campaign (2013) Tables and Figures, http://stateofthecampaign.org/2013-tables-and-figures/.

79. Microcredit Summit Campaign (2013) Tables and Figures, http://stateofthecampaign.org/2013-tables-and-figures/.

80. Nabarb (2014) Overview, https://www.nabard.org/english/OverView.aspx.

81. Grameen Bank (2014).

82. Bank BRI (2013) FY 2013 Financial Update Presentation, http://media.corporate-ir.net/media_files/IROL/14/148820/Full_Year_2013_Financial_Update_Presentation.pdf.

83. World Economic Forum (2012), Redefining the Emerging Market Opportunity: Driving Growth through Financial Services Innovation, http://www3.weforum.org/docs/WEF_FS_RedefiningEmergingMarketOpportunity_Report_2012.pdf.

84. Rich (2014) Safaricom Ltd., http://www.rich.co.ke/rcdata/company.php?i=NTU%3D.

85. FINO shop in Dharavi, India (2011), interview.

86. FINO (2012) Home page, http://www.finopaytech.com.

87. R. Gupta (2012), interview.

88. Bradesco (2014) Home page, http://www.bradesco.com.br.

89. C. Riquet (2012) "Technologie: Réduire les coûts pour les clients et les institutions en zone rurale," CGAP (Consultative Group to Assist the Poor).

90. GSMA (2009) Mobile Money: A US$5 Billion Market Opportunity, http://www.gsma.com/mobilefordevelopment/wp-content/uploads/2012/06/mmu_quarterly_update.pdf.

91. GSMA (2009) Mobile Money: A US$5 Billion Market Opportunity.

92. Juniper Research (2011) Press Release: Mobile Banking Users to Exceed 150m Globally by 2011 According to Juniper Research, http://www.juniperresearch.com/viewpressrelease.php?pr=120.

93. Informal employment outside of the agro sector made up 48 percent of employment in North Africa, 51 percent in Latin America, 65 percent in Asia and 72 percent in sub-Saharan Africa. Adding to those self-employed farmers puts the informal employment rates higher than 90 percent of the total labor force in India and most sub-Saharan African countries. International Labor Organization (2002) Men and Women in the Informal Economy, http://www.gdrc.org/informal/women.pdf.

94. International Labor Organization (2013) Global Employment Trends, http://www.ilo.org/wcmsp5/groups/public/---dgreports/---dcomm/---publ/documents/publication/wcms_202326.pdf.

95. Fairtrade (2012) For Producers, With Producers, http://www.fairtrade.net/fileadmin/user_upload/content/2009/resources/2011-12_AnnualReport_web_version_small_FairtradeInternational.pdf.

96. B. Bowonder, B. R. Raghu Prasad and Anup Kotla (2002), ICT Application in a Dairy Industry: The E-Experience of Amul, http://www.planningcommission.gov.in/reports/sereport/ser/stdy_ict/3_amul.pdf.

97. S. Naik (2011), interview.

98. eChoupal (2011), field visit.

99. ACDI/VOCA (2012) Growth-oriented Microenterprise Development Program, http://www.acdivoca.org/site/ID/indiaGMED/.

100. Hystra (2011) Leveraging ICT for the BoP, http://hystra.com/leveraging-ict.

101. Hystra (2011) Leveraging ICT for the BoP, http://hystra.com/leveraging-ict.

102. Copenhagen Consensus (2014) Home Page, http://www.copenhagenconsensus.com.

103. GAO (2010) For Profit Colleges: Undercover Testing Finds Colleges Encouraged Fraud and Engaged in Deceptive and Questionable Marketing Practices, http://www.gao.gov/assets/130/125197.pdf.

104. A. Smith, *An Inquiry into the Nature and Causes of the Wealth of Nations* (London: Methuen & Co., 1776) p. 196.

105. *Daily Mail*, 15 September 2007, http://www.dailymail.co.uk/femail/article-482012/Queen-Green-Roddicks-unfair-trade-started-copied-Body-Shop-formula.html.

106. C. Cahalane (2006) "I believe they are honourable and the work they do is honourable," *The Guardian,* http://www.theguardian.com/business/2006/nov/03/ethicalliving.environment.

107. The Body Shop (2014) Against Animal Testing, http://www.thebodyshop.fr/services/template1.aspx?topcode=AgainstAnimalTesting.

108. Oliver Wyman (2007) A Retailer's Recipe for Fresher Food and Far Less Shrink, http://ergoeditorial.biz/worksamples/OW%20grocery%20shrinkage.pdf.

109. European Commission JRC (2013) Trends in Global CO2 Emissions, http://edgar.jrc.ec.europa.eu/news_docs/pbl-2013-trends-in-global-co2-emissions-2013-report-1148.pdf.

110. United Nations, Department of Economic and Social Affairs, Population Division (2012) World Population Prospects: The 2012 Revision, Highlights and Advance Tables, http://esa.un.org/wpp/Documentation/pdf/WPP2012_HIGHLIGHTS.pdf.

111. BRAC (2013) BRAC At a Glance as of September 2013, http://www.brac.net/sites/default/files/BRAC-at-a-glance-September-2013.pdf; BRAC (2013) Annual Report, http://www.brac.net/sites/default/files/BRAC%20USA%20FY2013.pdf – see Chapter 10 for more details about BRAC.

112. R. Ali (2009), interview.

113. A Mourot (2012), interview.

114. New Profit (2014) Our Story, http://newprofit.com/cgi-bin/iowa/about/3.html.

115. K. Frischen (2012), interview.

116. National Venture Capital Association (2010) Venture-Backed Liquidity Events by Year/Quarter, 2004–2010, http://www.nvca.org/index.

117. Monitor Institute (2010) Breaking New Grounds: Using the Internet to Scale, a Case Study of Kaboom! http://www.monitorinstitute.com/downloads/what-we-think/kaboom/KaBOOM_Case_St.

118. D. Green (2012), interview.

119. G. Dench and K. Gavron (eds) *Young at 80* (London: Cacharet, 1995).

120. For more information on Open University, see www8.open.ac.uk; and on University of the Third Age, see www.u3a.org.uk.

121. For more information see http://www.which.co.uk/. Other organizations founded by Lord Young that are still running today include The Institute of Community Studies (1953–54), The Advisory Centre for Education (1959), National Extension College (1962), International Alert (1981), Open College of the Arts (1987), Language Line (1990) and Education Extra (1992), to name only a few.

122. Dench and Gavron, *Young at 80*; Daniel Bell, *The Sociologist as Man of Action*.

123. Dench and Gavron, *Young at 80*; Robert Gavron, *Making Money for Other People*.

124. Dench and Gavron, *Young at 80*; Tessa Blackstone, *The Birkbeck Presidency*.

125. K. Andrews (2012), interview.

126. Dench and Gavron, *Young at 80*; Malcolm Dean, *The Architect of Social Innovation*.

127. J. Billimoria (2012), interview.

128. C. Casey (2012), interview – see also www.kanchi.org.

129. S. Busari and E. Wither (2011) "African Dictators Warned: Your Time is Up," *CNN*, http://edition.cnn.com/2011/10/14/world/africa/africa-leader-prize/index.html.

130. V. Bali (2011), interview. Naandi (2008) Britannia, Naandi and GAIN: A Public-Private Partnership for Delivering Nutrition through Fortification in India, http://www.naandi.org/strategy_papers/PDfs/Naandi%20Case.pdf.
Indiatimes (2014) Britannia Industries Ltd., http://economictimes.indiatimes.com/britannia-industries-ltd/directorsreport/companyid-13934.cms.
Indian Biscuits Manufacturers' Association (2012) Industry Statistics, www.ibmabiscuits.in/industry-statistics.html.
Britannia Industries (2011) Health and Nutrition Initiatives, www.britannia.co.in/bnf/media/britannia-in-health-nutrition.pdf; Britannia Nutrition Foundation (2011) Charter, www.britannia.co.in/bnf/bnf-charter.html.

131. See Chapter 16 on financing social businesses for more details.

132. J. Tricoire (2011), interview.

133. General Electric (2009) "How GE is Disrupting Itself," *Harvard Business Review*, http://hbr.org/2009/10/how-ge-is-disrupting-itself/ar/1.

134. E. Faber (2008), interview.

135. E. Jardine (2012), interview.

136. *As Fundações Privadas e Associações Sem Fins Lucrativos no Brasil* (2002), produced by IBGE, GIFE, ABONG and IPEA. http://www.ibge.gov.br/home/estatistica/economia/fasfil/fasfil.pdf.

137. B. Drayton and V. Budinich, "A New Alliance for Global Change," *Harvard Business Review*, 2010.

138. L. Crutchfield and H. McLeod, *Forces for Good: The Six Practices of High-Impact Nonprofits* (San Francisco: Jossey Bass, 2012).

139. C.K. Prahalad and Stuart L. Hart, "The Fortune at the Bottom of the Pyramid," August 5, 2004, article published in strategy+business, First Quarter 2002, Issue 26, http://www.strategy-business.com/article/11518?pg=all.

140. Etude d'impact de l'entrepreneuriat social, http://rtes.fr/IMG/pdf/Etude_d_impact_de_l_entrepreneuriat_social_-_synthese.pdf.

141. *Danone Ecosystem Fund Newsletter*, 3, October 2010. See http://ecosystem.danone.com.

142. Drayton and Budinich, "A New Alliance for Global Change," *Harvard Business Review*, 2010.

143. World Health Organization (2014) Household Air Pollution and Health, http://www.who.int/mediacentre/factsheets/fs292/en/.

144. World Health Organization (2014) Water Sanitation and Health, http://www.who.int/water_sanitation_health/advguide/en/index8.html.

145. Hystra (2013) Marketing Innovative Devices for the BoP, http://hystra.com/marketing-devices; Hystra (2014) Marketing Nutrition, http://www.hystra.com/marketing-nutrition.

146. International Telecommunication Union (2013) Measuring the Information Society, http://www.itu.int/en/ITU-D/Statistics/Documents/publications/mis2013/MIS2013_without_Annex_4.pdf.

147. International Telecommunication Union (2014) ICT Facts and Figures, http://www.itu.int/en/ITU-D/Statistics/Documents/facts/ICTFactsFigures2014-e.pdf.

148. Hystra (2014) Marketing Nutrition, http://www.hystra.com/marketing-nutrition.

149. D. Barua (2012), interview; Bright Green Energy Foundation website, www.greenenergybd.com.

150. Pureitwater (2014) Home page, http://www.pureitwater.com/IN/about-us.

151. As of 31 December 2012, there were 116,000 MFI clients earning below $1.25 PPP per day out of 1.1 billion people in this income bracket. Microcredit Summit Campaign (2012), State of the Microcredit Summit Campaign Report 2012, http://www.microcreditsummit.org/resource/46/state-of-the-microcredit-summit.html.

152. Lighting Africa (2012) Market Trends Report. http://lightingafrica.org/resources/market-research/quantitative-research/.

153. Hystra (2013) Marketing Innovative Devices for the BoP, http://hystra.com/marketing-devices.

154. Hystra (2013) Marketing Innovative Devices for the BoP, http://hystra.com/marketing-devices. Gross margin is here defined for the whole downstream value chain, from distributor to end consumers, independently of the number of intermediaries. Gross margin = (price for end consumer – cost of goods sold for distributor) / price for end consumer.)

155. Hystra (2014) Marketing Nutrition, http://www.hystra.com/marketing-nutrition.

156. Deloitte (2013) Indian Retail Market: Opening More Doors, http://www.deloitte.com/assets/Dcom-India/Local%20Assets/Documents/Thoughtware/Indian_Retail_Report_Opening_more_doors.pdf.

157. K. Jerath, S. Sajeesh and Z. J. Zhang (2012) "The Coexistence of Organised and Unorganised Retailing in Emerging Economies," *Institute of Asian Consumer Insight*, http://www.aci-institute.com/uploads/pages/2012_09_05_15_33_13_FinalKin.pdf.

158. Hystra (2013) Marketing Innovative Devices for the BoP, http://hystra.com/marketing-devices.

159. FTE (on the graph) means full-time equivalent. If companies employ a full-time sales force, the sales per salesperson FTE equals the sales per salesperson.

160. Natura (2014) Bem Estar Bem, http://natura.infoinvest.com.br/enu/4781/Natura_DB_2014VFinal.pdf.

161. K. Muralidharan, P. Niehaus and S. Sukhtankar (2014) "Assessing the Scope for Cash Transfers in Lieu of the TPDS in Rural and Urban Bihar," *J-PAL South Asia*, http://econweb.ucsd.edu/~kamurali/papers/Other%20Writing/Bihar%20TPDS%20Pre-pilot%20Study%20Report%20(25%20May%202011).pdf.

162. European Venture Philanthropy Association (2014) Home page, http://evpa.eu.com. The European Venture Philanthropy Association is made up of European organizations interested in or practicing venture philanthropy and social investment.

163. McKinsey & Company (2011) New Ways to Fund Social Innovation, http://voices.mckinseyonsociety.com/new-ways-to-fund-social-innovation/.

164. Impact Investments, an emerging asset class, J.P.Morgan, 29 November 2010 http://www.rockefellerfoundation.org/uploads/files/2b053b2b-8feb-46ea-adbd-f89068d59785-impact.pdf.

165. This notably attracted the interest of philanthropists wary of the unsustainability of the social impact achieved by the traditional nonprofit sector, who saw in the financing of investment fund operating costs a way to invest their grants more efficiently.

166. For instance, Danone has created danone.communities and GDF Suez its own €100 million fund, Rassembleurs d'Energies.

167. Grassroots Business Fund (2014) Impact Report, http://www.gbfund.org/annual_report.

168. Aspen Network of Development Entrepreneurs (2011) Impact Report, http://www.aspeninstitute.org/sites/default/files/content/docs/ande/

ANDE-2011-Impact-Report-Final.pdf; 37 members invested $750 million in small and growing businesses in investment markets.

169. Monitor (2010) Building Houses, Financing Homes, http://www.mim.monitor.com/downloads/BuildingHouses-FinancingHomes-FullReport.pdf.

170. This includes social entrepreneurs, local companies, NGOs and large corporate-driven projects.

171. J. P. Morgan Social Finance (2011) "Insights into the Impact Investment Market," *Global Impact Investing Network*, http://www.thegiin.org/cgi-bin/iowa/download?row=334&field=gated_download_1;

172. Acumen Fund (2012) From Blueprint to Scale, the Case for Philanthropy in Impact Investing.

173. McKinsey & Company (2011) New Ways to Fund Social Innovation, http://voices.mckinseyonsociety.com/new-ways-to-fund-social-innovation/.

174. A. Carnegie, *The Gospel of Wealth* (New York: Century, 1889).

175. Foundation Center Database (2014), http://data.foundationcenter.org/.

176. V. Krause (2008) "USA Foundations: $652 Billion in Assets," Rethink Campaigns, http://fairquestions.typepad.com/rethink_campaigns/usa-foundations.html.

177. W. Meehan et al., "Investing in Society," *Stanford Social Innovation Review*, 2004.

178. Disclaimer: ASN was founded by Olivier Kayser during his years with Ashoka.

179. B. Brecht, *Life of Galileo* (New York: Penguin Classics, 1943).

180. M. Friedman, "The Social Responsibility of Business is to Increase its Profits," *The New York Times Magazine*, 13 September 1970.

181. In total, the US Department of Justice respectively fined $1 billion and $550 million in 2009 and 2010 for criminal antitrust. As for the EU Antitrust Commission, it imposed fines for a total amount of €1.5 billion ($2 billion) and €2.9 billion ($3.8 billion) respectively in 2009 and 2010.

Select bibliography

Akula, V., *A Fistful of Rice* (Cambridge, MA: Harvard Business Review Press, 2010).

Bishop, M. and M. Green, *Philantrocapitalism: How the Rich Can Save the World* (New York: Bloomsbury Press, 2008).

Brecht, B., *Life of Galileo* (New York: Penguin Classics, 1943).

Carnegie, A., *The Gospel of Wealth* (New York: Century, 1889).

Dench, G. and K. Gavron (eds), *Young at 80* (London: Cacharet, 1995).

De Soto, H., *The Mystery of Capital: Why Capitalism Triumphs in the West and Fails Everywhere Else* (New York: Basic Books, 2000).

Drayton, B. and V. Budinich, "A New Alliance for Global Change," *Harvard Business Review*, September 2010, pp. 56–64.

Hammond, A., "The Next Four Billion," World Resource Institute and the International Finance Corporation, 2005.

Hystra, Access to Energy for the BoP (2009), Leveraging ICT for the BoP (2011), Access to Safe Water for the BoP (2011), Access to Housing for the BoP (2012), all available at http://www.hystra.com.

London, T. and Hart, S. L., *Next Generation Business Strategies for the Base of the Pyramid* (Upper Saddle River, NJ: FT Press, 2010).

Polak, P., *Out of Poverty* (San Francisco, CA: Bennett-Koehlen, 2009).

Prahalad, C. K., *The Fortune at the Bottom of the Pyramid* (Prenti PA: Wharton School Publishing, 2004).

Smillie, I., *Freedom from Want: The Remarkable Success Story of Brac, the Global Grassroots Organization That's Winning the Fight against Poverty* (Sterling, VA: Kumarian Press, 2009).

Smith, A., *An Inquiry into the Nature and Causes of the Wealth of Nations* (London: Methuen & Co., 1776).

Townsend, P., *Poverty in the United Kingdom* (London: Penguin Books, 1979).

Index

Printed and bound by CPI Group (UK) Ltd, Croydon, CR0 4YY